Desperately Seeking
the Fair Go

Desperately Seeking the Fair Go

We know how to make
Australia a better place
and it's not that hard.

Geoff Davies

A BetterNature Book

Book 5 in the *Seventh Generation* series.

Thanks to Julia Green for reminding me
to keep some balance in my own life,
and for enriching it with her presence.

eBook first published 2017 by BetterNature Books, Braidwood NSW, Australia

Hardcopy published 2018
betternature.wordpress.com/my-books/

Copyright © 2017 Geoff Davies
Davies, Geoffrey Frederick, 1944-
Cover design: Timothy Pryor, Pryority Design Studio
Layout and production: Paul Cockram, Artplan Graphics

Version 4 February 2018
ISBN-13: 978-0-6482968-0-5

Praise for Geoff Davies

If change is going to come, it will be from other professions, like physics, engineering and biology, who are used to modelling the dynamic, unstable real world rather than fantasies of equilibrium. They should be emboldened by this crisis to step onto the turf of economics and take the field over from the economists. **Geoff Davies was one of the very first** to do this, long before the current crisis hit, and **his physics- and biology-inspired work is part of the promise of a future economics** that is actually useful–unlike the downright dangerous fantasies of today's neoclassical economists."

— Economist **Steve Keen**, author of *Debunking Economics*.

Praise for *Sack the Economists*

This book raises many interesting questions, most importantly, why does anyone take economists seriously when it comes to discussing the economy?

— **Dean Baker**, Co-Director, Center for Economic and Policy Research, Washington D.C.

With delightful wit and insightful analogies, geophysicist Geoff Davies dissects the inconsistencies — and the inanities — of mainstream economics. Don't blame Adam Smith, he makes clear, for the mess this mainstream has become. Blame the intellectually lazy and morally obtuse careerists who practice an economics that in no way, shape, or form resembles the science they claim it to be. In the end, *Sack the Economists* helps us understand, plutocracy never works — and neither does an economics that refuses to discomfort our plutocrats.

— **Sam Pizzigati**, Institute for Policy Studies, Washington, D.C., and author of *The Rich Don't Always Win*.

Praise for *Economia*

Imagine a much more equal and inclusive society than we have now. It has old-fashioned family values, solid local communities, and full employment in an efficient and sustainable market economy with a debt-free money supply and no executive plunder. Impossible? Perhaps. But Geoff Davies' project is distinguished by such common sense, hard science, practicality, surprise, fine writing and expert contempt for orthodox economics, it's a joy to read for visionaries and sceptics alike.

— **Hugh Stretton**, author of *Economics, A New Introduction*

Contents

1. From the Heart — 9
2. Challenges — 13
3. A Nation Half-Formed — 23
4. The Reign of the Radical Right — 43
5. The Failing Neoliberal Experiment — 59
6. Collateral Damage: Society, Land, Planet — 71
7. Back to Basics — 85
8. A Healthy Society — 95
9. Reclaiming Our Conversation — 105
10. Markets: Taming the Wild Horses — 119
11. Finance: Corralling the Feral Extractors — 133
12. Banks: Seeing Behind the Curtain — 143
13. Not Back to the Caves: Smart Ideas, Proven Practices — 155
14. An Economy to Support Society — 171
15. Not Wrecking Our Home: Working With the Land — 185
16. Sovereignty — 197
17. The Strength to Offer Hope — 213
18. Retrieving the Fair Go — 221
    Appendix: New Anthem Words — 229
    Bibliography — 231
    About the author — 243

1
From the Heart

The better angels of peoples and nations are ever present even if unseen, and even in times when our rancorous angels are more visible. Better angels need to be conjured from the fog of fear and cynicism. – Noel Pearson, 2017

In mid-2017 two hundred and fifty Indigenous Australians gathered at Uluru to consider their place in modern Australia. They used a word new to most of us, the Yolngu word *makarrata*, which refers to *the coming together after a struggle*. After three days they issued the *Uluru Statement from the Heart*, in which they voiced their wish to be heard, their wish for a First Nations Voice to be enshrined in the Australian Constitution.

The Uluru gathering was the culmination of a decade of debate, including twelve regional gatherings, seeking a way forward among diverse points of view, not all mutually compatible. They found that way forward, through respectful discussion, with only a handful feeling unable to support the final statement. The Uluru Statement, addressed to the rest of the nation, concludes 'We invite you to walk with us in a movement of the Australian people for a better future.'

The gathering also called for more discussion and for a 'fair and truthful' relationship with other Australians. They want a process of truth and reconciliation. Truth-telling and truth-accepting can be difficult and painful.

Therein lies a potential struggle for all Australians, if we choose to take up their invitation. Therein also lies a potential *makarrata* for the whole nation.

Noel Pearson says the constitutional reforms of 1967 that, among other things, allowed Aboriginal people to be counted in the census, left the job of accommodating Aborigines within the constitution and the nation 'half undone'.

We Australians have other unfinished business. We, the immigrant people, still have not managed to adapt ourselves fully to a land so very different from other lands. We are still careless of our effect on the land and the world around us. We have not learnt to fully claim Australia's place in the world, but still tend to defer to others. We once held it as important to give all of our people a fair go, but we have allowed other agendas to gain priority.

The aspiration for a fair go was not unchallenged, a century ago, and not even all-inclusive. Yet it was an expression of a growing idea, also expressed in the term *mateship*, that Australia could grow beyond the classes, hierarchies, excesses and deprivations of Europe.

Lately a hierarchy of wealth and power has re-asserted itself, but in a new form based overtly on the strange claim that selfishness is best. Since 1980 this idea has come to dominate the world. After decades of disruption of communities, of dispossession and suffering of the poorest, here and around the world, of unstable and mediocre economic performance and of degradation of the natural world many people are coming to question the reign of selfishness.

Lacking a clearly perceived alternative, some people have turned to demagogues and xenophobes like Donald Trump and Pauline Hanson, who at least promised to challenge the power of the wealthy. Those reactionaries will quickly fail in their turn because about all they have to offer is a police state version of what we are trying to escape. With them in charge we will just continue the descent into fear and division.

Yet there is another possibility. It is based not on selfishness and fear of others but on unselfishness, tolerance and the courage to act accordingly. We know it can work, because we used to work more together and be more welcoming of strangers. Many of us never stopped living unselfishly.

We can also change the goal of our society. The implicit goal now is to provide more and more stuff. We can instead work towards a society that supports fulfilling lives.

To support our better angels and a saner goal we can make more sensible use of the ever-increasing fund of human knowledge. To that end, we are learning how to get our energy, grow our food and manufacture things without fouling our nest. We also have better ideas on how to manage the economy so it supports the society we want to live in.

Unselfishness, tolerance, better goals and smarter organising can help us to finish our unfinished business. They can help us to heal wounds from our sometimes careless, selfish or brutal history. They can help us to reclaim the fair go.

Journalist Stan Grant said, during a *Q&A* discussion of the Uluru Statement, that our politicians sell us short, and there's truth in that. But we still, too often, sell ourselves short. A little over a century ago we didn't ask the world what it thought of our bold economic and social progress, we just did it. We (and the Kiwis) led the world. The world looked to us.

Then we dropped the ball. We let old habits take over. We thought like colonials. We felt second best, derivative, behind the times. We cringed. The best was always in London, or New York, or where ever. Our so-called leaders reverted to facilitating those, local and foreign, who were happy to run our affairs for us, for a handsome profit.

We know what it will take for us to grab the ball again, it has been said many times. Franklin Roosevelt said 'We have nothing to fear but fear itself'. Nelson Mandela, quoting Marianne Williamson, said 'Our deepest fear is not that we are inadequate. Our deepest fear is that we are powerful beyond measure. It is our light not our darkness that most frightens us'.

We can be stuck in our heads, thinking small thoughts, or we can listen to what our hearts really want. We can let our fear limit our lives, or we can push through it and let our light shine.

Much of this book is addressed to, and about, non-indigenous Australians. However indigenous Australians are very much in mind. The mess we are in is mainly a Whitefella mess. As we Whitefellas are extracting ourselves from the mire we will become more capable of respectfully supporting indigenous Australians to deal with their long-standing and urgent needs.

We have many blessings in this great south land. We have ample wealth and resources. We are (mostly) well-educated and speak many languages of the world. We can live healthy and active lives. We can be a land of opportunity and fulfilment. We can give our grandchildren the greatest gift: a long future in a healthy country and a healthy world.

Uluru is in the middle of our broad continent. Noel Pearson calls Uluru the spiritual centre of Indigenous Australia. Uluru can be the heart of a reborn Australian nation, one that eschews fear and division and chooses to live generously and from the heart.

Desperately Seeking the Fair Go

2
Challenges

We need to look carefully at our situation and how we currently organise and manage ourselves, so we can be clear what works and what is not serving us well.

Our present leaders discourage us from being well-rounded human beings. They would like us rather to be like reptiles – calculating reptiles. They may or may not realise it, but that is what they are asking. They want us to be individualists who look after number one. We should transact, not share. We should compete, not work together. We should be efficient, not have fun. We should feel no empathy for those less fortunate. We should be fearful and ever-vigilant.

If you would like to know where this leads, then consider the health system in the United States. Photographer and writer Michael Katakis, in *A Thousand Shards of Glass*, tells of when his wife developed a brain tumour. This took them 'into the bowels of a brutal and savage corporate medical business'. His wife was not seen as a patient but as a consumer. They were advised to *hire an advocate* to help them through the Kafkaesque maze. 'The promises made prior to an illness quickly evaporate at the most desperate of times to reveal a labyrinth of conditions, ever-changing rules and small print that not only fails to soothe or elucidate but terrifies instead.' It emerged, too late and despite assurances of 'complete' coverage, that the doctors at her hospital did not accept payment from her particular insurance company. How could that even be? Katakis and his wife were deluged with incomprehensible forms, and endless phone calls from strangers demanding more and more money. What purported to be a caring system instead was incompetent, obfuscating, unjust and above all callous.

Katakis' greatest resentment is that the medical industry robbed him and his wife of much of their remaining time together. He reminds us that the riches we possess are not the things we own, our riches are each other.

The abomination experienced by Katakis was turbo-charged by the neoliberal ideology that has dominated the world since 1980. This is the ideology that prioritises free markets and selfish, competitive behaviour. The signs are that this neoliberal project has run its course. It has never matched the performance of the postwar social democratic regime, a fact rarely noticed or noted. It has undermined democracy, which is being supplanted by plutocracy, rule by wealth.

Rising political instability is one consequence. In Australia we have unstable governments, a plethora of small parties, increasing vindictiveness in politics and growing divisions within our society. Globally there are the Brexit vote and political instability in the UK, the growing divisions in the European Union, the depression in the European periphery, and the anger in the United States that has propelled Donald Trump to the presidency.

The political confusion is fertile ground for fear-mongering demagogues like Trump, wielding simplistic slogans and promising security to the frightened masses. We know where this leads, we've been there before.

One path to the essence of our problem is to acknowledge we are highly social beings. We crave to belong and we sicken if we are outcast. We are empathetic. We compete *and* cooperate, and we must balance the two for a healthy life. We have passions. We like to have fun. We can override primitive urges: we can choose to act from love rather be driven by fear.

Instead we are presumed to be like that most dismal of creatures, the economist who knows the price of everything and the value of nothing. Worse, corporations have been created in the image of that economist, the epitome of the calculating reptile.

The neoliberal ideology harbours remarkable ignorance and folly, quite apart from its misplaced faith in selfishness. The theory that is supposed to justify free markets is so abstract it is irrelevant to real economies. Neoliberal economists are ignorant of how modern banks actually work, or of how computers allow us to extend economic models far beyond the limitations of old ideas. There is a pretence that mountains of debt do not matter, and an inability to construct a simple balance sheet when purporting to do national accounting.

The so-called neoclassical school of economics, the promoter of free markets, has become entrenched and dominant globally. It has yet to acknowledge that our behaviour is far more complex and subtle than a reptile's. Neither does it acknowledge other basic deficiencies of its central theory. If the neoclassical theory were true there would, for example, be no market crashes.

In the wake of the Global Financial Crisis the neoclassicists sit around like stunned mullets, mouthing the same old formulas and failing to grasp the monumental failure that was the GFC. They are utterly unwilling to loosen their grip on power, even as they demonstrate day after day they are incapable of doing things any other way.

A rising chorus outside the economics establishment calls for new economic thinking, but even most of those who recognise the inadequacy of free markets seem unable to offer a coherent alternative.

Political establishments are now populated by people who have known little else, and who clearly have little conception of what a serious alternative might look like, so they fiddle at the edges. However the signs of breakdown are now so obvious that even some of the mainstream commentariat are acknowledging the system is in disarray and we need some more fundamental kind of change.

Senator Bernie Sanders in the US and Labour Party leader Jeremy Corbyn in the UK turned to social democracy, and that is a defensible move. Without the exogenous challenges of the 1970s, like the oil embargoes and the Vietnam war, social democracy could once again do better than neoliberalism.

A better prospect even than social democracy will emerge in this book. Markets should not be left unfettered, they need to be guided, as wild horses need to be tamed and guided if they are to be useful to us. By managing the incentives under which markets operate we can harness their power to deliver what we want, instead of inequality, chaos and environmental destruction.

GLOBALISATION HAS BEEN a key part of the neoliberal program. In the neoliberals' conception of us as reptiles, we are all pretty much the same, and so the same nostrums can be applied globally. The world comprises seven billion consumers, and national and cultural borders only get in the way of efficiency. Giant transnational corporations are now big enough to dominate most governments, and they are happy to use the neoliberal license to extract profit from us, according to their reptilian natures. It is no surprise that global cultural diversity is being trampled and crushed.

But of course we humans are sophisticated social beings and our extremely diverse cultures are an expression of that. Why should every culture have to submit to doctrinaire claims that we all have to make our living in the same way? We don't of course, and the ability of each society and each culture to manage its material basis as it wishes will be elucidated in this book.

Australia has its own unique history and culture, and we can manage our economy so it supports our own aspirations. We can also heed some lessons from our history. Although we gained nominal independence in 1901, the colonial mentality has continued to flow strongly through our leadership class. Donald Horne, in *The Lucky Country*, 1964, was scathing of the complacency of our leaders. However our leaders also tend strongly to subservience. Spurred on by the neoliberal doctrine, this mindset is handing control of many of our affairs to foreign corporations and countries. It seems the Coalition's only conception of promoting our economy is to invite foreigners to do it for us.

The colonial mindset of our leaders, political and cultural, aggravated a serious inferiority complex we carried through the 20th century. It was called the cultural cringe. We were always better than that, and our artists have moved through it and strut their stuff to the world. However our politicians and economists are still very much in its grip.

A look behind the clichés of our history shows that in fact we were a remarkable society through much of the 19th century and into the early 20th. We were highly pragmatic and innovative, and we weakened the bonds of class, demanded a fair go for everyone, and set about getting it. We are still remarkable, having incorporated, relatively peacefully, people from many other cultures. Aboriginal culture is resurgent despite having been crushed by occupation and marginalisation. We have the opportunity to forge a joint future with them, one that heeds and celebrates wisdom from the oldest living culture in the world.

Such is our potential, but the old political parties are still fighting the battles of last century, and they have prostituted themselves to big money. They ignore the huge challenges of economic instability, inequality, global warming and growing floods of refugees worldwide. They propagate caricatures of our history and character.

We can move on from those old, limiting habits and stories. To do so we will need to reclaim the means of our national conversation. The media have been allowed to fall into the hands of a few self-interested people who limit our view of the world. They routinely promote dissension and feed us distortions and outright lies, as we will explore later. We can require responsible behaviour as the price of the great privilege of broadcasting to large numbers of us. We can also explore ownership arrangements beyond those of big money or big government.

For several decades we have been deluged with the mantra of selfish individualism. At the same time, and paradoxically, we have been encouraged into dependence and helplessness by commercial marketing and right-wing demagogues. In spite of these pervasive influences, we Aussies still have not capitulated to selfishness and inequality. Voters' resistance to extreme right-wing policies accounts for much of the recent political instability.

There is not yet a coherent political movement in Australia comparable to those Sanders and Corbyn have inspired. If one is to emerge then progressives need to identify compelling messages based on a clear understanding of our situation. That will include highlighting our full potential and fostering our innate decency. We may then be able to mute our divisions, work together, get creative, resume the task of giving everyone a fair go, and constructively face the big new challenges bearing down on us.

NOTHING PHYSICAL CAN GROW indefinitely in a finite world. It will eventually fill up the world or use up all its resources. Yet growth of 'the economy' has become the over-riding measure of success in managing our society. Much of the thing called 'the economy' is physical in its nature, so it follows that the economy cannot grow indefinitely, in its present form. Our so-called leaders deal with this problem by averting their eyes. We carry on as if there is no tomorrow.

Indeed, it seems Western culture has been losing its belief in a future. It is a curious paradox that even as we are exhorted to be modern, to keep up with ever-changing technology, to rat-race into the future, so the future we admit into our perception has become more and more foreshortened.

Our movies, for example, portray futures in which the natural Earth does not feature. There is mean, violent and artificial life in a future New York City, or space fantasies like *Star Wars*, or post-apocalypse dystopias in which humanity has been decimated and lives a mean and precarious existence (*Mad Max*). Some movies even claim to portray the end of humanity (*Armageddon, 2012*).

We seem to have no expectation of a future on our home planet. We have no vision of what world we might pass to *the seventh generation unborn*, as the Iroquois people so poignantly framed it. We can barely even conceive of the world our children might inhabit. Do you know of a movie, a book, a play, anything in which an indefinite future on a healthy planet Earth is even implied, let alone depicted?

So we do not expect a long future. It is as though our industrial civilisation is intent on delivering a future that is nasty, brutish and short, echoing Hobbes' ignorant caricature of the pre-civilised past.

A startling recent survey by Melanie Randle and Richard Eckersley underscores this perception. It reveals a widespread and profound fatalism. Broadly similar results were found in four Western nations: the US, UK, Canada and Australia. Overall, a majority (54%) rated the risk of our way of life ending within the next 100 years at 50% or greater. A quarter (24%) rated the risk of humans being *wiped out* at 50% or greater. The authors point out that these responses probably do not reflect carefully considered assessments, they are more like lurking gut feelings that are rarely examined or articulated.

People report three main kinds of response to their gloomy perception of the situation. Almost 80% agreed 'we need to transform our worldview and way of life if we are to create a better future for the world'. About a half agreed that 'the world's future looks grim so we have to focus on looking after ourselves and those we love', and over a third that 'we are facing a final conflict between good and evil in the world'. The proportions add up to more than one, so evidently some people hold more than one of these attitudes.

(By the way, references and sources of information such as this study will be identified sufficiently throughout the text so they can be located in the Bibliography.)

THE UNDERLYING PROBLEM that feeds this pessimism has been widely understood for many decades now. Our civilisation is not sustainable. The 1972 book *Limits to Growth* by Donella Meadows and others was only one of the more prominent warnings. Its message was that human use of natural resources was approaching the planet's capacity, and if we did not soon moderate our use the human population could overshoot and crash sometime within the following century (i.e. before about 2070). The book was widely maligned by pro-growth advocates, especially economists. However the criticisms were mostly based on misunderstanding and misrepresentation. We are in fact still following its projections rather closely, including the increasing signs of a badly overstretched planet. That is made clear in *Limits to Growth, the 30-Year Update* published in 2004.

Many others have recognised the problem, and many have been working on ways to reduce our heavy footprint on the planet. These efforts have been very successful. However their effect is still marginal and the old destructive practices are still dominant. The clean and healthy practices exist, and some are very well developed, but this new way of thinking and doing is struggling to gain traction against the entrenched old ways.

So we pretty much know what to do. We just have to get on and do it. The problem is not that we don't know what to do, nor that it is horribly expensive, nor that it will wreck our economy or our civilisation. A big part of the problem is that the good news is being buried under the torrent of distraction, distortion and propaganda that passes for news, discussion and information in the current regime. So one of our immediate challenges is just to get the good news out.

However another challenge is to understand and counter the underlying mindset of the current paradigm. This mindset is older than neoliberalism. It can be traced back not just decades but centuries or millennia if you trace its essence, probably back to the beginning of agriculture. It is the idea that we can dominate and control the living world around us rather than living as part of it, as we did in earlier times.

It is the idea we can be *takers* rather than *makers*. Rana Foroohar, in her 2016 book *Makers and Takers*, details how pervasively finance and big business *take*, not just from the natural world but from the productive part of the economy. Naomi Klein, in her 2015 book *This Changes Everything*, calls the current manifestation of this mindset *extractivism*. It attempts to *extract* wealth from everyone else, and everything else, rather than relying on our own resourcefulness, and the innate productivity of the natural world, to *create* or *renew* wealth.

IT IS EASY TO FEEL OVERWHELMED by the problems we face: global warming, degradation of the land, terrorism, refugees and a remote political class. We are in danger and, under current leadership, we sit in stunned immobility.

Yet the means to deal with our problems are known. If we put our will to it, it is quite plausible that we can dramatically reduce the damage we inflict within a decade or two. We could do this without great physical discomfort or suffering. In fact it is likely we would soon realise our quality of life was improving, as we eliminated many activities that don't really serve us, and as we learnt to live in a less frenetic and more fulfilling way.

It turns out most of us already want to go this way. In a 2016 study by Richard Eckersley people were asked which of two possible futures came closer to what they expected, and which of the two they preferred.

Scenario one was 'a fast paced, internationally competitive society, with emphasis on the individual, wealth generation and enjoying the good life'. Three quarters *expected* a future along these lines.

Scenario two was 'a greener, more stable society, where the emphasis is on cooperation, community and family, more equal distribution of wealth, and greater economic self-sufficiency'. 93% *preferred* this scenario.

So we don't like the path we are on, even if it had a future. We already prefer a society that would have a much better chance of surviving.

Ours is far from the first society to be led astray by harmful ideas. The Easter Islanders became obsessed with building giant stone statues. The Mayan leaders competed to build grand monuments even as the foundation of their society crumbled. In his 2005 book *Collapse*, Jared Diamond recounted the stories of many societies that faced crises – some of those societies collapsed through pursuing misguided ideas, whereas others survived by adapting.

Those societies that did survive their crises did so because a few people were able to perceive and articulate the problem and to influence or gain leadership. Those societies' survival would also have required most people to be willing to change their ways. It is even possible for a society to change against the wishes of its leaders. The power of the old East German regime evaporated once the people realised how many of them wanted change.

At present more and more people are becoming aware not only that we need to change, but that the means to live sensibly and sustainably are largely available. Our power will emerge when we realise how many of us want to switch to a better path.

The Eckersley study says 93% of us want a cooperative, sustainable future. Perhaps all we need to do is wake up to how many of us there are, and the power of the present regime will evaporate, just as happened in East Germany.

OUR MAIN CHALLENGE, as individuals, is to let go of our old ways of seeing the world and to reach for the world we want. The main challenge for our society is to persuade those in power to change, or to remove from power those unwilling to change. That applies not just to politics but to media, business and other institutions. Thus the main challenges are not in the physical world, nor from other societies. Our main challenges are within ourselves, and in our relationships with each other.

A century ago our adaptability and initiative helped to make us the wealthiest people, *per capita*, in the world, and we were world leaders in progressive social and political innovation. About that time we dropped the ball, and since then we have often manifested a national inferiority complex. The potential we showed early last century is there for us to take up again.

There are also darker aspects to our history and character. Indeed the national myths tend to gloss over the best *and* the worst in us and to propagate a rather superficial view of ourselves. We can all benefit from facing up to our truths, and reconciling with our pasts.

3
A Nation Half-Formed

Historian Paul Ham reckons Australia is a stalled work in progress. We live in a half-formed nation, he says, writing in the *Griffith Review*. We have lost the sense of direction that motivated our society in the years around Federation in 1901. We pursued a free and fair society, we had 'a willingness to experiment, to pioneer and to champion new ideas, which manifested in votes for women, political representation for workers, schemes for universal health and education.' We innovated, we made things, we believed in ourselves.

Julianne Schultz says, in the same issue of *Griffith Review*, 'The world watches and wonders what went wrong: why did Australia fail to fully live up to its early promise as a global leader with an innovative, egalitarian social democracy? The time is right to pick up this mantle and re-imagine what it might look like in the 21st century'.

The First World War had a profound impact on Australia. We suffered casualties as heavy as any European nation. But as well as the pain and trauma of those casualties, we became bitterly divided over conscription, and even over being involved at all in a conflict that is now widely seen as a sordid battle over trade and empire. Misguided loyalty allowed authority to be reasserted over a fractious democratic populace. The myth was established that our nation was baptised in blood and only truly formed at Gallipoli. The adventurous spirit and great accomplishments around Federation were overshadowed in our national mythology.

It may not be too much to claim that since then Australia's leaders have often acted more as agents for a foreign power, a hangover from the role of the colonial governors. Donald Horne, in his 1964 book *The Lucky Country*, offered a scathing assessment of our elites. The famous quote from the last chapter is 'Australia is a lucky country run mainly by second-rate people who share its luck'. He found our leadership class, political, business and academic, to be complacent, boring and uninterested in ideas. They were oblivious to the great changes then building, and so could not position Australia to take good advantage of coming technological changes. Even Horne did not foresee the huge social changes and political dramas that would occur over the coming decade or so, and no-one foresaw the oil shocks to come. By the mid-1970s Australia was already a rather different place.

It was one of Horne's great frustrations that so many people missed, and still miss, the intended irony in his title. A common interpretation is that we are lucky because we live in one of the richest countries in the world with a great climate and great lifestyle, so let's all relax and have a good time. He meant, rather, that we were *living on our luck*.

Today we are more divided socially and much more fearful than we need to be. We were not so fearful a few decades ago. Our economic performance is rather less impressive than is claimed, thanks in part to mounting private debt. Already impinging on us are the effects of humanity's overuse of the planet's resources. So again we and our leaders seem to be living on luck, luck that may be running out very quickly.

To build a more secure future we need to understand how we came to our present condition, and whether we have always lived only on luck. We need to be aware of the ideas that have prevailed in our brief history, and how successful they might have been. In the process we can get some measure of our strengths and our quirks.

The need for historical perspective seems particularly pertinent at present. Anyone younger than about 40 will have little personal memory of what Australia was like before 1983, when the modern economic paradigm was launched in earnest. As well, mainstream economic commentary seems to be oblivious to anything before about 1980, apart from misleading myths about the Whitlam years.

For many of us Australian history comprises convicts, explorers and gold rushes. The 20th century hardly featured in what I learnt at school in the 1950s, except for a very skewed interpretation of the effects of the Gallipoli campaign. It is easy to suppose that gold made us rich, perhaps aided by abundant 'free' land, or as the song says, these days with heavy irony, 'boundless plains to share'. There is much more to us, good and bad, than these caricatures.

AUSTRALIA WAS ONE OF THE FIRST countries to accomplish what is now called an economic miracle. The early convict settlements were amazingly devoid of the knowledge and skills required to survive in a little-known environment. The first fleet included no farmers, no engineers, few practical men or women, not even any ploughs. Any convicts with skills were put to use. One of my convict ancestors was a carpenter, and he did relatively well as a result.

Even after several decades life was still basically subsistence, although the soils and climate were yielding some good crops. Then, between about 1830 and 1890, Australians went from near-subsistence to being the richest people *per capita* in the world. The change has been described in *The Australian Miracle* (2006) by Thomas Barlow and *Why Australia Prospered* (2013) by Ian McLean, though here I don't always follow their interpretations.

What drove this economic miracle? The wealth from gold certainly helped, but there was more to it than that. The influx of people during the gold rushes also helped. Pioneer pastoralists took possession of rich grazing lands, though the quality of pasture soon declined.

Despite common impressions that settler Australia was populated by ignorant felons and yokels, many of the settlers from mid-century on were quite skilled and educated. Many moved from gold mining to farming. The local breeding of Merino sheep was certainly important, as it greatly increased the productivity and robustness of the breed in the Australian climate. Then an important further innovation was the combination of sheep raising with wheat growing. This combination made small family farms much more viable. Family farming displaced some of the sheep grazing that had become established early. Cattle grazing was established later, especially in the north. Forests were harvested for great profit, if brutally.

Not only gold, but other minerals contributed. New mining technologies were imported and adapted, and thus extended the early gold mining boom to deeper extraction, and extraction from more difficult kinds of rock. This was a key factor according to Thomas Barlow, as it provided a sustained contribution to prosperity rather than the transient flush that typifies many gold rushes.

Government policies also helped to capture longer-term benefits. The colonial governments were alert to the need for the new immigrants to stay on after their stint in the gold fields. To encourage them, governments converted lease-hold grazing lands into smaller lots more suitable for farming. This succeeded to a sufficient extent that many did stay, and many of those established themselves as farmers, though not without a lot of trial, error and tribulation. This not only added to the economic base of the country, but had significant social and political consequences as well.

According to Barlow, a key factor in building Australia's prosperity was the ability of people to import new technologies and make innovative adaptations to local conditions. Because much of the population had been born overseas, people were well-connected with the rest of the world and well aware of new developments. Australia's 'tyranny of distance' might have delayed the flow of information by a few months or years, but it did not stop it. Although some new technologies were developed in Australia, generally more important was the practical willingness and ability to adapt imported technologies.

The practicality was of an enlightened kind. Knowledge and learning were not disdained as ivory-tower activities, but valued as sources of useful ideas. This was manifest in vigorous memberships of scientific societies and mechanics institutes, in regular reporting of scientific developments in the major newspapers, and even in sponsorship of science and scientific advice by state governments.

Some manufacturing and processing industries also became established, despite the hindrance of small and scattered markets. Butter factories proliferated with the importation of efficient cream separators, and refrigeration later enabled exports of butter. Refrigeration and canning technologies also promoted meat exports.

Agricultural machinery became one of the largest sectors, with not only local manufacture but a great deal of local innovation. Particularly important were the locally-developed mechanical grain stripper, which may have been one of the first in the world, and later the combine harvester, a combination of stripper and mobile thresher. There were as many as 3000 factories of diverse kinds operating in 1891. On the other hand heavy industry, such as locomotive manufacture, was too disadvantaged to become established.

Barlow concludes that the greatest benefits from imported knowledge and technologies came from boosting the productivity of primary industries, rather than from promoting local secondary industries. Thus steam power was widely adapted in the latter half of the 19th century, and electrification proceeded apace in the closing decades, as did railway and telegraph construction. People were very receptive to new technologies, and typewriters, telephones, pocket watches, all the latest technological gizmos, were rapidly adopted.

The railways and many mechanical innovations were crucial to the profitable expansion of agriculture into exporting. Wool is relatively imperishable and so could be grown far from ports and markets and survive slow transportation by bullock dray. On the other hand wheat and, especially, meat are perishable and required the efficiency of rail transport to become viable as exports. Even so, wheat and meat were limited to being relatively close to ports, whereas wool production spread far into the interior.

Thus both mining and agriculture, the 19th century staples, benefited greatly from technological adaptation and innovation. Australian agriculture was among the most efficient in the world by late in the century. One result of this was that many people were displaced into the cities. By the end of the century Australia was already a highly urbanised society.

It seems then that the Australian miracle was driven by a synergy among many factors. The ready availability of pastures and gold certainly created a good beginning, but these were parlayed into greater wealth and a diverse society by the lively practicality and innovation of the rapidly growing population, and by some judicious government decisions. Government also played an explicit economic role, notably by building the railways.

Putting this another way, an industrial ecosystem grew up in 19th century Australia. In an ecosystem there is a great deal of mutual dependence, although there may be keystone species without which the system would degrade. This is a more useful perspective, because it gets us away from trying to find one or two 'causes' and allows us to see the growth of a more complex system in which all components play a role. The accomplishment then was not just a creation of industries, primary and secondary, it was the cultivation of the linkages that build an ecosystem. The ecosystem perspective is still sadly lacking in our leadership, which depends on tired old cause-and-effect clichés.

There was some element of luck. Australia was fortunate to have ready markets for its products during this period. Britain was the main market, but internationally conditions were conducive to the trade of primary products for technology and value-added products. The fact that Britain was the technological leader of the time also helped.

It is also true there was a great deal of trial and error, failure and privation, particularly among the poorer people. There were still great disparities of wealth and privilege. The sufferings of the poor were greatly aggravated by a savage depression and drought in the 1890s. Henry Lawson's stories of battlers do have a real basis.

ANOTHER REMARKABLE FEATURE of the transformation of Australia through the 19th century was that it became, for its time, one of the most egalitarian and democratic societies in the world.

Many of the poorer settlers, both convict and free, were desperate to establish their own lives and to escape the strictures and oppression of class-based English society. This was a double edged sword. On the one hand they slaved and suffered on their own behalf to get established. On the other hand they were ignorant of, and careless of, the people they were displacing and the land they were transforming.

In any case many of them were able to succeed in establishing independent livelihoods. The early gold mining, in alluvium, was more suited to small operators than to big companies, although only a minority of them gained significant wealth. Wheat and sheep farming, once established, was also better suited to small-scale family farming, in contrast to sheep grazing which was controlled mainly by the big land holders.

There were also very strong egalitarian sentiments among wage earners, must notably shearers and dock workers. There were major strikes by both shearers and dock workers in the early 1890s. The early strikes resulted in bitter defeats. The workers responded by forming labour unions, and ultimately the Labor Party.

This account may seem at times to be a paean to the Labor Party. However it is not so partisan. Rather it is a paean to anyone who championed the interests of ordinary people over the interests of privilege. Sometimes Labor did that, at other times it did not, including the present day. Nor is this a paean to socialism, as will become clear.

Parliaments had been established in the main colonies around 1850 and voting was later extended to all adult men. The goldfield rebellion of the Eureka Stockade in the 1850s gave an important impetus to these developments. The wealthy establishments that had been running the colonies realised they must concede some power to maintain order, according to Nick Dyrenfurth and Frank Bongiorno. By late in the century women were also gaining the vote in most colonies.

There was a major political struggle over land that gathered pace in the 1870s. Much of the land was leased by large land holders. Some had gained their spreads through patronage whereas others had simply moved onto large areas of land. Such was the scale of the land rush in mid-century that it was not challenged by overstretched authorities. Ultimately the extra-legal occupations were rubber stamped, to the extent that the occupiers were granted leases. These were the so-called squatters.

As the population grew, there was a growing demand for small farming properties. The squatters lobbied desperately to have their leasehold converted to freehold. Their first attempt fell short, as an Act in 1847 did not gain them freehold. Ultimately much of the leasehold was withdrawn and opened to selection for small farming. Most of the squatters still retained quite large properties, though smaller than the fiefdoms they had earlier claimed.

McLean notes that the British Government may have been an important restraint on the power of the squatters in mid-century, before the power of the small-holder and wage-earner constituencies developed. Had the squatters had a freer hand to dominate the governors and early parliaments, in proportion to their economic dominance, they might have entrenched the institutions of a landed gentry intent on self-preservation. Thus cheap labour supporting grazing fiefdoms might have been favoured over developing small-holder production and manufacturing, and Australia might have developed more like Argentina, a poorer agrarian society dominated by a very small wealthy elite.

The actual outcome, of more distributed ownership of land, was a significant victory for ordinary people, the selectors, over the would-be landed gentry, the squatters. It was a measure of the growing egalitarian temper of the colonies, and it strongly reinforced it, establishing a large constituency of ordinary people making their own living by one means or another.

Initially the political expression of this growing democratic impulse was through the generally middle class politicians of the liberal Protectionist Party. They believed that every man should be master of his own destiny. They opposed the domination of wealthy conservatives, but their concern was focused more on their own kind than on the poor. The growing numbers of small land holders and wage earners were impatient with the meagre concessions they were granted. Nick Dyrenfurth described in 2011 how Labor Parties were formed in several states to challenge the Conservative dominance. They gained significant representation in colonial parliaments, and even briefly formed government in Queensland, the first labour government in the world.

With Federation in 1901 Labor mounted a more coherent national campaign than did the other parties. To almost everyone's surprise Labor won nearly a quarter of the seats in the new Federal Parliament. The resulting three-way split in power between Labor, Protectionists and Free Traders was famously characterised by Alfred Deakin as three cricket teams (three 'elevens') trying to play in the same match. For the next decade the three parties jostled, forming uneasy alliances and minority governments. Even so, significant progress was made in building national institutions. Women were granted the federal vote in 1902, and industrial arbitration was instituted.

Labor's electoral strength grew steadily until in 1910 they achieved a stunning victory under the leadership of Andrew Fisher. They gained majorities in *both* federal Houses of Parliament, the first time a majority had been achieved in either house. Peter Bastian has described the extensive accomplishments of this government between 1910 and 1913. It established funding arrangements between the Federal and State governments, created a national currency, uniform postal rates and Australia's largest bank. It built the East-West rail link, established the national capital, developed coastal lighthouses and laid foundations for national library and art collections. A large proportion of the nation's armed forces and military training academies owe their existence to this government. It extended the industrial relations system, introduced maternity allowances and reformed the voting system. Not all of these policies were exclusive to Labor, but Fisher was the first to achieve majority government, and he pursued nation building with great vigour.

The Labor Party early in the 20th century was not particularly ideological. Although there were socialists in the party, Labor was never driven by ideology. Its approach was to work pragmatically to create a fair, fully employed and prosperous society. It was socially progressive in many respects. On the other hand it strongly promoted the White Australia policy. It characterised the Conservative opposition as the fat man, and used his image very effectively in political cartooning. This might now be called populism, and was important in reaching beyond the industrial unions of the city to small businessmen and the small land holders of the country, who were quite mistrustful of the city unions. Although there was some Republican sentiment, most people saw themselves as part of the British Empire.

Without romanticising this period of Australian history, it is still fair to describe it as remarkable for its time. On the negative side, it was strongly racist, Aborigines were treated with brutal contempt, women were still clearly subordinate even though they gained the vote, social mores were still rather moralistic and repressive, and people were very ready to go to war in the imperialist cause, as was soon to be demonstrated. On the positive side, ordinary people struggled for and attained political power, wealth was shared more equally through society, and women had more rights than anywhere else except New Zealand. A vigorous local culture was developing, exemplified not only by Henry Lawson and Banjo Paterson, but by artists and a local movie industry that was perhaps the most prolific in the world.

Andrew Fisher deserves greater recognition as an outstanding prime minister than he is usually given. Peter Bastian describes him as an underestimated man. Fisher's rather stolid character was somewhat overshadowed by the greater rhetorical flair of Edmund Barton and Alfred Deakin. He rose from very modest origins, having begun his working life as a pit boy in the Scottish coal mines. His very steady, honest and open character was an important factor in his success. He is described by some as uninspiring, but this does not seem to square with his stunning victory in 1910. He had a clear and practical vision for the new nation and worked conscientiously and effectively to bring it about. He held together a parliamentary Labor Party still trying to find its feet and define its direction, and which contained some very volatile personalities.

Andrew Fisher, three times Prime Minister

Labor interests had had very little input during the process of Federation, and the vested interests of the individual colonies made sure the

Commonwealth Government would not be too strong relative to the states. Fisher considered that the Commonwealth Government ought to have more powers. He campaigned vigorously to amend the Constitution, against considerable opposition. As a result Labor fell just short of retaining power in the 1913 election. However within a year instability among the other parties allowed Labor to regain power. By this time Fisher's immense efforts had taken a toll on his health, and he resigned in 1915 to become ambassador to Britain. The stresses of World War I were by then triggering great changes within Australia.

IT IS INSTRUCTIVE TO COMPARE this history with developments in the United States over the same period, recounted in Sam Pizzigati's *The Rich Don't Always Win*. The late 19th century saw the rise of great industrial empires based on railways, steel and other industries. The great wealth generated by these industries gave the industrial barons great power which they used to repress wages. Industrial workers in the cities were impoverished and largely powerless.

In the 1890s small farmers rebelled against banks and grain dealers who were keeping them impoverished. This rebellion grew into a political movement that became known as the Prairie Populists. It gained considerable political power and got a block of representatives elected to Congress. However the movement lost momentum and direction, and accepted a deal which led to it being absorbed into the Democratic Party.

The decades around 1900 are known in the US as the Progressive Era, but it never compared with the progressivism in Australia at the same time. It is true there were some significant restraints imposed on the untrammelled power of the industrial barons, but the common people gained much less than their cousins in Australia. There were no railway barons in Australia, because the railways were built by governments. The railroad barons in America were called robber barons for a reason, as gaining rights of way was a highly corrupt process that fed the formation of the plutocratic system.

It was not until the 1930s that poor people in the United States began to gain more political power, during the Roosevelt years. Although Roosevelt was better than the alternative, he was not a natural champion of poor people. He had to be pushed into seriously shifting wealth and power by the atrocious behaviour of the very rich, by the people acting collectively, and by the fear that together these could lead to communism.

During the time in which Australia was one of the most democratic and egalitarian countries in the world, conditions in the United States were almost feudal. There never has been a party for the ordinary people, and the United States has never had an egalitarian tradition like Australia's, despite the fine rhetoric of its upper- and middle-class Founding Fathers.

THE FIRST WORLD WAR caused serious divisions within Australia and within the Labor Party. There was great tension between loyalty to the Empire and the view that it was a war between capitalists. It was pointed out with bitterness that young men went to war and came back maimed, whereas 'money' went to war and came back fatter. It was true that many businesses profited greatly from the war effort.

On top of these divisive issues, Labor had to contend with volatile personalities, once the steady Fisher had departed. Both Billy Hughes and King O'Malley were impetuous men. Hughes became Labor leader after Fisher, and against the wishes of many of his colleagues began to campaign vigorously for conscription. Two conscription referenda were held and they bitterly divided the country, though both were narrowly lost. In the heat of these conflicts, Hughes quit the Labor Party and formed a government with conservatives.

The war inflicted great tribulation on Australia. Australian casualties were heavy, even compared with many European countries. As well, Australia ran up large debts to pay for the war effort, debts that burdened Australia for decades and became a major issue during the Depression. Whereas Britain forgave the debts of other allies, Australia's debts were never forgiven.

The remarkable energy, optimism and social progressivism of the early Australian Federation was dealt a body blow by the First World War. On top of the personal and national tribulations there was a shift in political power. Arguably, by triggering people's loyalty to the Empire, the war allowed the power of authority to be reasserted over the emergent democratic and egalitarian pushes of the preceding decades. Egalitarianism did not disappear, but it rarely regained the strength it had during Fisher's terms in office. Egalitarianism was a continuing positive influence, but has struggled ever since against a generally conservative press, conservative financial interests and some selective writing or rewriting of history.

One example of selective writing is the myth that Australia only really became a unified nation because of the disastrous 1915 Gallipoli campaign. No doubt the adversity drew the colonies closer together in some respects, but it also created or exacerbated great social divisions around conscription and more broadly around the conduct of Australia's war effort, including whether Australia should be involved at all. As well, soldiers and families were traumatised by the horror, and that trauma will have passed down the generations, reinforced by later wars and contributing a significantly fractious component to our society.

Australia was already a vigorous nation in 1913, with an established awareness of its unique identity. We don't need to glorify a disastrous war to claim the early Federation was a vital and distinctive nation. We didn't need the approval of the rest of the world. We didn't wait until someone else had shown it could be done. We did not have an inferiority complex. We had the confidence to lead the world.

A**FTER FISHER'S TIME** there was not to be an effective national champion of the interests of all the people for many decades, and then only for brief periods. The notable pre-Whitlam figures are Jack Lang and Ben Chifley. Because of the conservative dominance in politics and media, their contributions tend to be under-rated, like Fisher's. Robert Menzies was very different from the modern Liberal Party, and there was more to Gough Whitlam than the modern caricature, so they also deserve some brief review.

Jack Lang is notable for being one of the few leaders ever who understood banks and finance enough to challenge their power. His story has echoes in the subjection and humiliation of modern Greece. Lang was twice Premier of New South Wales, 1925-27 and 1930-32. In his first term Lang promoted social welfare and infrastructure, and later oversaw the building of the Sydney Harbour Bridge, seeing it as an important morale booster as well as an essential investment, despite the difficulties of the Depression.

By Lang's second term, the Depression was weighing heavily. Lang understood that much of the debt burdening Australia was a hangover from Australia's support for Britain in the War, and the debt was to London bond holders. He also understood that the deflation that occurred during the Depression magnified the debt, by reducing the purchasing power of Australia's money. With high unemployment and many people suffering great hardship, Lang reasoned that the bondholders could wait while his state helped its desperate citizens. He therefore sought to defer payments due on the debt. For his trouble Lang was pilloried by the banks, the Commonwealth Government and the entire Establishment. His name is vilified to this day. A more informed, balanced and nuanced account of events is given by Gerald Stone in his book *1932: a Hell of a Year*, and Lang's autobiography records his own views.

Contrary to popular myth, New South Wales Governor Sir Phillip Game did not immediately dismiss Lang for proposing to defer debt payments, but allowed Lang to battle his opponents for over a year, so long as all formalities were observed, and even though Lang indulged in some legal but highly unconventional tactics. Indeed the men had a respectful formal relationship. Game can be given credit for resisting the Sydney establishment's baying for Lang's blood, and refusing to dismiss an elected government without clear legal reason. Eventually Lang, perhaps exhausted by incessant tactical battles and tumult, refused to yield on a technically illegal move, and Game did dismiss him.

The policies imposed on Australia during the Depression were what we now call austerity: cut public services so the government can pay back its debts. It was self-defeating then and it is self-defeating now. When the government cuts spending, the economy is depressed further and government revenue falls further. This has been demonstrated again in the depressed economies of the European periphery, most notably in Greece. In fact there are some striking parallels between Greece now and Australia in the Great Depression, including leaders who abandon their left-wing party and join conservative forces. In Australia Joe Lyons abandoned Federal Labor in 1931, and in Greece Alexis Tsipras split his Syriza Party.

Also at issue is whether debt is excessive (in modern Australia it is not) and whether the burden of debt should fall heavily on the poor, who usually have little role in creating it, or whether the burden should be shared or borne by the rich, who generally create the debt.

Labor regained national government in 1941 under John Curtin. Curtin was necessarily focused on the exigencies of the Second World War, and he died before the war ended. He and his successor, Ben Chifley, had ambitious plans for the postwar development of Australia, many of which Chifley carried through. These included the Snowy Mountains Scheme, a national university, a new airline (Trans-Australia Airlines), a local car industry and a major immigration program. He also extended welfare state benefits, including sickness and unemployment benefits, and financially supported health, education and housing improvements.

Chifley introduced Keynesian economic management, a central part of which is for the government to spend during recessions and tax during booms. This is the opposite of austerity. It is meant to smooth out the ups and downs rather than exacerbating them. Chifley also believed private banks had excessive power and tried to nationalise them. He is therefore also among those few leaders, who include Jack Lang and Abraham Lincoln, with a good understanding of the strategic power that banks hold over a society. Naturally his ambitions were vociferously opposed by the banks and the conservative establishment. Unfortunately he had also allowed some wartime rationing to continue well beyond the war and he rather harshly suppressed a coal strike he believed was fomented by Communists to discredit Labor. He lost power to Robert Menzies in the election of 1949.

MENZIES NEEDS SOME QUALIFIED notice here because, compared to the mean-spirited lot who have taken over the Liberal Party he founded, he was relatively benign. However the 'statesman' tag that some anoint him with is certainly debatable. He had the good fortune to serve when economies were booming globally, and to inherit a reasonably well-structured economy. As well, he survived for so long as Prime Minister through deceit and some large doses of dumb luck.

It was Donald Horne's opinion that Menzies was a cunning and ruthless politician but he didn't have much idea what to do once he was in power. He left much of the running of the country to civil servants, and focussed on removing potential rivals within the party, and on outsmarting the Opposition. He let country drift and many opportunities slip by.

Menzies continued many of his Labor predecessors' policies, including the immigration program, the Snowy mountains scheme, and the expansion of the university system. In stark contrast to the received wisdom of the present day, he ran up government debt to pay for such projects, regarding them as a sensible investment. He also allowed the Government, socialist-style, to continue owning two airlines, a bank, the postal and telephone systems, and much infrastructure. He not only tolerated strong unions prone to frequent strike action but reportedly believed in legislative protection for collective bargaining.

Menzies survived 16 years and seven elections, but that endurance was far from a foregone conclusion. A Russian spy defected in 1954 and claimed there was a Communist spy in the Opposition Leader's office, thus feeding the anti-Communist paranoia of the time. Menzies set up an inquiry and called an election. The inquiry held hearings before the election, thus maximising sensational headlines, but did not report until well after the election. It found there was little substance to the sensational allegations. Menzies had been facing defeat, but the confected hysteria got him across the line, a feat notably repeated by John Howard in 2001.

The following year the Labor Party split. A Catholic and strongly anti-Communist faction formed the Democratic Labour Party, which thereafter supported the Conservative side of politics. As a result Menzies had an easier ride through several more elections. Even so, he barely won the 1961 election, by only one seat and a handful of votes, and against Opposition Leader Arthur Calwell, whose grating voice and old-fashioned views and manner could not be considered very attractive. Menzies nearly lost because there was a recession, and unemployment had risen to nearly 3%. He rebuilt his standing by taking over a number of Labor policies. After Menzies' retirement in 1966, the Liberal Party stumbled on under a succession of leaders until they were ousted by Labor under Gough Whitlam in 1972.

By today's standards Menzies would be considered leftist. A more objective assessment is that he presided over a period of mild democratic socialism, though his sympathies were certainly with the big end of town. Of course Menzies did not nationalise the banks, as Chifley had proposed, but he continued the Keynesian approach to economic management and thus presided over considerable 'intervention' in the economy, as was the fashion in the postwar decades. As just noted he left many enterprises in Government ownership and tolerated unions. According to today's received wisdom those policies should have ruined the economy.

The postwar period until the 1970s is noteworthy, instead, because it was the most economically successful period in the 20th Century, in all developed economies. Not only did the economy grow rapidly, but the wealth was shared more equally. The middle and working classes prospered as never before or since. This was no accident: Government policies, under pressure from the people, made it so. For example, high incomes were taxed quite heavily and the financial system was heavily regulated by today's standards, so it could not become as dominant, feral and parasitic as it is today.

ALTHOUGH AUSTRALIA was economically successful in the postwar decades, socially and culturally it was insecure and deferential to other countries, particularly Britain and later the US. These were my growing-up years, and I clearly recall the way everything was measured against current fashions in London. Any local accomplishment was not locally acknowledged until it had been anointed in London. Visiting 'overseas experts' were automatically presumed to be superior to locals. Reviews of shows in London's West End (whatever that was) were reverentially reproduced in our newspapers, as though we would all take a slow ship to England to see them ourselves. No doubt it was important for those on the cocktail circuit to have read the reviews.

In the early decades of the 20th century Australia had one of the most productive movie industries in the world, part of a vigorous local culture. The world's first full-length feature film, *The Story of the Kelly Gang*, was filmed in Australia in 1906. This thriving industry was killed off by depression, war and American distributors, who bought out local distributors and refused to distribute local movies (with the compliance of local politicians). An early demonstration of the free market at work.

I remember what a revelation it was for me to see movies like *Breaker Morant* and *The Chant of Jimmy Blacksmith* in the early 1980s (I was living in the US at the time). OMG, quality movies made in Australia! There, on the big screen, people who talked like me, places I knew, beautiful eucalyptus forest, cockatoos! Almost unheard of after a diet totally dominated by British and American movies. A mere handful of local movies was made between the 1940s and the 1970s, and often then with American stars.

Other countries had their own culture reflected on the big screen. We could watch only foreign cultures, as though we didn't really exist. In a push to revive Australian film, Philip Adams had written in 1969 'It is time to see our own landscapes, hear our own voices and dream our own dreams.'

The third computer in the world was built in Australia, at Sydney University. Australia was the fourth nation in the world to launch a satellite. Yet Bob Menzies convened a committee of overseas experts to advise on Australia's economic role in the world. They patted us on the head and told us just to get on with supplying raw materials, from mine and farm, and leave the sophisticated stuff to other countries. Righto, said Pig-iron Bob.

The term *the cultural cringe* was coined in 1950 by A. A. Phillips and it aptly captures the national inferiority complex we had acquired by mid-20th century. Other influences may have been at work, but the combined effects of the 1960s counter-cultural rebellion and the Whitlam Government were proximate triggers for breaking through those stultifying times. Now Australian arts of all kinds strut their stuff around the world. The cultural cringe is no more.

Except that in politics and economic policy we still act like colonials. We are afraid to step out and do our own thing, or anxious to know if the rest of the world has noticed us if we have done something a little bit daring. We kowtow to those bigger and richer. Our scientists and local experts are still shoved aside in the stampede to hang on the words of any 'distinguished' overseas visitor. We still have a lot of growing up to do. We'd have less to do if more of the spirit of the early Federation period had survived.

GOUGH WHITLAM is widely acknowledged to have been a visionary. He modernised the Labor Party and then set about waking the country from the long somnolence of the Menzies era. He accomplished a great deal in his tumultuous three years in office, though he still had much to do when he was dismissed. Unlike Lang's, Whitlam's dismissal was without clear legal basis. This time the howling conservative mob got its way.

The Whitlam Government is commonly charged with being economically incompetent, but this claim does not withstand scrutiny. It minimises the oil shock imposed by the OPEC oil cartel, which quadrupled oil prices and dramatically affected all Western economies. There was also a much-overlooked international credit bubble, documented by economist Steve Keen. Most significantly, the Australian economy outperformed most other developed economies 1973-75, according to Ian Verrender. The US and UK experienced long and painful recessions, whereas Australia had none.

Despite the hysterical opposition from conservatives and the press, Whitlam's Government was more about socially liberal reforms than socialist economic policy. His accomplishments, detailed by the Whitlam Institute, span health care and social security, women's interests and social reforms, the environment, culture and heritage, democracy, law, human rights, foreign affairs, defence and more.

Younger Australians might not be aware of how many features of modern Australia were established in the brief Whitlam years, though many have been eroded since. Among his most notable legacies are the creation of Medibank, now Medicare, increased school funding and the abolition of university fees, equal pay for women, no-fault divorce, the Racial Discrimination Act, abolition of the White Australia Policy, recognition of China, protection of the Great Barrier Reef, ratification of the World Heritage Convention, funding for arts, television and film (which triggered the renaissance in film), the National Gallery of Australia, extended sewerage to outer suburbs, *Advance Australia Fair* (replacing *God Save the Queen*) and the Australian Honours system. He returned traditional land to Aborigines and promoted their recognition and welfare, including the Land Rights Act.

Like Scullin and Curtin, Whitlam governed in difficult times, and his immense accomplishments are the more remarkable because of the challenges he faced. Of course it is regrettable that his program was so rudely truncated. Although many of his changes have been rolled back over succeeding decades, it was widely recognised after his death in 2014 that he had changed Australia permanently and for the better. He was certainly concerned for the welfare of all Australians, not just the rich.

Malcolm Fraser ousted Whitlam by the highly dubious tactic of blocking 'supply' (the Government's budget bills) in the Senate, an unprecedented tactic Menzies explicitly deplored. Then, echoing Menzies, Fraser continued many of Whitlam's policies. Ironically this included the centrepiece of the Whitlam Government's economic policy, its last budget. Fraser had little of Whitlam's vision. He was conservative and favoured big business, yet compared with later governments he did not do great harm to the interests of ordinary people. On the other hand he blocked the further improvements that Whitlam surely would have delivered.

Fraser had quite liberal social views, and perhaps their most significant expression was his decision to welcome political refugees from Vietnam, some of whom arrived on leaky boats seeking asylum following the collapse of the South Vietnamese regime. His decision was based not only on a general duty of care, but on his recognition of Australia's responsibility as a combatant in the Vietnam War.

SO OUR HISTORY until the 1980s is that we were at first remarkably innovative, co-operative, successful and self-confident, but we lost our way after the First World War. We became timid and subservient. We allowed ourselves to be more divided against each other. Our self-confidence abandoned us and we cringed before the world.

The reason mateship and egalitarianism have such a strong place in our mythology is that we were, not so long ago, one of the most egalitarian societies in the world. We helped each other, we cooperated. Our history also reveals we Australians can be tenacious, practical, innovative and adaptable. All of these qualities fed into the 19th century economic miracle that made Australia one of the wealthiest countries *per capita* in the world. Not only have we been wealthy, but the wealth became relatively widely shared, particularly after World War II.

Donald Horne's scathing portrayal of our country's leadership as conservative, backward-looking, self-centred, and fearful of change and of the future, has had more than a grain of truth for much of the 20th century and into the 21st. Conservative leaders typically serve the interests of the wealthy, and after the democratic push lost steam in the First World War they reverted to serving foreign money, mostly British.

However we, the Australian people, have also responded to more adventurous leadership, and to the dictates of necessity when the future forced itself upon us. At our best, we were willing to lead the world. There were still flashes of independence and leadership through the 20th century. The Chifley Government developed an Australian (i.e. not British) foreign policy. Labor leader Dr H.V. Evatt played a major role in the formation of the

United Nations. The Keating Labor Government established the *Canberra Commission on the Elimination of Nuclear Weapons*, with high-level international membership, to seek the total elimination of nuclear weapons.

It is sometimes claimed Australians are innately conservative. However our history shows we can be very adaptable, which is the opposite of conservative. We also became socially quite liberal, especially during the years roughly from 1960 to 1990. So there is good reason for believing we are progressive when our better angels are given half a chance.

Whitlam may have tested our tolerance for change, but the antics of recent governments ought to make us less judgemental of Whitlam's ministers, none of whom had any experience in power, and all of whom were perhaps overanxious to move on from the stultifying Menzies era. They were trying to get things done, they did get a great many things done, and the economic performance was much better than is reputed. In any case they were rather more successful than a hysterical conservative establishment claimed at the time.

The reasons Australia has been politically conservative for much of the 20th century are arguably more to do with a consistently right-wing press and a strongly entrenched conservative establishment. It hasn't helped that progressive forces in our society struggle to organise consistently to gain and retain political power. The Labor Party suffered three disastrous splits, two while in power, when Billy Hughes and Joe Lyons quit and joined the conservatives, and the third in 1954 while out of power.

Major political parties are always uneasy alliances of diverse groups. They need a clear and strong vision and narrative to hold themselves together. Progressives have allowed themselves to be divided by various issues, including the loyalties of Empire, conservative scare mongering and egotistical, divisive or impulsive leaders.

Our more recent history shows that we're still very adaptable, as our society has been subjected to quite radical change of a different kind. Modern Australians are more educated and cosmopolitan than one hundred years ago and, in the absence of systematic scare campaigns, are comfortable with our ethnic diversity and willing to face the big challenges of the future.

Of course the record of tolerance has been quite patchy. The White Australia policy was originally in part a reasonable reaction to the importation of dark-skinned islanders as cheap indentured labour in the cane fields, and also reflected a not-implausible fear that Australia's small and isolated white population could be overwhelmed by nearby Asians. However it also reflected the common view in the British Empire that Whites were superior to all other races and the British were the best of the Whites. This attitude was sharpened by the conflict with Aborigines, who were not uncommonly regarded as subhuman and treated with contempt and cruelty.

Despite this unpromising history, Australia in the 1980s was a remarkably diverse and tolerant society, though still with notable blind spots. It is tragic that fears of difference have been fanned and exploited for profit and power, often based on overt lies about those targeted, such as that asylum seekers are illegal and that most Moslems promote violence. Recent policies promoting financial and employment insecurity also created conditions conducive to greater intolerance.

Even so, compassion and tolerance still run strongly through our society, co-existing with the cultivated upsurge of xenophobia and racism. We often pull together, through disasters and trying times. We can even rally for foreigners, as our response to the 2004 Indian Ocean tsunami demonstrated.

Our mixture of xenophobia and compassion may seem paradoxical, but it is not useful to try to label a person or a society simply as being racist or not racist. We're all capable of racist behaviour if our fear of some group is triggered, and if we allow that fear to drive us. We're also capable of overcoming such a fear and reaching out to people. Thus it is more accurate to speak about racist behaviour than racist people. This means racism is not a static, ingrained thing, it can change if we choose to change it.

There is ample reason in our history to believe Australia can again change direction and resume its trend to being a more tolerant, adaptable and equitable society, with better prospects of surviving and thriving as dramatic global political and environmental changes loom. What we require is to break out of the present passivity and negativity, and to develop the organisation and leadership to take us in the new direction. We need to believe again in ourselves, without worrying what the rest of the world thinks.

We also need to understand how far we have been dragged in the wrong direction over the past few decades.

4

The Reign of the Radical Right

We left our national story at the end of Malcolm Fraser's prime ministership. A distinct era followed, an era in which the radical prescriptions of neoliberalism were aggressively and progressively imposed, though never with the full endorsement of the Australian people. The neoliberal era, still persisting, changed the character of Australia's economy, politics and society.

Although the full force of the changes that began in Australia in 1983 was not evident at the time, it was certainly widely perceived that there was a sharp break with the approaches that had prevailed since Federation. Since 1983 a series of choices was made that moved us progressively further away from the fair, open, democratic society to which we used to aspire. Different choices could have been made. We might be a less fearful and divided society if they had.

The change of direction was not unique to Australia. It was most pronounced in the Anglophone countries but also affected many European countries and impinged harshly on South American and other Third World countries. The change was widespread because the US and Britain dominated international finance, and because it was promoted internationally by well resourced intellectuals. Economists Friedrich Hayek in Europe and Milton Friedman in the US were among the most prominent developers of the emergent neoliberal ideology.

The super rich had fared relatively poorly through the Great Depression and World War II, so that in the postwar years their share of wealth had dropped considerably, and in the US they were subjected to income taxes as high as 90%. They were still very wealthy but had lost significant power. Complementing their reduced circumstance, which most of us would have been happy enough to endure, a postwar boom, unprecedented before or since, spread wealth within the developed countries to a degree also unprecedented. The reduced inequality and the boom were not unconnected.

The rich and powerful of course always defend their position. To lose power and influence to the common ruck apparently is a violation of the natural order, to be remedied at the first opportunity. For nearly three decades they worked behind the scenes, until at last the postwar boom faltered.

The economic disruptions due to the Vietnam War and oil shocks in the 1970s were deftly exploited by followers of the neoliberal ideology. They misrepresented the nature of the economic problems. For example they blamed inflation mainly on excessive wage claims while ignoring excessive spending on the Vietnam War combined with a real rise in the price of oil, which flowed through to a real rise in the cost of most other things. They made grandiose claims that their policies would fix everything, even though similar policies had precipitated and prolonged the Great Depression. It was obvious at the time that reduced government involvement in the economy would favour big business and the rich at the expense of ordinary people.

There had been some moves to 'open' the Australian economy before 1980. A significant one was a 25% reduction of tariffs by Whitlam in 1973, which does not quite fit the caricature of socialist buffoon and satan. However the rise of neoliberalism was resisted by the conservative Malcolm Fraser, who regarded it as simplistic and who disliked the selfishness it promoted. Ironically, it was taken up enthusiastically by Labor's Bob Hawke and Paul Keating. Hawke took leadership of Labor in an internal pre-election coup, and then won power from Malcolm Fraser in the 1983 election, appointing Keating as Treasurer.

THE HAWKE-KEATING GOVERNMENT effectively took over the policies of Labor's opponents, and set about 'deregulating' the economy at a much more rapid pace than had been happening previously. Subsequent governments followed up with more deregulations and other social changes, so the cumulative effect after three decades is a substantial change, not only in the structure of the economy, but in the character of Australian society. Those changes are still playing out.

Hawke and Keating between them governed from 1983 to 1996. They implemented much of the neoliberal agenda by privatising many publicly-owned, and profitable, enterprises, deregulating business and finance, imposing by decree an artificial 'competition policy' on non-commercial organisations, and diminishing the rights and power of employees. Hawke was described by some as Australia's best Conservative Prime Minister, only partly in jest.

Labor did not ignore social welfare, but it made economic restructuring its first priority and pushed social welfare into a more distant second place than it had been. Labor implemented Medicare and broadly continued other social welfare policies, but they were pared back. Its industrial relations changes shifted the balance of power away from employees to employers.

Beyond those explicit policies, which it presented as trade-offs to gain greater prosperity, Labor seemed oblivious to the way free-market policies would systematically subvert its social policies, and indeed its whole reason for existing, by favouring the rich at the expense of the poor. That blindness within Labor persists to this day.

During this period one could search political commentary in vain for a clear justification for the dramatic policies being implemented. There were plenty of claims that the changes were for the best, but the criterion was always to make the economy more 'open' and 'competitive'. In other words the ideology of free markets was taken as self-evidently true. It seemed never to occur to all the breathless commentators that there was any need to explain why, exactly, free markets were so obviously correct. Most economic commentators are employed by commercial media and big financial organisations, so their bias is not surprising, though not excusable. The ABC did not even have that excuse for essentially sharing the bias.

Nor did the commentary pay any heed to the actual performance of economy. The recession of the early 1990s was widely acknowledged to be the most severe since the Great Depression. Interest rates reached 17% and unemployment 11%. It had lasting negative effects on our politics and society, for example by pushing many older men permanently out of the workforce, a point we'll pick up below. It followed a wild binge by financial 'entrepreneurs' who took advantage of the deregulated financial system to run up huge debts for themselves and the economy. Prominent among the entrepreneurs worshipped by the financial commentators were Alan Bond, who ended up in jail, and Christopher Skase, who fled to Spain to escape prosecution. The overall performance of the economy never matched the postwar years, as we'll see later.

L IBERAL JOHN HOWARD eventually succeeded Hawke and Keating in 1996. Howard pushed the neoliberal agenda to greater extremes, when it suited him. However he was a cunning and adroit politician who did not hesitate to do anything that would continue his hold on power. His social and cultural actions revealed him to be as much a reactionary as a neoliberal, quite intolerant of liberal and progressive voices. That reactionary streak was to take our society in a new and darker direction.

Howard was also a big-taxing, big-spending Liberal, because he implemented the regressive Goods and Services Tax (GST), passed most of the proceeds to the states and spent the rest to electoral advantage. Government revenues peaked on his watch, according to Peter Martin. Labor utterly failed to exploit this chance to reverse the usual charge of 'big-taxing, big-spending socialists'.

The GST was highly unpopular and Howard would almost certainly have lost the 2001 election were it not for the unprincipled advantage he took of asylum seekers and terrorist attacks. These episodes, being more recent, are presumably better remembered than our earlier history, but they are important because of their lasting negative effects on our society.

Hard times always prompt some people to seek scapegoats, and the 1990s recession was no exception. A vocal minority of reactionary xenophobes emerged, including many older men cast into long-term unemployment by the recession, who blamed their troubles on a small flow of refugees. Pauline Hanson became their chief spokesperson. This was the context in which, in August of 2001, Howard suddenly decided to block the access of (legal) asylum seekers to Australian territory, starting with his unsuccessful attempt to prevent the Norwegian vessel *Tampa* from delivering rescued refugees to Christmas Island.

Howard then subtly encouraged the vilification of the asylum seekers. This culminated just before the November election in what became known as the Children Overboard Affair. Howard's Government alleged that refugees had thrown their children overboard to force the Australian navy to rescue them. This was a whopping lie built on an early misunderstanding. The misunderstanding was quickly corrected by navy personnel but the

Government did not want to know. The election was held in the midst of the ensuing hysteria.

It became clear after the election that there had been a conspiracy among some senior military, public service and government people to preserve the appearance that Howard did not learn the truth before the election. It would have been easy for Howard to ascertain the truth, but it was more useful politically to continue the lie, and later to pretend ignorance of the truth. None of those involved in this 'truth overboard' was ever brought to account, by Liberals or Labor.

Howard's cynical actions set Australia on a slippery slope. Distortion and manipulation were far from unknown in Australian politics, as we've already seen, but Howard raised them to a new level, and at the expense of some of the most vulnerable people in the world. Once started, such deception must continue and escalate, because the truth tends to leak out eventually and it must be continually countered. Cynicism and alienation of citizens is the direct and inevitable consequence. As the level of misinformation and untruth rises, so our democracy sickens. Xenophobia and paranoia are dark and powerful forces, easy to unleash, difficult to restrain.

True to this form, after the '9/11' September 2001 attack on the World Trade Centre in New York Howard enthusiastically fanned (not unreasonable) concern about terrorist attacks into more unreasoning Australian hysteria. He left unchallenged claims by xenophobes and his own ministers that refugee boats might carry terrorists, as if terrorists would choose such an arduous, risky and visible means of entry when they could quietly fly in (along with many other asylum seekers). Howard became adept at the *dog whistle* – the use of code phrases that were known to trigger the reactionary Right – to stir the political and media attack dogs while appearing to stand above the fray.

Meanwhile Labor under the leadership of Kim Beazley had made a fateful choice to support Howard's anti-boats refugee policy. This infuriated and disillusioned a significant part of Labor's support base, already very uneasy over Labor's implementation of right-wing economic policy over the previous two decades. A steady decline in party membership accelerated, along with a drift of votes to the Greens.

Howard won the 2001 election, but only narrowly. He replicated his hero Robert Menzies' use of fear and hysteria, most obvious in 1954, to fall over the line.

Subsequently Howard implemented a draconian regime of 'anti-terror' laws, with only minor quibbles from Labor. Fundamental legal protections dating back hundreds of years were rapidly jettisoned, according to Human Rights Watch. Courts that dissented were vilified by the Government. Laws that were inconvenient were changed, finessed or ignored. International treaty obligations were serially violated and associated international organisations vilified. Dissenters were vilified and accused of supporting terrorism. The independence of the ABC was compromised by the appointment of quite extreme ideologues to its governing Board. Electoral procedures were manipulated to the Government's advantage. Australia's borders became comically elastic, moved every time a refugee boat reached a new destination, all to deny refugees fundamental legal process and human rights. Innocent refugees, men, women and children, were interned in remote and inhospitable inland 'detention centres' that are more accurately described as concentration camps, typically for many years, while their cases allegedly were being processed, very slowly.

John Howard's dark leanings were manifest in two other fateful actions, both military in character. He enthusiastically committed Australia to blindly supporting the US response to 9/11, including George W. Bush's 2003 invasion of Iraq. Howard thus exposed us to the attentions of Middle Eastern terrorists. The 2002 and 2005 Bali bombings, the 2015 Sydney Lindt cafe siege and Parramatta police killing can be attributed in whole or part to Howard's commitment.

The Iraq invasion was unjustified and illegal. This was known at the time and has been documented clearly, most recently by the Chilcot report in the UK. There were no weapons of mass destruction. Al Qaeda was not based in Iraq because Saddam Hussein kept them out. The invasion was perpetrated by governments, principally the US, UK and Australia, against the wishes of their citizens, clearly expressed in polls and mass demonstrations prior to the invasion. Even in the US public opinion was split 50-50. The invasion and subsequent civil war killed nearly 300,000 Iraqis. Iraq descended into anarchy, later followed by Syria, and that anarchy gave birth to Islamic State, the most brutal and threatening terrorist organisation so far. The invasion was utterly counter-productive.

Howard's other dire action was the 2007 Intervention in indigenous communities in the Northern Territory. Howard implied child abuse was widespread, but the report he invoked, *Little Children Are Sacred*, had found its occurrence to be scattered. Howard ignored the many recommendations of the report and brought in the army to impose draconian restrictions on the communities. Those restrictions comprised hundreds of pages of regulations, making it clear the action was long-planned and the report was only an excuse.

In conjunction with the Northern Territory Government, community supports were withdrawn and people were encouraged or required to move to towns, where disorder, drunkenness and crime quickly rose. The Government did offer some improved housing, but only in return for a 40 year lease over land previously ceded to indigenous communities. Removal from their country had devastating cultural, spiritual and health impacts on the people. It is all too plausible that this was another phase of land clearance for the benefit of mining and other interests. Similar actions in 2015 by the deeply pro-mining Western Australian Government fit the same pattern.

Another of Howard's most lasting accomplishments was to appoint right-wing ideologues throughout the Government, semi-government and not-quite-autonomous bodies within his reach, including the High Court and an increasingly under-funded, intimidated and blinkered ABC. He also promoted the so-called culture wars, particularly in denigrating what he called the 'black-armband' view of Australia's treatment of Aborigines, and favouring a sanitised chronicle of heroic white settlers. In this way Howard, obviously with clear purpose, entrenched the Right in our governing institutions, complementing the Right-dominated media and business lobbies.

John Howard unleashed dark forces that have only gathered strength since his departure. His grovelling adherence to misguided US policy put us in harm's way by making us a much more obvious target of terrorism, as well as making Australia complicit in the crimes of a disastrous illegal war. He attacked some of the most vulnerable – boat-borne refugees and Aborigines – for his own political advantage, encouraging the vilification of both groups. He facilitated the conflation of refugees and terrorists, fanning fears of both. He also ensured that his followers took greater control of our stories, stories of who we are and how we can be.

ALTHOUGH LABOR regained power in 2007 it had by then jettisoned most of its reason for existing and seeking power. Having adopted neoliberalism, it confined itself to softening some of the sharper edges and putting bandaids on the wounds inflicted. Having failed to make a stand against the mistreatment of refugees and our involvement in the Iraq invasion, it left itself no principled ground and was vulnerable to being wedged ever-further to the Right, for fear it would be portrayed as soft on security and terrorism. With most of the neoliberal economic agenda implemented by Keating and Howard, it seemed to have little agenda left. This left it vulnerable to conflicting egos within.

Howard was never popular. He scraped in in 1998 and 2001 and he would have lost in 2004 had Labor been able to produce a credible leader with a clear program. There was an initial surge of interest and support when Mark Latham became leader, claiming to set a new direction, but the support fell away as Latham's erratic behaviour and insecure grasp of the issues became clear.

Kevin Rudd provided the appearance of a solid leader and a decent person, and he easily beat Howard in 2007. He was helped when Howard over-reached and proposed draconian restrictions on employee rights, in the name of the neoliberal notion of 'labour market flexibility', which means treating employees as disposable commodities.

The Rudd and Gillard Governments of 2007-2013 slowed the rightward drift in some respects. However they continued with the Iraq occupation and the NT Intervention. They did very little about Howard's institutional and cultural changes, and indeed seemed oblivious to any need to reverse what Howard had done, if only for their own self-preservation. Were they afraid of the self-interested reaction of the Murdoch press? In significant respects they were wedged further to the right.

Rudd actually described himself as conservative, and he continued Labor's right-wing policies, but with two exceptions, one directly contrary to the neoliberal program. In an eerie echo of the victory of Scullin's Labor in 1929, the Global Financial Crisis broke soon after Rudd attained office. Almost uniquely in the world, Rudd implemented a vigorous stimulus program of government spending, and saved Australia from the severe and protracted recession that hit most other countries.

Rudd even argued explicitly in a 2009 article for a decisive break from neoliberalism and a return to Keynesian economic policies, renouncing 'free-market fundamentalism, extreme capitalism and excessive greed'. As so often with Rudd, and with modern Labor, the latter claim turned out to be empty rhetoric. His stimulus was a welcome but one-off deviation from neoliberal doctrine. All the other neoliberal policies continued.

Rudd's one other outstanding accomplishment was his apology to the stolen generations of Aboriginal people. It was symbolic but highly important, and he did it in the face of vigorous objection from the reactionary Right.

Otherwise Rudd seemed to be incapable of the politicking required to carry out such ambitions as he had, which were not very evident. This was obvious fairly soon in his term to anyone observing closely, as his main actions in his first year were to establish enquiries and to convene a summit of Australia's best and brightest, whose suggestions he basically ignored. However his high standing in opinion polls continued until early 2010.

Rudd's undoing came when he walked away from his attempts to slow emissions of the greenhouse gases causing global warming, which he had correctly called 'the greatest moral challenge of our time'. His poll approval collapsed, as people judged he was mostly hot air. He attempted to recover by proposing a tax on mining super profits, a very sensible idea, but the big miners attacked him with a deceitful advertising blitz claiming the tax would cause the sky to fall. A spooked party dumped him and installed Julia Gillard as leader and prime minister.

Rudd's economic stimulus program has been acknowledged by many internationally as best practice, and Australia was the only developed economy to avoid recession after the GFC. Nevertheless within Australia Rudd and his Treasurer Wayne Swan have been pilloried ever since by neoliberals and the commercial media for allegedly running up massive Government debts. In fact the debts, as a fraction of GDP, were quite modest compared with most other developed economies, and much smaller than Australia's dangerously high private debt.

Julia Gillard, as prime minister, displayed admirable perseverance in a difficult and hostile situation, but she was often quite inept politically, and the net effect was to continue Labor's drift to the Right.

Gillard failed to acknowledge straightforwardly why she went back on her pre-election promise that there would be no carbon price in the coming term of Parliament. She did so because she faced the quite unexpected situation of a hung Parliament, and needed to secure the support of the Greens and independents to form a minority government. By glossing over her change instead of frankly explaining it, Gillard opened the way for an interminable campaign labelling her 'Ju-liar', though all politicians lie and John Howard was one of the more prolific practitioners, infamously distinguishing his 'core promises' from his 'non-core promises'. Howard has now been surpassed by Tony Abbott, who quickly broke a string of promises central to his election campaign.

Another of Gillard's crucial missteps was to announce the carbon price without announcing, until many months later, how the resulting revenue would be fed back to consumers, particularly the poor, so that most people would not be seriously affected. The Greens must also bear responsibility for this blunder. Even former Liberal leader John Hewson marvelled at how Gillard had given the Opposition a free kick every day for many months, until details were spelt out, by which time it was far too late. The resulting disingenuous 'no carbon tax' slogan was central to Tony Abbott's successful election campaign in 2013.

Gillard was also wedged further to the Right on asylum-seeker policy. After trying to sort out Rudd's confused attempts to be firm but not totally draconian, she abandoned any pretence of compassion and instituted an offshore-processing policy that involved extended, abusive detention in deficient facilities in third-world countries for innocent men, women and children. Such policies had, since at least 2001, been in clear violation of the spirit of Australia's international agreements on refugees.

WHEREAS LABOR'S internal conflict was basically between egos within a party lacking a clear vision or ideology, the conflict that soon emerged in the Liberal Party was between ideologies that had never been compatible: the liberal and neoliberal push for individual liberty and radical change, and the conservative and reactionary resistance to change and suppression of disapproved views. Of course the Liberal conflict was spiced with fierce ego rivalries as well.

Labor's policy and leadership disarray led to its loss in 2013 to Tony Abbott. Although the character of the Abbott Government fits a broadly predictable and predicted trajectory, wrought by neoliberalism and Howard's xenophobic policies, it nevertheless represented a distinct jump in its ideological extremity, its arbitrariness and its rapidly manifested authoritarianism. It is tempting to describe it also as incompetent, and it was certainly politically inept, yet it rapidly implemented many parts of its agenda, mainly by cutting, withholding or redirecting funding, with already rather dramatic consequences for our society.

Although brief, its record is clear in its disregard for the rule of law and the needs of democratic process. Also clear are its fear-mongering, its reactionary views, its hostility to informed and rational debate, its incivility and wild exaggerations, and its callousness or even malevolence towards the disempowered.

Perhaps the most chilling development was the Abbott Government's attitude to the rule of law, which it not only played very loose with, but seemed not even to understand. A 'law' to strip citizenship that is administered by a politician is not a law, it is a tyranny. Claiming decisions can be appealed to a court of law is of little practical relevance to someone who can't set foot in the country and on whom the onus of proof would lie. Similarly, a 'law' that is infinitely malleable is no law at all. Every time a legal challenge to government abuses of innocent asylum seekers looked like succeeding, the law was changed to get around it. This has been going on since John Howard bent our borders to deny asylum seekers their legal rights.

Early in 2015 Australia was listed by Human Rights Watch among some of the world's notorious human rights abusers for its treatment of asylum seekers, excessive limitations on freedom of information, draconian laws and other problems.

The Abbott Government, in other words moved to greater neoliberal, libertarian and reactionary extremes. Foundational institutions and conventions of democracy, the rule of law and citizen rights were trampled and our open democratic society was increasingly threatened.

The Abbott Government's post-election honeymoon was possibly the briefest ever, terminated by Abbott's brazen breaking of a string of pre-election promises and reinforced by a budget, in May 2014, widely and accurately perceived as being highly unfair to the poor and vulnerable while pandering to the very rich. Thereafter his Government consistently lagged in the polls.

The most widespread reaction to the eventual ousting of Abbott and his replacement by Malcolm Turnbull in September 2015 was relief. Turnbull, with obvious intention, immediately adopted a calming tone, avoiding exaggerations and provocations. Even when a terrorist event occurred, with the shooting of a police worker in Parramatta, he urged Australians to avoid blaming our Islamic community.

However it soon became apparent that most of the hard-right agenda remained. Evidently Turnbull had sold his soul in order to gain the support of the party's Right for him to replace Abbott. His Government was undisciplined and right-wing, and its initially high popularity declined steadily in consequence. He barely survived the election and will be vulnerable to internal and external forces, unless he has the gumption and skill to defy the Liberal extremists. It seems Australia's experience of unstable political leadership is not over yet.

It is tempting to see the Abbott-Hockey 2014 budget as the high water mark of right-wing extremism in Australia. That budget was largely rejected in the Senate. The Government's persistence with its right-wing agenda caused it almost to lose the election, so the people's continuing resistance to neoliberalism was manifest. The Coalition's options have been to persist and guarantee electoral oblivion or to drift aimlessly, hacking at anything within reach, which is what they have done, under both Abbott and Turnbull. However it is also true that the 2016 election returned another assortment of reactionaries to the Senate, along with some more sensible groups like the

Nick Xenophon Team. Whether Australia uses this time to set a more deliberate course for moderation and sense remains for us to decide.

THE REALITY AND SEVERITY of the shift in the Right over recent decades is attested by conservatives themselves. Former Prime Minister Malcolm Fraser resigned from the Liberal Party in 2009. The occasion was the ousting of Malcolm Turnbull as leader in favour of Tony Abbott, but this was only the last straw, according to Margaret Simons writing in Crikey. Fraser had been disgusted by Howard's failure to condemn the xenophobic views of Pauline Hanson in the 1990s and by Howard's co-opting of Hanson's ideas in the blocking of the Tampa and subsequent treatment of asylum seekers. Over a longer period he had been disturbed by the Party's shift towards market fundamentalism and libertarianism.

Fraser saw himself as liberal (in the classic sense, not in the American sense of leftist). For him the Liberal Party had been an anti-communist bulwark that could also be socially progressive. With the fall of the Berlin Wall and the passing of the communist threat he perceived threats from other directions. One was an unreasoning faith in free markets as an organising principle in human affairs. Another was Pauline Hanson's xenophobia, whose ideas, he wrote, posed an 'extraordinary danger to the unity and cohesion of a fair-minded, democratic Australia'.

John Hewson, leader of the Liberal Party 1990-94, was a regular and sometimes trenchant critic of the Abbott Government. Robert Menzies, founder of the Liberal Party and longest-serving prime minister, might well also have resigned, were he still around, and if he didn't he might be thrown out for advocating, or at least tolerating, the social-democratic ideas by which he governed. In fact, just as Fraser was disgusted by John Howard's exploitation of vulnerable refugees, Menzies had been disgusted by Fraser's trampling of long-established convention when he blocked Whitlam's supply bills in the Senate in 1975, according to George Megalogenis.

The shift to the Right in Australia parallels that in other countries. As is often true, the trend is more extreme in the US, as described by Nick O'Malley. US Republican economist Bruce Bartlett said of the domination of the Republican Party by Tea Party extremists 'They have descended from the realm of reasonableness that was the mark of conservatism. They dream of anarchy, of ending government.' David Frum, the Bush II speechwriter who gave us the term "axis of evil" writes that allegedly smart, sophisticated people, including canny investors and erudite writers, believe President Obama is driving the US to socialism, and that "No counter-evidence will dissuade them from this belief: not record-high corporate profits, not almost 500,000 job losses in the public sector, not the lowest tax rates since the Truman administration.'

There seems to be only a limited perception of how much our politics and society have changed since 1983. Certainly the major political parties and vested interests want to legitimise themselves by claiming to be merely the continuation of the traditional Australian project.

They are aided by compromised, lazy or ignorant journalists. A few years ago the prominent, chummy commentator Annabel Crabb referred to a couple of prospective members of a Labor Cabinet as 'hard left'. Well no, Annabel, there has not been a hard left member of Parliament for decades. Some of the Whitlam Cabinet could be called socialists, but the last seriously socialist policy was probably Ben Chifley's failed attempt to nationalise the banks, in 1949. The left and liberal elements of both major parties have dwindled pretty much to extinction.

The dramatic, even radical nature of the changes that have occurred in Australia since 1983 are further obscured by simplistic usage of the terms *Left* and *Right* to characterise our politics. If we insist on a simplistic one-dimensional picture, then it must be said that both major parties have shifted well to the Right of their earlier attitudes. However commentators commonly use Left and Right only in terms *relative* to the parties at any given moment, so the big change is obscured. The old and new meanings of Left and Right are sketched in Figure 4.1.

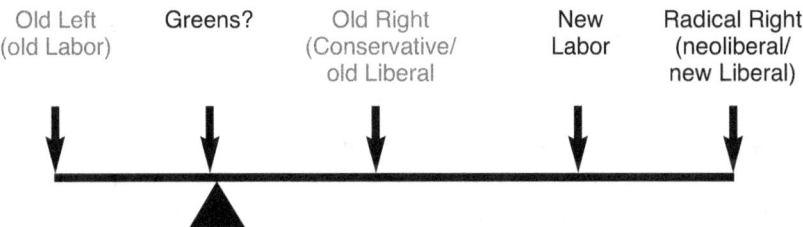

Figure 4.1. Sketch of old and new meanings of Left and Right

According to the usage of the previous era, there are now no significant parties of the Left. Labor is Right and the Coalition is far right. The Greens, whose policies are more social democratic than socialist, are more Centre than Centre-Left, and possibly closer to Menzies than modern Labor, which is well to Menzies' right.

The sketch provides some perspective on claims by the Liberal Party and the commercial media that the Greens are extremists. It also gives perspective to calls for the ABC to be 'balanced'.

'Left' used to refer to socialist, though old Labor was only partly socialist. The old Australian Left could be taken simply as promoting the interests of ordinary people.

The old Right was a mixture of liberal, conservative and reactionary elements. Liberals champion individual autonomy and seem to have originated in opposition to the old monarchies. Conservatives, who seem to have originated in opposition to socialists, claim to value stability and tradition. Evidently that includes the tradition of their own wealth and power. Reactionaries tend to be afraid of change and to favour regulation or suppression of personal and social behaviours they disapprove of.

Neoliberals have taken liberal ideas to the extreme of favouring anarchic markets and minimal society based on asocial competitive individuals. The modern Right in Australia comprises neoliberals, reactionaries, and scant few remnant conservatives and old-style liberals, people like the late Malcolm Fraser.

Neoliberalism is neither conservative nor simply reactionary. It can be called right wing, in the sense of favouring established wealth and power, but it is pro-active rather than conservative or reactive. It *actively displaces* traditions and old securities. Thus neoliberalism is certainly not conservative, it is *radical*.

THERE IS AN APHORISM that people get the government they deserve. It is a lazy copout that fails to take account of institutional inertia and the heavy influence of special interests, including the media.

The major political parties have become deeply entrenched in our society, so they are very difficult to change or displace. It is simply true that most people vote tribally, for the group they have traditionally identified with. Even so, in spite of this strong tendency, the primary votes for the major parties have been dropping steadily. Many people clearly are not satisfied with the choice available. If an alternative were to appear that people perceived as a viable alternative government, it is likely they would flock to it.

The political commentariat seems to be mystified by the current political instability, with its frequent changes of leaders and governments. They cite the 24-hour news cycle, or globalisation, or the internet shrinking the world.

Or they cite the viciousness and superficiality of modern politics, or the personalities and deficiencies of leaders, though they don't usually explain why these things have changed or become dominant. Some even claim it is really our democratic system that is failing, because governments can't make the necessary tough decisions and survive.

The reason for the political impasse seems rather obvious. It is that both parties are on the nose. Voters do not want what is being offered. The Labor Party, having swallowed the neoliberal ideology and capitulated to special interests, lost sight of the needs of ordinary people. Having failed to defend the vulnerable, it has joined in tormenting them. It has lost all reason for being, except to gain and hold power. The Liberal Party has become so extreme in its pursuit of ideology that, finally, it may be exhausting the tolerance of voters. Both parties live in fear of the media, which pursue a mixture of ideology and exploitation of our fears, for profit. Both parties have become dominated by second- and third-rate careerists obsessed by power or ideology or both.

5

The Failing Neoliberal Experiment

Chairman Mao used to say imperialism is a paper tiger. It looks fierce, but it is a flimsy construction. We may say the same about neoliberalism. The 'Left' has been thoroughly intimidated by it, but when one looks closely there is very little to it. Its performance is rather less than is claimed. The theory behind free markets is a bad joke. Its view of people is a crude parody. We'll look at its performance here and cover the other aspects later.

We would have recovered from the shocks of the 1970s anyway. Subsequent economic performance globally has comprised mediocrity masked by rising debt, and instability leading into disaster. Australia was fortunate to escape the worst of the Global Financial Crisis, by briefly abandoning neoliberal doctrines. Our economic situation is still precarious, and our prospects are deteriorating, due both to external factors and to continuing mismanagement.

Economist Stephen Bell's was a rare voice of knowledge and clarity amidst the neoliberal love fest of the 1980s and 90s. In his 1997 book

Ungoverning the Economy he gave a more plausible account of the crises of the 1970s, and he documented the already-evident failure of neoliberal policies to match the postwar era.

Bell portrays postwar economic history in terms of the competing interests of employees, business and government. The power of business and finance had been reduced by the Depression and by centralised government during the war. The success of postwar democratic socialism increased the power of both labour unions and government, relative to business, and business perceived its profits and power being increasingly encroached. The so-called Bretton Woods arrangements had also strongly regulated postwar international finance, and the financial industry was largely confined within national borders so national economies could be more readily managed. This enabled governments to channel more wealth into infrastructure and to employees. Because employees generally spend their money with little delay, this created a virtuous circle of rising demand and rising prosperity, supported by improving infrastructure, health and education.

By the late 1960s the rising workforce claim on wealth, led by ACTU President Bob Hawke, was beginning to provoke price inflation, as employers chose to pass on wage increases through higher prices. This fed a wage-price spiral that, it is rarely noted, is as much the responsibility of employers as employees. Inflation was then considerably exacerbated in the 1970s first by the US policy of paying for the Vietnam War by printing money, and then by the oil cartel quadrupling oil prices. Business was looking for a way to regain power, and unions were also learning painful lessons, from inflation and particularly from the recession of the early 1980s.

Some rebalancing among competing interests was widely seen as necessary, at least until the economy stabilised. Bob Hawke, wearing his new hat as Prime Minister, negotiated an Accord between labour, business and government that was very much in this spirit, and it was a substantial success for a time. However the Hawke Government also vigorously pursued the neoliberal approach of deregulation of the economy, driven mainly by Treasurer Paul Keating. This was seen as part of the rebalancing as it returned power and profit to business.

However deregulation was based on the naïve idea that markets generally promote equilibrium. Neoclassical economists thought, and still think, market forces would automatically rebalance the competing interests. Business interests were not so naïve, but they were happy to ally with the economists, because it gave business the means to start regaining power.

The reduced bargaining power of unions, and employees in general, has substantially reduced employment security, increased working hours and casualised the workforce, with a large increase in part-time, casual and low-paid service jobs. The neoliberal myth of 'labour market flexibility' holds that employees will simply bargain with employers and arrive at fair working conditions. However Adam Smith knew, and today everyone but the ideologues knows, that employers always have the greater power, so the relative power of owners and employees did not automatically reach a balance. The power of business increased steadily, and only began to be limited by political means, for example when John Howard's invidious WorkChoices policy was rejected in the 2007 election.

The greater insecurity of employment has reduced family and community cohesion and promoted divisive attitudes that have been further exploited in the fear-mongering campaigns about refugees and terrorists, so the social consequences of these misguided policies have been very serious. On the economic side, the deregulation of finance has had far-reaching and destructive effects that are still playing out locally and globally.

THE ECONOMIC 'REFORMS' OF THE NEOLIBERAL ERA are proclaimed almost every day to have delivered us from a sick and declining economy and ushered in an era of unprecedented prosperity. Reality begs to differ.

The economy since 1980 has never equalled its performance between about 1950 and the early 1970s. The numbers are shown in Table 5.1. The *average* unemployment from 1953 to 1974 was a paltry 1.3%. Bob Menzies very nearly lost the 1961 election because unemployment had risen over 2%. Growth of the Gross Domestic Product (GDP) averaged 5.2% from 1960 to 1974. According to modern economists such numbers are virtually impossible, because unemployment below about 4% will result in runaway inflation. However inflation from 1953 to 1974 averaged just 3.3%.

The corresponding numbers for the early neoliberal years, 1983-93, after the difficulties of the 1970s had waned, were unemployment 8.4% (vs. 1.3%), GDP growth 3.4% (vs. 5.2%) and inflation 5.6% (vs. 3.3%). More recently the numbers have been unemployment around 5%, GDP growth 2-4% and inflation 2-3%, still not as good as the postwar period, despite a mining boom described by some as equal to or bigger, in relative terms, than the gold booms of the nineteenth century.

This superiority of the postwar decades is not just an Australian phenomenon, as the nations of the Organisation for Economic Cooperation and Development (OECD, essentially the rich nations) show a similar contrast (Table 5.1).

Table 5.1 Economic performance, pre-1974 and post-1974. From Bell, 1997.

	Pre 1974	1974-83	1983-93
Australia			
GDP annual growth (from 1960), %	5.2	1.8	3.4
Inflation (CPI annual increase, from 1953), %	3.3	11.4	5.6
Unemployment (from 1953), %	1.3	5.6	8.4
OECD			
GDP annual growth (from 1960), %	4.9	1.6	2.8
Inflation (CPI annual increase, from 1960), %	4.5	11.1	6.8
Unemployment (from 1953), %	3.2	6.4	8.4

Even globally the contrast is evident. A compilation for over 100 nations, reported by Mark Weisbrot and others in 2005, shows GDP growth prior to 1980 averaged 2.5%, whereas after 1980 it averaged 1.1%. Global growth more recently has been a little faster, but this is due mainly to rapid GDP growth in China, pursuing decidedly non-neoliberal policies.

In the US, the homeland of neoliberalism, such growth as there has been under neoliberalism has benefited mainly the very rich. In fact median hourly wages in the US have nearly flatlined since 1980, growing by only 13% in 30 years, whereas productivity nearly doubled and incomes for the top 20% increased by 55% (up to 2010).

The change brought about by neoliberalism in the US is so dramatic it is worth showing in graphical form, Figure 5.1. The darker line effectively shows total wealth rising steadily from 1950 until 2010. The lighter line effectively shows a typical worker's income, which rose steadily through the postwar years until around 1980 but which has hardly risen since. After Reagan the wealth did not trickle down. The very rich in the US have creamed off most of the extra wealth generated by the steadily rising productivity per person, as revealed by the income gains charted in part (b) of Figure 5.1.

The United States is being hollowed out. The rich put their money into speculation rather than into productive investment, so the economy only stumbles along. The obsession with cutting taxes on the wealthy, which is one of the main ways in which the rich have harvested more of the wealth, has left US infrastructure declining to the point where major bridges have collapsed and paved roads are being returned to gravel. Public education and hospitals are struggling. Frightened and confused citizens have turned to scapegoating. There has been a noticeable rise in racism, particularly evident through police shootings of black people. As the US turns in upon itself conditions become ripe for simplistic demagogues. Donald Trump, hypocritical billionaire, fulfils the role.

The flow of benefits has not been so unbalanced in Australia, because neoliberal ambitions for 'labour market flexibility' have been resisted by an electorate still not as cowed as in the US. Even so, inequality of income has increased substantially, according to 'Possum Comitatus' in 2011.

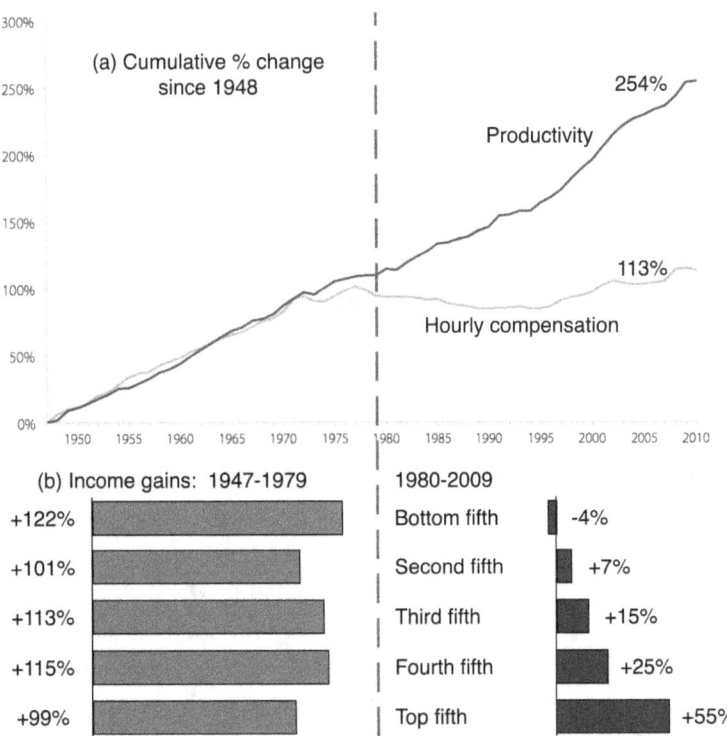

Figure 5.1. Wages (Hourly compensation) in the US have hardly risen over the past 30 years. If wealth had been shared after 1979 as it was before, the median 'Hourly compensation' curve would have continued to rise along with productivity. If it had, average Americans would now have much higher incomes. Instead, wealth has been creamed off by the rich. From Reich, 2011.

If the contrast between pre-1980 and post-1980 economic performance is mentioned at all by apologists for the neoliberal regime, it is brushed off as an after-effect of World War II. Supposedly, consumer demand was suppressed during the war, and the postwar bounce in consumer demand produced anomalously high economic growth. This explanation does not withstand scrutiny. First, is not plausible that a postwar transient effect would last 25 years.

Second, it overlooks the huge stimulus of war spending that operated during the war. Economies respond to both consumer demand and government spending. It was government spending during the war that lifted Western economies out of depression, something consumer demand had failed to do for a decade. There was in fact serious concern at the end of the war that Western economies might return to depression, as the stimulus effect of war spending ceased, according to Ian McLean.

Economies were deliberately structured and managed so as to maintain activity. Government spending on sound investment in productive infrastructure was a crucial ingredient. Wage, tax and other policies ensured the wealth was shared around. This in turn ensured new wealth was spent back into the economy, rather than being squandered on speculative money games by the rich. So sound government spending on infrastructure provided a base, and consumer demand was sustained on top of that. The result was the prolonged postwar boom that yielded the greatest gain in wealth of the most people to that point in history.

EVEN THE NUMBERS JUST SHOWN overstate economic performance in the neoliberal era. Growing instability is obscured by the use of long-term averages, and the source of that instability, rising private debt, is left out entirely.

The deregulation of the Australian financial industry, including the banks, led to a dramatic rise in business debts through the 1980s as banks competed to expand their own business. It does not take a genius to understand there is a limit to how much debt can be carried before businesses start to default. One default or bankruptcy can trigger other defaults and lead to a cascade, so the whole debt house of cards collapses. This is the cycle that operated in Australia through the 1980s. So-called entrepreneurs, in particular, took on high levels of debt for their corporate game playing, which was more about financial manipulation and extraction than investment in real production. The debt binge culminated in the collapse and recession of the early 1990s, which was the most severe in Australia since the Great Depression. It still holds that distinction.

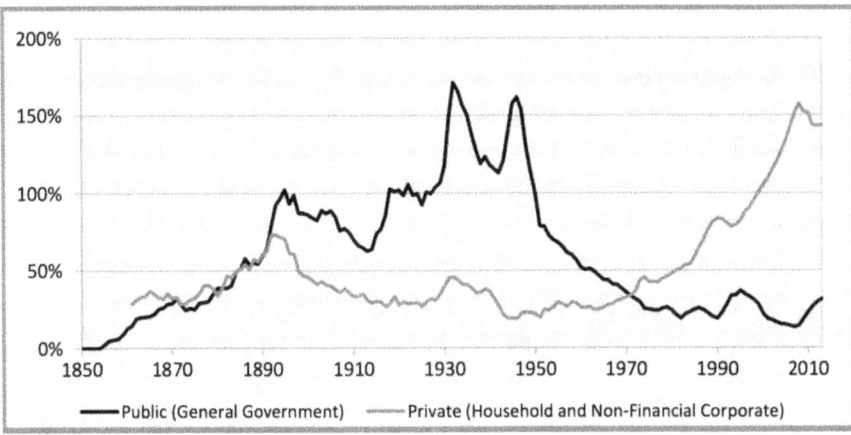

Figure 5.2. Public and private debt in Australia, as a percentage of Gross Domestic Product. Public debt includes Federal and State Government debts. From Egan and Soos' 2014 *Bubble Economics*

Private debt is pretty much ignored by mainstream economists, for a strange reason that we will get to later. So it was up to the unconventional economist Steve Keen to plot some numbers compiled by the Reserve Bank and to point out the alarming implication. Figure 5.2 is a later plot by Paul Egan and Philip Soos that includes government debt as well as private debt.

The 1980s rise in private debt was part of a longer-term trend. A long upward swing of private debt began in the 1960s and peaked in 2008. Total private debt by then was over 150% of GDP, and very much higher than previous peaks associated with the booms and depressions of the 1890s and 1930s. At the same time government debt was below 20% of GDP. Not only is government debt much smaller than private debt, but Australia's government debt is much smaller than that of most other developed nations, whose government debts are mostly in the range of 80-150% of GDP.

The rapid rise of private debt in the 1980s was followed by a drop during the recession in the early 90s. The boom and bust is visible as an extra bump on the overall upward trend in Figure 5.2. After the early 1990s recession, growth in private debt resumed with a vengeance until it peaked in 2008.

Now here is an alarming feature of this graph: during 2007 private debt increased from nearly 140% to nearly 160% of GDP. In other words private debt increased by 20% of GDP in that one year. Think of it as the national credit card: in that year *20% of our national income was borrowed*. Without that borrowing binge, the Australian economy would have been in severe recession.

The appearance of prosperity was an illusion. A faltering economy was kept afloat by taking on a lot of debt. We all know you can't live that way for long, and indeed the boom soon came to a bad end. The problem is not close to any resolution, as governments attempt merely to keep the debt bubble inflated.

THE RISING LEVEL OF DEBT took us from mediocrity to disaster. The debt not only masked the weak performance of the real economy, but it was a time bomb. Debt was rising in all the developed countries, and especially in the US. The Global Financial Crisis that started in 2007 was a direct result of neoliberal deregulation of financial markets, as was well argued by Stephen Keen in 2009. Basically too much debt was accumulated, as it had been in Australia in the 1980s, though the details were different in 2007.

The global financial markets had become dominated by speculation. The rate of financial trading increased about fifty-fold compared with the previous regulated era, and compared with what is required to service the productive economy, as I have argued in *Sack the Economists*. This means only about 2% of trades are useful, the other 98% are gambling.

Financial operators invented many new kinds of 'instruments'. These instruments amounted to bets on whether prices would rise or fall over some future period. The instruments also amounted to a promise, or a debt. The operators persuaded themselves they could insure, or hedge, against any future rise or fall of the market, so the bets were safe and profits were guaranteed. They became careless. They gave mortgage loans to people with drug problems, people who were unemployed or, as the joke went, anyone with a pulse. They created *$600 trillion worth of debt*, more than 20 times global output for one year.

Eventually, of course, people started to default on their debts. By this time the dodgy financial instruments had spread through the entire global financial system. The early defaults triggered more defaults and began a cascade, a collapse of the enormous debt house of cards.

Suddenly everyone realised that much of the debt had become worthless.

Each of the big banks didn't know if the others were still solvent. They didn't even know if they were solvent themselves. Some collapsed. In the US, where the trouble had started, the government pumped trillions of dollars, much of it taxpayers money, into the banks' coffers to prevent complete collapse of the financial system.

There was a downward spiral of debt and prices. In the US, many home owners found their home was worth less than their mortgage. The Government did little to help them. Rather, the Government rescued bank shareholders, by effectively buying their worthless financial instruments at nearly face value.

The GFC has visited immense harm on much of the world, with much of Europe and parts of the US sinking into depression. Recovery in the US has been slow and feeble, and depression persists even now in the periphery of Europe, due to the rigid neoliberal policy of austerity being pursued by European authorities. The problems in Europe have been exacerbated by a faulty structuring of the Euro currency system, which magnified the difficulties in the peripheral countries.

To quote commentator Rob Parenteau on the Greek situation: 'Austerity has proven to be a disaster on nearly all fronts. Firms have been bankrupted, households have dropped into abject poverty, banks have lost capital to loan losses, tax revenues have come up short or have been hijacked to service debt (debt that was ultimately issued to socialise bank loan losses), and government debt to GDP ratios have *risen*. Economies are evidently not drawn to full employment growth paths [by EU policies], ostensibly so that prices are free to adjust to market forces. ... this *fatal neoliberal conceit in the self-adjusting properties of unfettered markets* was the central premise, as well as the fundamental design flaw, behind the European Monetary Union.' [Emphases added.]

AUSTRALIA ESCAPED THE WORST EFFECTS of the GFC by explicitly departing from neoliberal doctrine and indulging in some Keynesian government spending, much to the credit of the Rudd Government. We were helped, over a longer period, by the huge mining boom. So we were lucky, again.

However we're still vulnerable. Private debt in Australia is still very high, and Steve Keen has shown in *Debunking Economics* that the greater part of it is mortgage debt. A housing price bubble has inflated prices well above historical norms compared with household incomes and the Gross Domestic

Product. The bubble is not really in the price of houses, it is in the price of the land the houses stand on.

The bubble is driven by excessive bank lending. Banks' main source of profit is from the loans they issue, so they have an incentive to lend more than is prudent. As people obtain more and bigger loans, they bid up the price of land. As the price of land goes up, banks use it as security for even bigger loans. So prices and mortgage debts spiral upwards, disconnected from the real worth of the land. This is a market failure, a basic malfunction of our financial system, due to insufficient regulation of the banks. It creates a Ponzi scheme, effectively a pyramid scheme in which land prices must keep rising and people must keep borrowing more and more to prevent a collapse.

The money that people have borrowed from banks keeps the economy bubbling along nicely. Governments have kept the housing bubble inflated by subsidising first home buyers, tax breaks and other such devices. However if the economy slows, as it is now doing with the end of the mining boom, then house prices might start to fall. This could trigger the kind of collapse locally that the rest of the world has already experienced, resulting in a serious recession.

Much of the proceeds of the mining boom were squandered by the Howard-Costello Government in the form of tax cuts for the middle class and the wealthy. Kevin Rudd tried to tax the mining companies, to recover more of the wealth, but his party did not have the spine to carry it through. The mines are mostly foreign-owned, so much of the profit flows overseas. We're left with little long-term benefit from one of the greatest mining booms in history.

The mining boom actually harmed manufacturing and other export industries, because it pushed the value of the Aussie dollar above $US1.00. This made our exports expensive for other countries so our non-mining exports fell and many manufacturers went broke. This has been called the resources curse, in which an abundance of natural resources stunts the growth of a more rounded economy. So not only did we not wisely invest the mining-boom bonanza, but the rest of our economy emerged weaker.

Then the Abbott Government made things even worse. As the mining boom eased in 2014, local car manufacturers, already subsidised, requested more help to keep their Australian operations viable after the difficulties of the high Aussie dollar. Subsidies of course are against the simplistic neoliberal religion, so the Abbott Government said 'So sorry, we don't do that. Bye.' By the time Ford, Toyota and Holden have departed, many suppliers will lose a primary market, so the loss will resonate through our high-value-added manufacturing. The effect is to hasten our de-industrialisation.

The government preference for unfettered markets, and the markets' preference for financial manipulation over productive investment, have left the economy poorly structured. Too much of our economy depends on borrowing and unsustainable extraction. The extraction applies not only to mining, but to industrial agriculture that effectively mines the soils, to excessive harvesting of forests, and to a general disregard for the fragile Australian environment. We are also mining ourselves, because we work much longer hours than we did 30 years ago. We're working harder rather than smarter. We're paying a heavy price in our families, communities, and social cohesion.

NEOLIBERALISM HAS NEVER BEEN POPULAR with Australians. We did not want our job security undermined, working hours extended and government services reduced. We have not approved of the greater inequality that has resulted. Always sceptical of the motives of big business and politicians, we have become more cynical about both. We were always uneasy about privatisation of public assets.

After experiencing the results of many privatisations, our views are loud and clear. Several state governments have lost support or lost government entirely attempting to privatise electricity and other assets, going all the way back to the Victorian Kennett Government in 1999. A telling survey by Essential polling in 2011 showed not only that people oppose privatisations and other neoliberal policies, but we would like some of them reversed. We would like to buy back Telstra, Qantas and the Commonwealth Bank. By a large majority we would like to increase trade protection. We are strongly opposed to privatising Medicare. A more recent survey by Woods and Lewis shows we think utilities like water and electricity supply are too important to be sold off. By large majorities we think privatisations increase customer costs and mainly benefit the corporate sector.

In other countries there is also strong public support for reversing privatisations in energy and transport. About two thirds of voters in Britain support public ownership, whereas less than a quarter support private ownership. Germans have been actively reversing privatisation of energy companies as part of a strategy to move to clean energy. We'll get to that later.

The Radical Right's great experiment in social engineering is failing. The mainstream world just hasn't figured it out yet. The Right persists in power because it has such a stranglehold on the media, the economics profession and major political parties, and because people are reluctant to break old allegiances.

6

Collateral Damage: Society, Land, Planet

The neoliberal era has not made Australia a nicer place, more 'relaxed and comfortable', as John Howard deceitfully promised in his 1996 election campaign. There is rising social unease. A materialist addiction has intensified. Politically we are more corrupted, more polarised and less effective. The liveability of our land is worse, and of our planet is disturbingly worse.

NEOLIBERALISM PROMOTES PERSONAL AND BUSINESS INSECURITY. It does this under the guise of promoting competition, which allegedly increases economic efficiency. That claim can be readily challenged on economic grounds, but the negative social and other consequences of insecurity are obvious and important.

Neoliberalism explicitly promotes 'labour market flexibility', which means treating employees as just another cost and commodity, to be disposed of at the whim of the employer. Employees need not be given any acknowledgement, need feel no loyalty, and their knowledge and experience are (supposedly) irrelevant or replaceable. As a result, employment is not only less secure, there is less reason to commit to the work or to make a job one's own. One is in competition with fellow employees, and the workplace is less socially engaging. So employment is less secure, less engaging and less fulfilling. It follows that, on average, employment has become more stressful.

Josh Fear and Richard Denniss of The Australia Institute have reported that full-time workers in Australia work an average of 44 hours per week, more than in either the US or Japan. This is far from the aspiration of forty years ago, which was to reduce the standard working week from 37.5 hours to 35 hours. Furthermore a significant fraction of modern work is in the form of unpaid overtime. Excessive working hours contribute to poorer health and less time with family and community. Family and community, it is increasingly recognised (or remembered), are central to our physical, social and spiritual wellbeing. As our supporting social network is weakened, so our anxiety rises.

Insecurity is also cultivated at the level of firms and industries. Industries have been required to compete internationally with little or no subsidy or protection, even though many foreign products are subsidised in their home country. The unfair competition is most obvious in agriculture. Agricultural subsidies in Europe and Japan are infamous, and the US subsidises many of its products. High-fructose corn syrup is protected by tariffs in the US which keep out cheaper Australian sugar. This corn syrup is used in many food products, unnecessarily, and is a major contributor to the obesity epidemic sweeping the Western world, according to Richard Manning. Corn is subsidised in the US in other ways, along with tobacco and many other agricultural products.

A number of primary and secondary industries have been eliminated or greatly reduced. Even if there were a case for some of these changes in strictly financial terms, social, strategic and national considerations were largely ignored.

As well as unfair foreign competition, farmers have faced pressure to get big or get out, as agribusiness has aggressively promoted itself, with the aid of compliant governments. Agribusiness is more concerned with financial results than with the health of the land. Family farms, often held by a single family for many generations, necessarily care better for the land, to protect their future. Many such farmers have been forced off the land. Commonly, they have known no other life and, as well as the disorientation of losing the source of their livelihood, they feel they have betrayed the family tradition.

Many regional and rural areas have been in prolonged recession or depression as a result of such policies. Suicides among farmers and regional youth have risen alarmingly according to the National Rural Health Alliance.

At the same time as employment has become more problematic, support from Government services has been declining. The effects of the loss of support services are often less visible than, for example, unemployment or farm bankruptcy, but they contribute to broader assessments of wellbeing and societal health. Richard Eckersley in 2012 described a very broad decline in people's wellbeing and their perception of the future, a decline most evident in the Anglophone world. The decline is manifest in a deepening pessimism and, disturbingly, declining mental and physical health is most evident among young people. According to a 2009 survey quoted by Eckersley in 2012, 'While 77% said Australians' material standard of living was higher than 20 years ago, 58% felt that emotional well-being was lower.'

People are angry and anxious about the way the Western world has changed, according to Eckersley: 'The concerns include excessive greed and selfishness, consumerism, too much competition and too little compassion, the loss of community, growing pressures on families, and drugs, crime, and violence.'

There are concerns about physical and mental health of youth, including suicide, drug and alcohol abuse, depression and other mental health problems, and crime. They also include excessive weight and obesity and their consequences on other aspects of health, especially diabetes.

People feel conflicted. One the one hand, they like having their stuff. On the other hand they recognise there ought to be more to life than material things, and we can't keep mistreating the Earth. A symptom of this inner conflict is that people complain it is hard to make ends meet, and life is a rat race. Economists and moralists tend to scoff, pointing out that Australians are among the richest people in the world, and getting richer. They overlook the daily deluge of manipulative marketing designed (very skilfully) to induce people to want more stuff, regardless of their material wealth. People are both very rich in dollar terms and stressed by their personal economic and social circumstances. This internal conflict is the paradox of the materialist addiction promoted by neoliberalism.

FEAR UNDERLIES MANY current social phenomena. If you dig below negative emotions and attitudes, such as suspicion, racism, aggression and anger, it is commonly fear that is the underlying emotional driver. Insecurity itself is a form of fear. The fears are close to apocalyptic among a substantial fraction of the population, as was noted in Chapter 2. This level of fear is striking, because Australia is still one of the most favoured places in the world.

If you make people insecure, you make them fearful. If they're fearful, they start looking for someone to blame and find scapegoats. Social division, racism and xenophobia may follow. These tendencies can be held in check by responsible politicians and media, or they can be fanned and exploited by irresponsible politicians and media. After World War II and during the 1970s responsibility concerning immigrants and refugees prevailed. Unfortunately irresponsibility has been the norm for the past couple of decades.

Fear is most explicit among xenophobes, and others I have called reactionary, to the point of irrationality. For example, refugees arriving by boat have posed only a moderate challenge to Australia. The image of a leaky boat full of desperate, alien, often Moslem and allegedly terrorist refugees is the lightning rod of the reactionaries' fear.

The Abbott Government promoted fear of Moslems relentlessly, and a worrying rise in the activity and visibility of extremist hate groups has been an obvious result. Moslems, it is claimed, are trying to take over our society and impose Sharia law, though they comprise just a few per cent of our very diverse population, and only a very few of them evince extreme views.

We have more to fear from fear mongers like Abbott than from Moslems and other minorities. A senior police officer has listed far-right extremists and their marches and rallies 'which encourage divisive notions of us and them' as some of the biggest challenges facing the police. He expressed concern about upcoming rallies by the anti-Islamic group Reclaim Australia. 'There is definitely activity on the extreme right wing of politics and people using events around the world to [justify] events in Sydney,' he said. Rachel Olding reported in 2015 that in the US more people have been killed since 2001 by right-wing extremists than by Moslem extremists.

These levels of irrational fear can be called paranoia. They are most developed and best illustrated again in the US. Both Bartlett and Frum, mentioned earlier, believe a lot of it is fomented by right-wing media like Fox News (owned by Rupert Murdoch). Frum says the billionaires who fund the extremists are not just playing a cynical game: 'They watch Fox News too, and they're gripped by the same apocalyptic fears as the Republican base.'

Bartlett says '[We] public policy analysts aren't meant to make comparisons with the 1930s, but it is beginning to look like the Weimar Republic.'

NEOLIBERALISM HAS PROMOTED CORRUPTION of our democracy. Its economic rationale is to liberate capitalist entrepreneurs to grow their businesses, allegedly for the benefit of everyone. However the corporate sector has benefited in less legitimate ways. Many examples could be cited. During the Howard years a group of industry lobbyists was essentially writing Government energy policy, according to Clive Hamilton in 2007. The group represented the worst greenhouse polluters: coal, oil, cement, aluminium, mining and electricity. One of the lobbyists bragged 'We know more about energy policy than the Government does ... we know where every skeleton in the closet is - most of them we buried.'

On the other hand when Kevin Rudd proposed to tax super profits from mining he was attacked by a deceitful advertising blitz run by three of the biggest mining moguls. After Julia Gillard replaced Rudd, she 'negotiated' with the miners and introduced a tax system designed by them. It was so well designed it collected virtually no tax. Yet Don Henry reported in 2011 that fossil fuel industries in Australia are *subsidised* with more than $10 billion of taxpayers' money every year.

The media also have a heavy hand in our political process. Any Labor or Liberal politician who aspires to lead his party seeks an audience with Rupert Murdoch. Murdoch controls 70% of Australian newspapers, plus other media interests, and he uses his editorial control blatantly to influence politics. The major parties hesitate to do anything of which Rupert seriously disapproves. Murdoch's papers have led the way in vilifying asylum seekers and climate scientists, and generally in raising the level of fear within our society.

Bob Hawke and Paul Keating bear a lot of responsibility for this situation, for they are the ones who announced in the 1980s that they would restructure Australia's media laws. They were of course immediately beset by lobbyists. I remember thinking at the time it was as though they had put 'for sale' signs outside the offices. It was this reform that handed Murdoch control of so much of our print media, according to Robert Manne in 2013.

In recent years there have been major corruption scandals involving state governments, particularly in Queensland and New South Wales. Such overt corruption makes big headlines, and of course it is a shocking betrayal of our democratic system.

Yet our democracy is *systemically* corrupt. Every government for many years has done the bidding of the very rich and powerful. The rich and powerful routinely make large donations to the major political parties. They thereby create a threat that if a party should displease them the funds will be cut off. If that threat does not suffice, and then a hostile media blitz may ensue. In this way the rich and powerful buy favours, big favours, from the government. Yet this is considered legal, and so unremarkable there is virtually no discussion of it. Our democracy has been corrupted and subverted to its core.

John Menadue is a former head of several Federal departments, including Prime Minister and Cabinet. He has given a chilling account of the numbers of lobbyists operating in Canberra, many of them hidden from public scrutiny.

This corruption certainly did not begin with the neoliberal era, but it has been greatly magnified by the reduction of regulation and supervision of business and the overt encouragement to make money by whatever means people can get away with. There was a series of big scandals in the late 1980s, as the first wave of entrepreneurs took advantage of their new license. The scandals at the national level have been less overt more recently, but they have been bigger and more insidious. If this sort of thing occurs in third-world countries it is called crony capitalism.

CYNICAL MANIPULATION has become the norm in our politics. Politics has always been an imprecise business, and consistency is not a notable feature of its products. Yet many major policies and strategies in the past have had an identifiable basis in facts and reasonable sense. Intrigue and deception have always been part of our politics, yet our politicians and political institutions usually maintained some connection to due process, beneficial conventions and even integrity. Today however, our politics has strayed very far from facts, due process and integrity.

One feature of our modern politics is the use of code words to disguise what is happening, or to frame the debate in a way that determines the outcome. We've already seen how the meaning of the terms Left and Right have been changed to disguise the dramatic shift to the political Right over the past several decades. Other terms have been given a derogatory meaning, and regularly applied to critics of neoliberalism.

Redistributing income downwards, or providing social services to the poor, is called *social engineering*. Yet the neoliberal program has manipulated the economic system to redistribute wealth upwards. It has been the most dramatic social engineering in our history.

Anyone who complains about the obscene levels of wealth, and the unearned power it confers, is accused of practising *class warfare*. Yet the rich have systematically undermined the middle class and poor.

Anyone who objects to discrimination, or racism, or public vilification of individuals or groups is accused of *political correctness*. Yet anyone who criticises the neoliberal program is likely to be set upon by the attack dogs of *right-wing political correctness*, the shock jocks, political knee cappers and media enforcers.

Discussion of the economy, and indeed of our whole society, is framed in neoliberal terms: the need for *efficiency, growth* and *jobs*, and to be *open* and *internationally competitive*. Anyone who objects is thus implied to be arguing for waste, stagnation, unemployment, isolationism and backwardness. Yet our economy is extremely wasteful of resources, it could employ more people in clean energy industries than in coal mining, rich foreigners are taking over more and more of it, and unemployment represents a huge inefficiency, as the contribution of the unemployed is foregone and they instead have to be supported, at however niggardly a level.

IS DESTROYING THE LAND and planet we depend on the only way we can make a living? Why does a question like that even come to be asked?

We are totally dependent on the natural living environment for our own survival. Taking care of our *life support system* is not just a middle-class indulgence or a conspiracy of deep greenies.

The degradation of the natural environment proceeds apace. Losses are reported on practically a daily basis, but the frequency and magnitude of losses are increasing. In a brief period in 2016 *nearly a quarter* of the Great Barrier Reef was killed and, we learned later, a vast stretch of mangrove was killed in the Gulf of Carpentaria. Vast kelp forests have disappeared off the coast of Western Australia in recent years. These are dramatic ecological collapses. Many ocean species live or breed in these habitats. Their loss will rapidly deplete the ocean of its living diversity. That will rebound on us in many ways, some of which we may have little notion of at this point.

The neoliberal business model is to extract profit wherever it might be found, and to have it show in the next quarterly profit report. It is the *extractivist* mentality, the old paradigm, the imperative to dominate the world and use it, the *takers'* creed. Neoliberal economists talk about 'rational economic man' and claim to practice a rational science. Neoliberal practice is not rationality, it is insanity.

So we have coal mining that scars the land and will push the world into overheating if it is allowed to continue. We have coal seam gas extraction that pollutes groundwater, disrupts wide areas of productive land, and leaks 'fugitive' greenhouse gases that may make it a worse emitter than coal. Globally fossil fuel companies are pursuing ever-more dirty and dangerous reserves in the deep ocean, in the Arctic Ocean, and in huge, filthy tar pits in Canada. As a result we have monster crude oil spills, despoiled fisheries, homelands and wilderness, and ever-greater emissions per litre of fuel gained.

Agribusiness extracts water from our fragile rivers at unsustainable rates and assaults the soil with old-regime chemical and bio-engineering methods, reducing fertility and resilience and breeding tougher pests in the process. Industrial agriculture promotes loss of biodiversity, greenhouse gas emissions, soil degradation and soil erosion. River runoff carrying excess synthetic nitrogen fertilisers causes around 200 large marine 'dead zones' where the rivers enter the sea. Reserves and parks are under constant political threat of reversion or invasion for the short-term profit the parks allegedly 'lock up'.

According to the 1996 UN Environment Report about one third of the original topsoil of the US is gone, and much of the rest is degraded. Herbicides, chemical fertilisers, monoculture cropping, even ploughing disrupt and destroy soil micro-ecosystems. More soil is being destroyed by salination associated with the removal of natural vegetation and with irrigation. Of the 11% of the Earth's land surface that was considered arable in 1990, little remains really healthy, most is stressed and losses are accelerating.

In poor countries the problems are amplified by the clearing of unstable hill slopes and the slash-and-burn destruction of forests for one or a few years' worth of cash crops, crops that are needed to service debts created by the pathological global financial system. Corporate agriculture's baleful influence is redoubled because it reduces prices and forces small farmers also to exploit their own land just to survive. Family farms in Australia are a declining species, squeezed by agribusiness on one side and the retail grocery duopoly on the other (as we'll see later).

Even an intergovernmental report by The International Assessment of Agricultural Knowledge, Science and Technology for Development in 2008 has acknowledged fundamental problems. Most of the world's farmers are very poor. Yet it is farmers, more than any other group, who are the immediate trustees of the biosphere's health and continued productivity.

Unless small farmers receive a decent income they will not be able to care properly for the land.

GLOBAL WARMING is the most dire threat. Most Australians are aware global warming is already having real effects. Unusually strong droughts, floods, cyclones and bushfires are not necessarily decisive evidence, but for most people they are the dramatic reminders that underline the warnings scientists have been giving for decades. Actually public opinion was clearer on this in the early 1990s. There was even some bipartisan political agreement that the problem existed and what should be done about it. However a concentrated disinformation campaign by industry, think tanks, media and some politicians confused the public so much that uncertainty rose, as told by Maria Taylor in 2014. Even so, more people are again acknowledging the problem. However our governments still lag well behind public opinion.

I will not take much space here to argue that global warming is real and caused by human activities. The reality of global warming has been obvious for decades. The so-called pause in warming never existed. It was an artefact deliberately and dishonestly created by taking 1998 as the base year, but 1998 was far above the long-term trend because of a particularly strong El Niño that year. Warming was noticeably a little slower until 2013, but there were earlier slow periods as well, so it was nothing remarkable. Now warming has resumed with a vengeance. The years 2014-2016 have seen the most rapid temperature rise in the 136-year record, and the temperature is now well above the trend since 1970. The signs are alarming. Temperatures are approaching the upper limit recommended by scientists, 1.5°C above pre-industrial temperatures. That wasn't supposed to happen for decades yet.

Those who deny the reality of human-caused global warming really have only one resort left, and that is conspiracy theory: the climate scientists are trying to scare everyone so they will get more grant money to support their research. It is hard to convey how wildly implausible this claim is. Every scientist knows that lasting fame would come from showing global warming is not happening, or that we are not the cause. They scrutinise each other's arguments closely. Organising scientists is like herding cats. The amount of money at stake would be around 10,000 times less than the trillions fossil fuel companies have at stake, which means the fossil industry turns over the annual climate science budget *in about an hour*. Are we to believe the scientists are all corrupted and wicked whereas the motives of the fossil fuel companies are pure as the driven snow?

Science is far from perfect but it has a well-developed bullshit filter. Over time the crazier ideas and poorly-based bandwagons get found out, and dropped. The media and many politicians, self-appointed experts, have very inefficient bullshit filters. The media pride themselves on being sceptical, but they do a very selective job, overlooking huge piles of bullshit generated by politicians and special interests.

There is a clear consensus among climate scientists that the warming is caused by human activity. The proportion of climate science papers that argue people are *not* causing global warming is somewhere between 3% and 0.17%, depending on who's counting. The latter percentage comes from 24 papers out of 13,950 examined by J. L. Powell in 2012. Let me put that another way: the level of consensus among climate scientists is between 97% and 99.83%. In any other context that consensus would be hailed as 'overwhelming' or 'virtually unanimous'.

The need now is to avoid a crucial tipping point beyond which the warming goes into uncontrollable runaway and rises as much as 4-6°C above present temperatures. It is not clear where such a tipping point might lie, but there are a number of known mechanisms, any of which could turn out to be the culprit. Even the official target of no more than 2°C warming would be very damaging, and on present indications a tipping point might well be crossed below 2°C. Some very serious consequences are now unavoidable, but we must still do whatever we can to avert catastrophic runaway.

The problem is both more urgent and more soluble than governments and media portray. A later chapter will outline the many things we can do right now, at modest cost, that would immediately start to reduce our greenhouse gas emissions. Reducing energy wastage is the quickest and most cost-effective action, but technologies to harvest the energy of the sun and wind are also cost-effective, taking account of their lifetimes and likely costs of fossil fuels. This is becoming widely known, as large numbers of people install solar hot water, photovoltaic panels, battery storage and other technologies that are rapidly progressing. It is governments and media that are lagging behind everyone else.

The effects of global warming are not just somewhat warmer summers, a bit less snow in winters, slightly lower crop yields and a bit snipped off the GDP. The effects include more frequent and more intense storms, floods, droughts and fires. With each degree of warming the effects will be *much* stronger. They will double, and double again, and possibly double again. Even if we stopped greenhouse gas emissions tomorrow warming would continue for another two or three decades because of delays built into the ocean heat system. It is hard to see how the Great Barrier Reef can survive the warming that is already inevitable.

Climate zones will move towards the poles, but plants and animals can't just pick up and move. Some will, some won't, and in the process ecosystems will be torn apart. The disruptions will upset many local balances, and the result will be extinctions of some species and plagues of others. Already forests in North America are being decimated because insect pests that used to die in the winter cold are surviving and chewing up the trees. The plagues will include microorganisms, which may cause pandemics.

Then there's sea level rise. Present indications from polar ice studies are that it may be more rapid than previously estimated. It will go on for centuries, rising at least metres and possibly tens of metres. We can't know the details of what may happen in a warmer world, but we can very plausibly project severe effects of one kind or another.

Neoliberal policies came along at exactly the wrong time. Not only have they promoted many activities that exacerbate global warming, but they have greatly interfered with our ability to politically control what we are doing. On top of that they have promoted the rise of reactionaries whose fearful gut responses override any appeal to facts and rationality. In Australia, exhibit A would be Tony Abbott.

MECHANISTIC, OLD PARADIGM ATTEMPTS to solve these problems commonly only multiply them. There are two alternative approaches. One is to stop our harmful behaviour, if we don't really need to be doing it. This would go quite a long way. The other approach is to carefully mimic biological strategies. The biological world solved such problems long ago, so if and as we follow its lead we are discovering approaches that really do work.

The fossil fuel industry provides a striking example of compounding problems. As the more easily accessible fossil fuels are used up, the industry chases ever-dirtier, more remote and more dangerous sources. Oil companies drill in deep ocean water where oil, methane and sediments take more unstable forms in the deep cold and the high pressures. This is the underlying reason for the 2010 blowout of BP's Deepwater Horizon well that poured filthy pollutants into the Gulf of Mexico for three months. There are active moves to drill in the Arctic Ocean and other remote and dangerous places. There are active programs to drill the deep water of the Great Australian Bight, still one of the more pristine regions of ocean, home to whales, great white sharks, fishing fleets and an immense diversity of marine life.

The failure to address the urgent need to wean ourselves from fossil fuels allows the logic of the present strategy to drag us into ever-more-rapid degradation of the Earth. As Naomi Klein puts it: 'What industry calls innovation, in other words, looks more like the final suicidal throes of addiction.'

Natural gas is claimed to be a bridging fuel because it releases fewer greenhouse gases per unit of energy than does coal. However its emissions are still large, and the large investments required to deliver it require many years to pay off, so the companies only wish to prolong their activities, and to take market share from the new, clean energies that are the real solution. As Naomi Klein asks, when would any industry agree to facilitate its own extinction?

Technological proposals to reduce the atmospheric concentration of carbon dioxide or to directly counter global warming are even more dangerous, fantastical and probably vastly expensive. So-called carbon capture and storage (CCS) is supposed to remove carbon dioxide from the chimneys of coal-burning power plants and bury it deep underground. However no large-scale demonstration has been accomplished, it still removes only some of the carbon dioxide, it requires huge amounts of water and would undoubtedly be extremely expensive. The Earth's crust is riven with fractures so finding sites that would hold huge amounts of pressurised gas for very long times is difficult. A leak could blanket countryside with asphyxiating gas, as has occasionally happened near some volcanos. CCS looks more like political window dressing to delay the shutdown of coal burning rather than a serious proposal. Naomi Klein notes other schemes, like sulphur in the stratosphere or mirrors in space to deflect the sun's heat, that are yet more fantastical and their complex effects on weather, climate, ocean and life systems extremely difficult to anticipate.

Some ideas go beyond counter-productive and into the realm of the bizarre. Unfortunately that description applies to current fossil fuel policy. We pay a fortune in subsidies to maintain our fossil fuel addiction and thereby trash our planetary home. David Coady and others in 2015 estimated the global subsidies, direct and indirect, of fossil fuel to be $US5.2 trillion a year.

Biological approaches, on the other hand, might draw down significant amounts of carbon dioxide with positive side effects instead of negative. Thus regenerative farming, which we'll look at later, can build up soil carbon relatively quickly and thus help to get some carbon back out of the atmosphere, as well as improving soil fertility and water retention. The carbon storage is long term, because *mycorrhizal* fungi create a protein encasement that has a thousand-year half life. Grassland protection and forest management can also contribute. Forest management tends to focus on the above-ground carbon, but the sub-surface carbon, including fungi, are as important, perhaps more so.

The best approach is of course not to emit the greenhouse gases in the first place. The feasibility of reducing fossil fuel use to very low levels by 2050 at quite modest cost has by now been argued by many studies, for example by Amory Lovins' *Reinventing Fire*. McKinsey and Company presented detailed analyses for both the US in 2007 and Australia in 2008. *Beyond Zero Emissions* argued in 2010 for the feasibility of zero fossil fuels in Australia within a decade.

For many years we have continued wasteful uses of energy even though many efficiencies would have immediately saved us money and others would have quickly paid back a modest investment. We are still investing in old systems and technologies that are or will soon be superseded in direct cost by clean energy. On top of all that we are shaping to export the fuels that will almost certainly tip the climate into runaway and possibly catastrophic warming.

THE NEOLIBERAL ERA indeed has not made Australia a more relaxed and comfortable place. Rather, Australia is in a lather of fear and insecurity. We are more divided, more selfish and more afraid. Our society is less democratic and our civil and human rights are being erased.

We are losing the fair go, and the hard-won tolerance of a few decades ago. We are even starting to become less healthy, and lately it is being said the young adults of today will be the first generation to be less well off than their parents. We are going backwards, except in the narrowest material terms, and even that cannot be sustained for much longer. The land continues to degrade and the planet is on the way to becoming a much less congenial place.

The longer the Right survives in power the more authoritarian it must become, to disguise its failure and retain its power. However the fear and force it increasingly uses will not be dislodged by reacting in kind, with more fear and force. That will only feed the spiral. Rather, its power will evaporate when we have the courage to step off its path and choose to relate to each other and the world in a healthier way.

7
Back to Basics

Troubled times always bring out those with fear-driven reactions and simplistic agendas. Fear spreads quicker than hope. So it is proving in the wake of the poor deal many people have had from neoliberalism. Uninformed reactionaries like Pauline Hanson and Donald Trump have no trouble finding scapegoats, but their misdirected anger only makes things worse. It takes a little longer to understand the real sources of the problems, and to identify constructive solutions, but we have no choice if we are to retrieve a fair and open society.

Despite the rise of some reactionary elements, there are also encouraging signs of grassroots pushes for a more positive and constructive political culture. To flourish they will need a vision for a positive, open society. To succeed they will need to challenge self-serving commercial media and come to grips with economic mechanisms that can be turned in our favour. Earth-friendly practices will soon become central to all but those defending old concentrations of wealth and power. These topics are covered in the rest of this book. We start by looking at encouraging developments in politics.

The political culture in Australia has been slow to change, but it is changing. The changes are shifting the makeup of Parliament and the nature of campaigning. The old parties' grip on power is still fairly strong, but slipping, and grassroots political activism is growing. Face-to-face connection is beginning to usurp mass media campaigning, and it is more effective at encouraging people into progressive attitudes.

THE OLD PARTIES, Labor and the Coalition, have been in decline for some time. Between them they got 77% of primary votes for the House of Representatives in the 2016 election. That means nearly a quarter of voters, 23%, gave their first preference to other parties. The informal vote was about 5%. There is also a part of the population that fails to vote or that is not registered to vote. It is hard to find good estimates for the latter, but they would amount to at least 5% of the eligible population.

This means at least a third of the eligible population, 33% or more, does not want the old parties. When discontent starts to approach 40%, tipping points can occur. We may not be far from a major shift in our politics. This would be the first major realignment since the Labor and non-Labor division emerged from the jostling of the first decade of Federation.

This situation has been developing for decades. There is a clear downward trend in the total vote of the old parties starting sometime around 1980. The formation of the Australian Democrats in 1977, when they received 11% of the primary vote, would have contributed to this change, but minor parties existed before then. For example the Democratic Labor Party was active from 1955 until 1978. The Democrats, and later the Greens, have been the most consistent in attracting votes away from the major parties, but more recently the number of minor parties has multiplied. In 2016 the Greens vote was just 10%, whereas the combined vote of other minor parties and independents was 13%.

The rise of the minor parties is reflected more clearly in the Senate because of its proportional representation voting system. There has been a handful of independents and minors for many years but in 2013 the Palmer United Party gained four seats, along with several other minor parties. In 2016 the Nick Xenophon Team gained three, One Nation (Pauline Hanson) four, and several others gained seats.

Even in the house, where it is much harder for minors to gain a seat, five seats went to non-majors in 2016: the Greens, Xenophon Team and three independents. Several more non-majors came quite close. A modest rise in say the Greens and Xenophon votes could, if they exchanged preferences, see a dramatic rise in the number of non-majors in the house.

So far the successful minor parties signify more of a protest than any clear political trend. They are a disparate lot. Only the Greens have a broadly coherent platform. Nevertheless among them all there is a strong theme of resistance to the neoliberal program of free trade, trickle-down economics and privatisation. Some object to such things as corruption of the political process and excess ideological zeal. The Nick Xenophon Team perhaps exemplifies this group best. Some represent fringe groups, such as Family First and other fundamentalist Christian groups, and the Liberal Democrats (who are really libertarian). Pauline Hanson is explicitly xenophobic and a climate denialist, but she is among those resisting globalisation.

So it cannot be said that the drift away from the old parties represents a clear move away from neoliberalism. The flavour in recent elections is more reactionary, though perhaps with less of the ideological extremism of the Liberals. On the other hand they still leave us vulnerable to fear-driven politics, and may still enable some of the xenophobic and anti-knowledge policies of the Liberal extremists. On the progressive side, the Greens held their ground, and Labor, if it counts, gained slightly.

The disaffection with the major parties also shows through increasing volatility of the electorate. Recently two state governments have been thrown out after only one term, despite having large majorities, and this is quite unusual in Australian political history. Federal leaders have become highly unpopular well before their terms finished. The 2010 federal election famously resulted in a hung parliament and a minority Labor government, and the 2016 election came close to being hung. The irony of the return of minority government just 100 years after Labor's Andrew Fisher had achieved the first majorities in both houses was little noted.

If we look overseas we see some analogous changes, much more pronounced in some respects, but still not showing a clear direction. On the one hand, Jeremy Corbyn in the UK and Bernie Sanders in the US explicitly advocate a shift to democratic socialism, and they gained a great deal of support. On the other hand the Conservatives won the 2015 UK election with their austerity policies, and Donald Trump gained even greater support than Sanders in the US, though with an anti-globalisation message. The Brexit vote in Britain seems to have come out of neoliberal neglect of those less well off, but it is expressed through a mixture of xenophobia and economic protest.

Thus the old order is breaking down, but it is unclear whether people will move to more authoritarian or more egalitarian positions. Despite the lack of a promising overall trend, domestically there are some positive signs in particular results and in the way campaigning methods have shifted over the past two elections. In such volatile times the outcome can depend much on who steps up to leadership positions: demagogues or leaders with a clear vision.

POLITICAL ACTIVISM IS INCREASING, and taking new forms. Grassroots campaigning is changing, and some strong resistance movements are bringing diverse groups together. Resistance to coal seam gas extraction or 'fracking' led to the Lock the Gate movement that has brought city people to join with country people directly affected. It includes conservative rural people and environmental activists, young and old, White and Black, the Knitting Nannas and online campaign specialists.

The influence and potential of social media has been much discussed. Until 2016 that influence was mainly on single issues and did not obviously translate into broader political action. The Greens in 2013 pioneered a combination of personal contact, information gathering and sophisticated targeting of contacts through door knocking, phone calls and social media. It was adapted from experience in the United States, where lack of compulsory voting requires a much greater effort to get the voters out. This style of campaigning got Adam Bandt elected in the lower house federal seat of Melbourne. In 2016 it was taken up by Labor, the unions and the online group *GetUp*.

The Greens' 2013 campaign featured an 'army' of on-the-ground volunteers. The campaign door knocked targeted residences identified by data crunchers, and volunteers sought to engage people in conversation about their concerns, listening and gathering information about their views in the process. The raw numbers are significant. Roughly 46,000 residences in the electorate were visited during the campaign. There were about 23,000 follow up phone calls made to constituents. On the last weekend before the election an army of 385 volunteers visited over 10,000 residences in the electorate. A comparable campaign got Bandt re-elected in 2016, despite the loss of major-party preferences.

In 2016 the unions and Labor picked up on the lessons from the Greens and the US and brought even larger numbers of volunteers to bear, in combination with similar sophisticated information gathering and targeting. In a first, the non-partisan online group GetUp conducted a political, though not explicitly partisan, campaign against members of Parliament whose extreme views most obstructed policies advocated by GetUp members. It is claimed these campaigns succeeded in winning a significant number of marginal seats and in removing some of the more extreme ideologues from Parliament.

The Liberal Party has a small membership, and its support base in small and big business is more inclined to write a cheque than to turn out personally for door knocking and handing out how to vote cards. In 2016 the Liberals made no attempt to match the ground campaigns run in opposition to them, and some in the party admit this hurt them significantly.

It is not really clear what was the relative influence of Labor's policy stance and the figurehead campaigning of leader Bill Shorten, *versus* the direct contact campaigns. Yet the Greens' experience, in particular, indicates that the grassroots campaigns are an important component that will need to be part of any successful progressive political campaign.

FACE-TO-FACE CONTACT is the most effective way of changing people's minds about major issues, it seems. Joshua Greene, in his 2013 book Moral Tribes, says some of the strongest determinants of people's views are the views of other people in their community. The grassroots campaigns just described, involving personal, though brief conversations, are a step in that direction. A greater level of social contact has been used in what are called 'kitchen table conversations', and they have been very effective. These had their origin in the reaction to the ruthless neoliberal State Government of Jeff Kennett in the 1990s.

In 1998 in Victoria, six community organisations launched *the purple sage project*, which set about gathering the views of disaffected people across the State through a series of kitchen table conversations. (Sage signifies wisdom, and purple is one of the colours used by the suffragettes a century ago).

Beginning in 1992, the Kennett State Government's policies included a massive restructuring and outsourcing of community services, the forced merging of local governments, the sale of many public assets including the state's highly profitable electricity industry, the closure of 380 schools, the firing of some 50,000 public employees, and unprecedented cuts in education and health. Both public and private services were rapidly reduced in rural areas and country towns, at the same time as farmers faced lower prices and were forced to compete internationally, often against subsidised products.

At this time record numbers of people became long-term unemployed. Suicide among young and mid-career men rose to be the highest in the world. Inequality rose dramatically. Premier Jeff Kennett was also, infamously, personally arrogant and rude, refusing to respond to media who were critical, and personally abusing the Director of the purple sage project when she raised people's concerns in his presence at a conference.

Many people felt ignored, alienated, angry and despairing. Social commentators reported a heightened sense of anxiety, a sense of disengagement, and deep distrust of mainstream politics. Women were especially affected.

This was the context in which the Victorian Women's Trust organised the Purple Sage Project on behalf of the six community organisations. They proposed a dialogue process and called for group discussion leaders. Over 600 people responded, three quarters being women. They led small discussion groups across the state in homes, halls and club rooms. Thousands of people took part. They were encouraged mainly to raise their concerns, rather than to debate issues, and to respect diverse points of view. Discussion summaries, much more detailed than the organisers had expected, were compiled into a draft document. This was to be returned to the discussion groups for comment, after which it would be finalised.

However the Premier happened to call an early election before the final discussions had occurred. At the urging of participants, the project leaders published a summary of the issues that had emerged. Even though the election campaign was only three weeks long, both sides of politics noted many of those concerns in their campaigns. There was an unexpectedly large swing against the Government, and eventually a minority Labor government emerged, supported by three independents. The backlash against the Kennett Government was particularly strong in rural areas, and at least one commentator credited the Purple Sage Project with substantial influence.

The Project did issue a final report. Just as importantly, it galvanised many people, and the lessons learnt have flowed into other political contexts. Community discussions were organised across Australia on the issue of water management, around which there are many contentions among farmers, communities, cities, States and environmental needs. The kitchen table process was refined, and a report issued in 2007. *'Watermark Australia* reframed the debate around water, emphasising the social, cultural and environmental context of water use.'

The methods have been taken up in election campaigns, most notably in the rural Victorian electorate of Indi, where the organisation *Voices for Indi* promoted independent candidate Cathy McGowan AO, who unexpectedly unseated Liberal MP Sophie Mirabella. Mirabella had been called 'nasty', and 'Tony Abbott's bomb thrower'. That success attracted attention across Australia, and a great deal of interest in the grass-roots methods used.

John Davis, writing on the Voices for Indi website, asks 'where in the current political process are there clear avenues for listening and discerning, for respect and for the appeal to our better selves?' He says they are 'now embarking on a much broader agenda. Something as big as 'reclaiming values in Australian politics. Values like transparency of intent, about agreed principles of good government, about re-examining the ways we interact with each other politically.'

WHEN THE PURPLE SAGE conversations began, people were excited. Most had never done anything like it before. The reports from the meetings revealed an acute sense of people unloading a burden: venting their worries, anger and frustration, and registering deeply felt values and community attachments. They also appreciated the opportunity to describe their preferred vision of the future and they did this with clarity and a deep sense of humanity and decency, according to the final report. They were buoyed by being able to share with others troubled by similar issues. People began talking and listening outside the groups, to family, friends, workmates and acquaintances. The Voices for Indi group has continued to be very active in promoting their approach. One of their activities was 'Country Hall Conversations', a follow-up focussing on improving the political process.

Some telling themes have emerged from these grass-roots processes. There is a strong support for increased awareness and education about the democratic process and for finding new ways for citizens to actively participate in our democracy. Politicians should be encouraged to fulfil their responsibilities ethically. The current practice of politics has been judged harshly: *corrupt, disrespectful, abusive, lying, cynical, punitive, cheap*. On the other hand it was recognised politicians who model good behaviour should be supported and acknowledged publicly.

People want to explore strategies to challenge the political party structure, which was seen to provide little opportunity for MPs to be free to truly express the views of the electorate ahead of the Party position, except for rare conscience votes.

Strong support is expressed for all people, including politicians, to use respectful language, to listen to opposing views, acknowledge differences of opinion and work towards collaboration.

The importance of the media has been noted, particularly the value of quality work that is well researched and which has a useful purpose. Too often, the national media and our political representatives are viewed as a poor reflection of each other.

Many issues resonate more broadly and are still highly relevant. People were disturbed by what they saw as an erosion of our democratic culture.

There is undue secrecy in government financial dealings, and much of this is done on the pretext of it being 'commercial in confidence'. Watchdog bodies like Auditors General are downgraded, defunded or even privatised. State governments have been removing or forcibly merging democratically elected local governments; they have the legal right, but that doesn't make it good practice.

Communities were being weakened. Local services, both public and private, were withdrawn. School class sizes were increasing and there were reports of sick people waiting days on hospital trolleys.

People are angry at the loss of public assets, especially to overseas owners. These assets were built up over generations by public taxes and voluntary efforts. People generally have a good nose for false economies. Many of the so-called savings being effected now will cost the community down the track. There are limits to the role of competition, and there are aspects of the breadth and quality of services that are incompatible with the drive for private profit.

People want an inclusive society, not one of winners and losers. They want a society where everyone matters. Environmental care and protection are also a high priority. They should not be sacrificed to increase the profit of an international company. Massive road projects are not the way to deal with urban air pollution and traffic congestion. People value parklands and wilderness as breathing spaces, rather than as areas to be annexed for commercial gain.

People are respectful of differences in culture. They see diversity as enriching and something to celebrate. They yearn for genuine reconciliation between Indigenous and other Australians.

A broader vision of society emerges from such discussions. People consistently identify values of *justice, cooperation, compassion, care, safety, inclusiveness, equality, tolerance, responsibility, multiracial and multicultural understanding, peace and happiness.*

There is a deep-seated understanding in our communities of the different complimentary ways we create social cohesion; a working knowledge about how communities grow and maintain their strength; a realisation that people are social beings with an urge to belong and relate to others. The ethos is mutual support, trust and respect.

People have a no-nonsense understanding of the roles and responsibilities of government in a democracy. Even in difficult times there needs to be stewardship of public assets, accountability, transparency, consultation, ethical conduct, governing for all and protecting the vulnerable.

Likewise there is a clear sense of the role and responsibility of businesses and their shareholders. The profit motive need not be incompatible with social responsibility, environmental care, safety and workplace justice.

The call for politics to be conducted with more respect and more constructively is a strong and persistent theme. Some members of Parliament do it or have done it. Independent MHR Peter Andren was a striking voice of sanity until his untimely death in 2007. He spoke for regional issues and against the Iraq invasion.

In the aftermath of the indecisive election of 2010, the manner of independents Tony Windsor and Rob Oakeshott, in a TV interview, was in striking contrast to the usual posturing of the major party politicians. They spoke with passion and integrity. They shared their concerns and gave thoughtful reasons for the difficult decision they were about to make, on which party they would support to form a Government. They alienated some of their conservative supporters by supporting Julia Gillard, and they were pilloried by the right-wing establishment, but their judgement was that Tony Abbott was not prime ministerial material. Perhaps they have been vindicated. Regardless of that judgement, the examples of Windsor and Oakeshott serve to show that thoughtful and respectful politics is possible.

Beyond the efforts of individual MPs, we might contemplate changes in procedure and even changes in Parliamentary structure, to reinforce and extend the efforts of individuals.

OUR DEMOCRATIC SYSTEMS, imperfect as they are, have been hard-won. It is instructive to read a short history of the formation of the Australian Labor Party by Dyrenfurth and Bongiorno, or of the see-sawing balance of power between people and plutocrats in the United States recounted by Sam Pizzigati and Howard Zinn. Grassroots movements are an essential part of a healthy democracy.

There is little prospect that Australia's major parties will seriously reform themselves, or the current functioning of our political process. If they respond at all, it is likely to be in response to the rise of a threatening alternative. This was well demonstrated in the 1990s and early 2000s when the Liberal Party scrambled to take over the reactionary policies of Pauline Hanson, after her party started pulling 15% or more of the vote in state elections.

The campaign that installed independent Cathy McGowan in the Federal Parliament gained national attention because her win was unexpected, and went against the national swing to the Coalition. It caught the attention of many dissatisfied people across the country because it was a grassroots campaign that broke the stranglehold of the major parties in that electorate. Not only that, it demonstrated the power of respectful, face-to-face discussion.

There are a couple of other notable features of the Purple Sage campaigns. They were strongest in rural areas and attracted a predominance of women. Rural areas and women are among those more disenfranchised by our mainstream politics, so we might have expected them to grasp this opportunity more energetically.

However the predominance of women in creating and running these campaigns surely also anchored the respectful tone in which they have been conducted. Plenty of men are also respectful and considered, and plenty of women can be nasty, as McGowan's opponent amply demonstrated. However plenty of other men too easily let their testosterone and adrenaline run away with them, as we see pathetically demonstrated every day in mainstream politics.

Many of the concerns that emerged in these campaigns would be described in mainstream commentary as *leftist*. Yet Independent Cathy McGowan, who was re-elected in 2016 with an increased majority, would probably describe herself as conservative, and offered to support a Coalition government if it was in a minority. The reflexive labelling of anyone with more compassion than Genghis Khan as *left wing* is a measure of how far to the right our politics has been dragged, and how much our public dialogue has been perverted.

The Purple Sage and Indi campaigns are heartening and instructive because they straightforwardly formulated and articulated values and issues that promote a strong social fabric and a fuller life for everyone. Indeed they are effective in promoting progressive attitudes because they walk the talk: they epitomise the personal connection and local community that is the foundation of a healthier society.

I use the term 'progressive', but the issues and attitudes described here cross the old left-right spectrum and cross party identifications. A progressive in this sense might identify as Liberal, National, Labor or Greens.

8
A Healthy Society

The point of politics is to organise ourselves. It is the way our society decides what to do, and what we do collectively determines the kind of society we live in. There is a lot of discontent with the way our society has been developing. But what kind of society do we want? It is worthwhile to step back for a bit of perspective.

At the same time it is important to be not too prescriptive. We cannot anticipate future circumstances, and we should not try to impose too much on our children and descendants. Nevertheless there are some ingredients that seem at this point to be important. Every generation does acquire some wisdom that can be passed on, just as every generation takes lessons from its forebears. The following thoughts are offered in this spirit, and as suggestions rather than prescriptions.

There is a strong sentiment emerging that we would like a more caring and inclusive society than we have at the moment. This does not mean we want a suffocating nanny state, just a better balance between individual responsibility and helping those who are struggling. The example of country people is instructive: they are generally very independent, but they do not hesitate to pitch in when someone can use some help or when a community needs to pull together. Also a better balance would result if the rewards of our collective efforts flowed more fairly, a topic that will be covered in later chapters.

There is also a strong sentiment that the role of government is important. There are some things that cannot be done individually, nor by private enterprise because the benefit flows to everyone. The provision of what used to be called natural monopolies, such as electricity and water supplies, are clear examples. It is worth remembering that our railways were built by governments, and that Australia thereby avoided the abuses that the United States experienced from its railroad robber barons. Government provision of social services like schools, hospitals and basic welfare support is also highly valued, and regarded as an important part of a cohesive and inclusive society.

It is a simple reality of life on Earth that we must ensure our life-support system, the natural world around us, continues in healthy condition. At present it is degrading rapidly, so we are committing slow suicide. Therefore we need to modify the material basis of our society, so we earn our living in a way that ensures the natural world continues and thrives. This is not radical, it is how people have lived for most of human history. Later chapters will summarise many ways that allow us to live well as we reduce our heavy footprint on the Earth. The changes are mostly in what is regarded as the economy, but the health of our life support needs to be a central recognition by and assertion of our society. As ever, the economy needs to be subservient to our society.

SOME INSTITUTIONS are granted special status because of their key role in our society. The legal system is a prime example. It is deliberately given considerable independence from government, politics and commercial activity, because of course it is required to adjudicate on disputes in other parts of our society. We need to re-assert respect for the courts in the wake of vindictive Abbott-Turnbull Government attacks on them.

The Armed Forces also require a special status, so it is clear their job is to defend the country, not to run it. Unfortunately there has been some blurring of this line as the Howard and later Governments have involved them rather closely in the politics of the day. We would be wise to redraw the line more clearly, remembering that many armed forces in the world are used against their own people.

In the same spirit, we would do well to recognise that *the media* also play a critical role in our society. In technical terms they are the main social signalling system, beyond the small local communities where people actually know each other, and thus have a fundamental influence on the character of our society. We'll pick this up in the next chapter.

Government itself needs to be recognised as serving legitimate and obviously important roles. Our written Constitution goes some way to defining its nature and role, but there is a great deal of less formal understanding that determines how it functions. We can reinforce those conventions that are positive, and add to them if needed.

We might note *education* as having some special status as well, as it is one of the main ways in which the vast fund of our society's knowledge and culture are passed along, and thus ensure our society's continuing viability and health. Education perhaps requires less formal acknowledgement, but the current denigration of knowledge by the reactionary Right requires that we re-assert the central importance of education.

There may well be other institutions and functions in our society worth highlighting. This brief discussion is just meant to highlight the broad question and to remind us to be aware of the health and status of important institutions of our society.

REFORM OF OUR POLITICAL SYSTEM is an obvious need. Just bringing a somewhat more generous spirit back into our parliaments could make a substantial difference. At least it could lift us out of the third-rate slanging matches, sloganeering and fear mongering that typify present performance. Some important improvements can be made without any fundamental changes. However we don't have to be tied to structures and procedures dating from the 18th and 19th centuries. We should not lightly change things, but circumstances have changed, and we do now have greater knowledge and wisdom to call upon, as well as new technologies.

Although our political system is commonly referred to as being a two-party system, there is nothing in the Constitution or elsewhere that requires two dominant parties. Many local councils operate as a single body, without dividing themselves into Government and Opposition. There is no reason parliaments cannot function more flexibly and cooperatively, even if they still retain the formalities of Government and Opposition. Party discipline is much looser in the US Congress. Of course there does need to be a governing cabinet. There is precedent in the formation during wartimes of governments of national unity drawing from all parties. So our parliaments do not have to be as confrontational and combative as they are at present.

The systemic corruption of our present parliaments needs urgently to be addressed. It is a flagrant conflict of interest for political parties to receive money from wealthy special interests. I see no option other than to prohibit private individual donations greater than say a few hundred dollars, and to prohibit all donations from any kind of business. All donations should be promptly and readily open to public scrutiny. Government is meant to be of, by and for the *people*. Election campaigns would need to be funded basically with public money, although there are some creative proposals such as to match private individual funding with public money. Nothing is perfect, but there are options that would be vastly better than the present corrupt farce.

We have the right to know who is trying to influence our governments. There ought to be complete transparency regarding the many lobbyists who spend time with our representatives. At present the reporting requirements are minimal, very belated and quite insufficient. Every contact, no matter where it takes place, should be documented promptly and publicly. Modern technology makes this quite feasible. Perhaps there needs to be a code of appropriate, formalised contact, with such things as dinners and golf games with business interests banned.

Governments ought to see it as central to their job to ensure they hear from all who are affected by contemplated policies. This ought not to need saying, but it is an idea that seems to be totally absent from current politics. Governments have at times practically boasted that they just consult the 'experts', meaning the vested interests. The Howard Government had the *chutzpah* to charge tens of thousands of dollars to anyone who wanted to be in on the Australian approach to the Kyoto Protocol on global warming. The charge was flagrantly designed to ensure only the voices of rich vested interests were heard.

We should require government practice to be the reverse. All interested parties should be sought out. Those who cannot afford it should be paid to attend parliament so they can put their case. The rich should be given no more time and attention than others. All newly-elected governments piously proclaim their deep respect for the voice of the people and their intention to govern for the interests of everyone. Let's hold them to it for longer than it takes them to step off the podium.

Traditional lobbying is being balanced somewhat by web-based advocacy groups such as GetUp. They operate very publicly, so there is less concern regarding inappropriate influence, but there is no reason their activities cannot also be publicly summarised. In fact they tend to do this already, in promoting their own cause.

Some people advocate forms of direct democracy, such as are used in other parts of the world. Switzerland allows direct voting by the public on certain issues. California allows issues to be voted on during elections if a sufficient number of signatories supports them. These approaches are not without problems, but they can certainly be considered and debated.

The American idea of checks and balances can be taken further. Some improved governance structures have been developed that can be used in businesses or in public affairs. One idea proposed by Shann Turnbull in 2003 is to have additional, cross-linking bodies in the governing structure. For example, there might be an elected body whose role is to monitor the main governing body, such as the Lower House, to ensure it is functioning the way it is intended. Outright lies could be called out, such as when politicians claim asylum seekers are illegal. The Abbott/Turnbull Government even made it a requirement that the term 'illegals' be used by the public service.

There might also be some constraint when governments verge on improper actions, such as using taxpayer money to promote their own party. Governments have always fudged such 'information' campaigns, but the Howard Government dramatically raised the stakes when it used public money to fund a TV advertising blitz promoting its health insurance policies. (Labor then happily and hypocritically followed the example.) The increasing trend of modern Australian governments to trample the rule of law might also be discouraged by a monitoring body.

Shann Turnbull cites some cooperative businesses that bring employees, suppliers and customers into a governing or advising forum. An analogous idea for government would be a body comprising a rotating group of citizens who might also monitor the main bodies' functioning, or who might comment on some of the more far-reaching issues. Something like this has already been proposed to give indigenous people a stronger voice in the many issues that affect them.

THE NEED TO RE-ENERGISE healthy local community is a theme that emerges persistently among people looking for a better way of living on our planet. We have a hierarchy of communities and societies, from neighbourhoods to nations, and the balance of power has shifted too far to the biggest: the biggest nations and the biggest corporations. Our local communities, in whatever modern form they take, can provide essential support, physically, socially, psychologically and, for many, spiritually. Yet they are disempowered, and too much power is remote from our daily lives.

We need to rebalance: not to eliminate the big organisations, but to reduce their overbearing power. We can and will communicate around the world, and coordinate many of our activities, but it needs to be more in the spirit of voluntary federation, not dictatorship. In other words we need to tilt the balance of power substantially back towards smaller groups.

In later chapters we will note how markets and money can work better in small communities, and how better-organised communities can reduce our heavy footprint on the planet. Local small businesses, locally owned, will be essential to returning some autonomy and health to local communities.

We can strive to create or recreate healthy small communities as the basis upon which all larger social structures are built. Such communities might take new forms, but if they are to serve our basic needs they must provide regular personal contact, supportive relationships and a sense of belonging and being valued for our humanity and our individual uniqueness.

A HEALTHY SOCIETY must always keep in sight the need to ensure its own continuance and health. It may be degraded or threatened by selfish people, by other societies or by changes in the natural world. It must be vigilant and always willing to adapt. The best way to maximise its adaptability is to maintain an open discussion of its situation and options. This means it is not wise to limit the number of voices heard in the discussion.

It is also fundamental that all dealings be conducted as respectfully as possible. In principle, those angry or fearful voices that *are* raised need to be heard respectfully, but the speakers also need to be encouraged to better manage themselves before their voices can become widely influential. Those who seek to inflame the passions of others need to be appropriately discouraged. Obviously we are a long way from that kind of practice. At present the inflammatory are encouraged by the media's practice of seeking extreme views. Even the ABC's *Q&A* program persists in giving megaphones to extreme or obnoxious viewpoints. We won't quickly change current practice, but we won't change it at all if we don't keep in mind what will make for a healthy society.

Certainly no-one should be able to *profit* from inflaming the passions of others. Nor should those with a megaphone of money or power be able to shout the rest of us down. Some other societies, for example in Europe and especially the Nordic countries, seem to do rather better than we do, so it is certainly reasonable to expect we can do better. The role of the media is so important it will be covered in more detail in the next chapter, but the need for a free and respectful flow of ideas involves more than the media.

Much of this book is about neglected, obscured, denied or suppressed knowledge, knowledge not used because it is fairly recent and not well known, or because some people have become attached to abstractions or myths, or because it is inconvenient to powerful people. It is essential that we promote and widely disseminate the most currently pertinent knowledge, and ensure that the vast funds of knowledge we have accumulated are not neglected and lost.

There is a range of reasons why some knowledge is resisted. Where knowledge is inconsistent with people's sincerely held religious or moral beliefs, the best approach is respectful persuasion, arguing that the knowledge can lead to beneficial results. However when knowledge is denied in defence of wealth and power we must resolutely insist that knowledge takes precedence. This is especially so if the sources and disseminators of knowledge come under attack, as universities and the ABC have.

The philosopher Karl Popper, in *The Open Society and Its Enemies*, argues that the goal of a liberal democracy ought to be to maximise the creativity of its citizens and the openness of its debates. His reasoning is that a society in which the flow of ideas is restricted will have fewer options to draw upon as its circumstances change, and the society may eventually be overcome by some unexpected development. A society that encourages and canvasses the widest range of options will thus have the least chance of overlooking options that will keep it viable.

We can recognise here the cultural equivalent of maintaining a diverse gene pool, which improves a species' chance of surviving change: we need to cultivate and maintain a diverse pool of 'memes' or ideas. Popper proposes that the implementing principle of a liberal democracy needs therefore to be the maintenance of openness. Interestingly, he distinguishes this from majority rule. The reason is that majorities sometimes vote to restrict the openness of society.

In Australia the fundamental protection against arbitrary and secret imprisonment was hastily weakened by an elected government, with the full support of the opposing major party, and now people can be secretly imprisoned for up to two weeks without the government having to show cause (the centuries-old protection of *habeas corpus*). With that precedent established, it would be easy for a future government to extend the duration of secret imprisonment.

Popper argues that the maintenance of an open society might sometimes require a minority to defend the institutions of a liberal democracy against a majority. The surest way to entice people into giving up their freedoms is to make them fearful. This was Hitler's tactic, and it has been the tactic of those who currently exaggerate the threats of refugees and terrorism. With the false cry of freedom on their lips they have not only invaded other countries, they have systematically assaulted the institutions of freedom in their own countries, notably in Australia, Britain and especially the United States. The test of their real devotion to freedom is that those who attempt to debate their policies have been routinely labelled sympathisers with the enemy. Tony Abbott invoked 'Team Australia', which you are necessarily against if you do not join it wholeheartedly.

Such demagogues are threatened by knowledge and by informed debate, and their antipathy to either has not infrequently reached the level of paranoia, as they see conspiracies in every failure of people to bend automatically to their will. They betray everything they claim to stand for. The betrayal is no abstraction. The actions of US President George W. Bush and his ilk only provoked more resentment and more extremism in the countries they assaulted. This has magnified the cycle of violence on both sides.

Popper also makes the point that personal freedom can be limited by too little regulation as well as too much regulation. Neither dictatorship nor anarchy promotes personal freedom. Rather, freedom is maximised by an *optimum degree* of regulation. His reasoning is that anarchy gives free rein to bullies, who proceed to limit other people's freedom. Dictatorship, obviously, installs one bully who limits others' freedom.

The intrusion of corporate power into politics and the closely related rise of anti-democratic demagogues, like financial, media and mining magnates, are manifestations of the under-regulation of our society. They are the bullies and economic warlords spawned by anarchy, and they severely limit the options of our society by limiting the expression of alternative views and of new ideas.

The assault on liberal democracy and the assault on our planetary life support system are both symptoms of those limited views and restricted options, and they have reached the point of endangering the continued existence of our society. We must therefore defend and extend the institutions of liberal democracy, in the broadest sense developed here, in order to retrieve a future for our society. This will require some re-regulation, particularly in finance, the media and some areas of commerce, to restrain the current destructive excesses, topics that will be taken up later.

Short of dictatorship, there are those at present who seem to take pride in ignorance, to be supposedly just part of the common ruck. You don't need to properly inform yourself, you have the right to shout your ignorance. Science is disdained, or at best treated as just another demand on budgets. The disdain for systematically pursuing knowledge manifests strongly in the global warming arguments. This attitude cultivates illusion, the comforting belief that the world is as we want it, but an illusion is ultimately a lie.

Jane Goodall (the writer and Australian Professor, not the primatologist) reminded us after the death of Czech intellectual and former president Václav Havel in 2011 that he pointed to the deeper effects of the communist oppression of his people. Oppressed people become so used to living in a lie that it infiltrates every aspect of their lives, until they can't deal honestly with each other, or even with themselves. We are not as oppressed as the Czechs were, but we are similarly fed a manipulated reality.

As Goodall observes 'A form of democratic politics that is conducted through the tabloid press, focus groups and opinion polls is one that ultimately fails democracy. An electorate dominated by resentment and punitive impulses can easily vote its way back into totalitarianism.'

Havel understood that only if we are willing to speak the truth, in public, to each other and to *ourselves*, can we hope to keep or extract ourselves from the mire of oppression. Havel suffered imprisonment and risked his life to do so. Goodall further notes 'Havel spoke always from a conviction that civic intelligence is the most valuable commodity in any nation, and its erosion is the greatest danger.'

9
Reclaiming Our Conversation

Australians are often said to be conservative, but how would we know? The commercial media have always promoted right-wing views, and they have only become more extreme. The Australian media are arguably the most powerful political force in the country, more powerful than the political parties. Even so there is an ugly synergy between the major parties and the commercial media that has driven the downward spiral into mindless slanging, divisiveness, arrogance and cynicism. Any movement to restore a more inclusive, fair-go Australia must come to grips with the media's role. Their real motives and nature need to be recognised and acknowledged.

Whenever our commercial media are questioned they react in horror and self-righteously portray themselves as *quality media*, essential to the preservation of free speech, which any kind of regulation would surely extinguish before you could say *socialist conspiracy*. In truth, their quality is abysmal, they greatly impede the free flow of information and ideas in our society, and they systematically cultivate and exploit divisions among us. The commercial media exercise great privilege, and they need to be held to corresponding responsibilities.

L̲ET'S STEP BACK and consider what the role of the media might be in a modern society, at its most fundamental. Language is one of the defining human characteristics. When you put people together in a group, what happens? Talk. Chatter. Discussion. We can hardly help ourselves: if we're with each other we talk to each other. Talk is a big part of what binds a community together, a central part of our intensely social nature. Talk serves this purpose in small communities, communities up to one or two hundred people, communities small enough that we can know everyone and meet them eye to eye.

Modern societies are much bigger than this, numbering in the millions. We cannot talk directly with each other so we use technology. Over the millennia we have used writing, printing and broadcasting. These technologies do not completely fulfil the role that talking does in a small community, but they do go a long way towards allowing us to communicate across our large societies. They do play the same role, however imperfectly, of binding our societies together. They are therefore a very special, critical part of our society. Ask any systems analyst and she will tell you the nature of the signalling mechanism within the system critically determines the system's behaviour. A sensible society would therefore do its utmost to ensure its media function as well possible, and in the interests of everyone.

Instead, we have allowed a few powerful people to control much of our media. Australia has had the great privilege and benefit of a publicly funded broadcaster which has played a role much closer to the one I just described, the role of facilitating society's conversation. However for some time now the ABC has been subjected to bullying by those who wish to control our conversation, and effectively to occupation by the Liberal Party. The commercial media have required no such bullying, their proprietors have ensured only an approved range of communication passes through their media. To be approved, such communication must not threaten the profits and power of the proprietor. The best way for a reporter to advance his career is to provide material that startles or alarms us, so we break into a frenzy of chatter.

M̲Y PARTNER AND I happened to witness the Great Australia Day Riot at The Lobby restaurant near Parliament House in Canberra in 2012. You might not remember much about it, but you will probably remember the dramatic pictures of Prime Minister Julia Gillard being dragged by a security man from the clutches of a howling mob, shielded by a policeman in full riot gear.

We had attended a nearby gathering marking the 40th anniversary of the Aboriginal Tent Embassy, then had some lunch at the cafe adjacent to the restaurant. We noticed some kind of formal function through the glass walls of the restaurant. As we finished lunch we noticed people running towards the restaurant, and emerged to find people streaming from the Tent Embassy rally and surrounding three glass-walled sides of the restaurant. We were told the Opposition Leader, at that time Tony Abbott, was inside and he allegedly had said the tent embassy should be removed. We also learnt Prime Minister Julia Gillard was inside. The demonstration soon became rowdy, with people chanting slogans and some beating time on the glass walls. Perhaps 200 people were milling around. Many were spectators like ourselves, and we were never more than metres from the action. Neither were we concerned for our safety. After a time more police and security men arrived, one dressed in full riot gear with transparent shield.

We did not actually witness the extraction of the VIPs from the side of the restaurant, but we did see them hustled into cars and driven away. There was a bit of pushing and shoving, but not close to the VIPs, and a couple of people tried to impede the cars, but soon desisted.

This was the event almost universally portrayed by the commercial media as a riot, implying violence. TV news personalities shook their heads in faux bemusement at the shocking and outrageous behaviour of a group of unruly Aborigines, threatening the safety of our country's leaders.

The police reported scuffles, but that no arrests would be made. They said there would be an internal investigation. *Three months* later they conceded there had been no injuries and no property damage. Of course this news was not given any screaming front page headlines.

The famous picture of the dragged Prime Minister came about because the security man was spooked and seriously over-reacting. He so rushed the PM that she lost a shoe, stumbled and nearly fell. You can see in the background Tony Abbott and others walking normally. None of the VIPs was under any immediate threat. The cameraman made sure the one policeman in riot gear was prominently in the foreground, to make the picture more dramatic, as they do. Was this why it was called a riot?

After the VIP cars departed, security made a show of linking arms across part of the road in front of the restaurant, with their rattled boss stalking up and down behind them and shouting at them to hold the line. It was quite farcical because you could freely walk past either end of the line in either direction. However it gave a focus to the still-angry demonstrators and provided more footage of yelling aborigines.

Not everyone was fooled by the hysterical media coverage. Quite a few people noticed the images did not really support the lurid language. There were no demonstrators close to the VIPs, and Tony Abbott was walking normally, if briskly. A few eye witness accounts, including my own, appeared on internet media sites disputing the substance and tone of the media coverage.

However the mainstream media were far more interested in whether someone in the PM's office had falsely reported Tony Abbott's alleged remarks about removing the tent embassy. They charged off in pursuit of the latest gossipy political intrigue, utterly uninterested in the latest example of gross misreporting, or the resulting slander of Australia's indigenous people.

THIS EPISODE ILLUSTRATES one aspect of the abysmal state of Australia's media. You could of course choose from hundreds of other examples. It is just the normal way they operate. They want conflict, colour and movement. They are not informing, they are entertaining. They are not interested in the truth, they just want drama. If what they report is shown actually to be a lie, as the above alleged 'riot' was a lie, they are studiously silent, or they feign outrage and threaten legal action. If innocent people get hurt by what they report, they deny it. If vulnerable groups are maligned, they're not interested.

On the other hand if the commercial media are challenged they are the most thin-skinned of all. They have submitted themselves to a so-called voluntary code of conduct, a flimsy gloss policed by a toothless body of their own creation. When it was suggested the code should be marginally improved, and actually made enforceable by an independent, non-government body, they went into paroxysms of betrayed innocence and outrage that anyone should question the integrity of the 'quality press', and at the supposed threat of a police-state ban on freedom of expression.

Rupert Murdoch owns around seventy percent of Australia's newspapers, along with a huge global media empire. His tabloids regularly splash gross distortions and inflammatory exaggerations across their front pages. His flagship, *The Australian*, indulges in self-proclaimed political campaigns (such as to 'destroy' the Greens) and regularly conducts campaigns of personal attack and vilification of anyone who attracts its disapproval. It so freely mixes editorial comment with its so-called reporting that it gives the impression of no longer understanding the difference. Much of its commentary comprises fact-free rants. Robert Manne in 2011 undertook the thankless task of documenting hundreds of its abuses over a period of months. Of course *The Australian* says he's a biassed lefty who is the one who commits all the things he falsely accuses them of. Like all the shock jocks, attack dogs and internet trolls of the reactionary right, it cannot perceive the difference between a gut-fuelled, fact-free rant and an informed, evidence-based commentary – or perhaps it chooses not to.

Murdoch's News Corporation displayed all these vices in its dealings with the Australian Press Council, which oversees 'voluntary' regulation of the media and is funded by the commercial media – hardly an independent body. Irked by a ruling that went against it in 2014, News Corp went on the attack. 'The attack consisted of the standard News Corp tactics of ridiculing the person, creating stories where no story really existed, promoting these stories well beyond any objective assessment of their news value, and publishing associated editorial commentary prosecuting the underlying agenda driving the exercise in the first place' wrote Denis Muller in 2015.

One cannot really call such a media organ as *The Australian* a newspaper at all. It is a propaganda rag. Murdoch's Fox News TV network in the US led the world in presenting rants as news, and Murdoch journalists and newspapers in Britain indulged in systematic, massive and illegal hacking of private phones, all in the name of sensation and scandal for the greater profit and power of the Murdoch empire.

There are a few rather basic requirements before media can describe themselves as *quality*. News reports must not contain editorial comment. That means they must not even contain judgemental terms, such as 'leftist' or 'radical', terms that were routinely applied to Yanis Varoufakis, the short-lived Finance Minister of Greece, though he was only proposing actions that were normal a few decades ago.

It should not need stating that reporting should not be persistently incorrect or significantly misleading. Yet *The Australian* in particular is persistently incorrect and misleading on the matter of global warming. I do not mean that aspects of global warming cannot be debated. I mean that if a sceptical point of view is reported then it should be made clear that only a tiny minority of climate scientists think humans are not causing global warming. By omitting this perspective, *The Australian* persistently and deliberately misrepresents the balance of scientific opinion.

THE AUSTRALIAN ROUTINELY GOES FURTHER, and flagrantly injects a point of view into what purports to be reporting. It is worth spending a little time on one example to be clear just how deficient is the product of this so-called newspaper, if you will bear with a bit of finicky analysis for a few paragraphs. It is a bit hard to believe so many mistakes and misrepresentations could be packed into one brief report.

On the 22nd of February 2014, *The Australian* ran a piece headlined 'Ice ships that sank the warming idea'. It reported that a number of ships had recently become stuck in ice in a particular part of Antarctic waters, where the sea ice was thicker than usual because of the presence of an unusually large iceberg offshore. It also wove in comments on a recent, unrelated scientific study documenting the retreat of Antarctic ice at a rate that significantly contributes to the rise of sea level. The newspaper report claimed the presence of some locally thicker sea ice, where the ships got stuck, was 'casting significant doubt' on the conclusions of the scientific study, and wrote that claim into the headline.

There were some other scientists on one of the stuck ships (not the authors of the report noted above). The newspaper report claimed a statement those scientists released said 'the Antarctic ice was expanding'. It then quotes from the statement, which concludes 'Sea ice is disappearing due to climate change, but here ice is building up.' So the reporter's supposed paraphrase is the exact opposite of what the scientists actually said. This fails elementary reporting standards.

There are multiple problems with this report. The unnamed but obviously untrained and unscientific reporter presumes to be a better scientist than the specialists. Even the facts and quotes included in the report contradict the reporter's interpretation, because it is clear the thicker sea ice was local, and due to the presence of an iceberg, not to the falsity of global warming. There are elementary factual errors and the article was not even properly copyedited. The reporter confused sea ice (a metre or so thick) with icebergs, claiming the ships were 'left stricken on massive icebergs', conjuring a picture of ships perched high out of the water. The source of the scientific study is not properly identified, as there is no prominent magazine called *Science Journal* - perhaps they meant *Science*. The name of a ship was left uncapitalised. Any reputable newspaper would fail a cub reporter who produced rubbish like that.

The report is larded with judgemental and emotive words. For example 'the scientists *further ignited* the debate'. Well, they presented their conclusions, and you can't *further* ignite something. Perhaps the illiterate reporter meant *further inflamed*. '*The cold hard facts* from the recent number of vessels ...', presumably as distinct from the limp warm facts of the scientists. 'The *battered* cruise ship and its *bruised* passengers *limped* to New Zealand'. There is no suggestion that the ships or their passengers were damaged or injured, let alone 'stricken'. They were merely delayed, so this sentence is pure fabrication.

THE PROBLEM IS NOT LIMITED to *TheAustralian*. Far-right commentators are thickly sprinkled throughout all of our media. Many of them have connections with the Institute of Public Affairs and other right-wing think tanks, which are conduits for rich vested interests. Even the ABC has had the IPA's Chris Berg as a regular commentator. Why? There are plenty of his kind in the commercial media. John Howard used to complain that the ABC should have a right winger to balance Philip Adams. Again, why, given the hordes of right-wingers in the commercial media?

It is not as though there is a large contingent of actual socialists always banging on in our media. By traditional measures, as portrayed earlier in Figure 4.1, there are no really left-wing commentators in the mainstream media. As with our political parties, there are a few in the centre and a lot on the right. There are others who merely give informed commentary that does not have much overt political flavour. It is only the right-wing extremists who perceive everybody else to be leftists.

It is pretty clear there has been a long-term concerted campaign to place far-right people in strategic positions throughout our society, in the media, the public service, semi-government bodies and politics. They have come close to taking over the Liberal Party. This is the way the Right has operated for a long time here and abroad. They are well funded and that is why they have become so powerful.

THE IDEA OF INFORMED BALANCE is absent from our media. Robert Manne, in his 2011 essay on *The Australian*, documented hundreds of items that were misleading, incorrect, or, through selective publishing, giving an unbalanced impression of important issues. If newspapers were required to have a licence, the way electronic broadcasters are, then there would be ample grounds for withdrawing *The Australian's* licence. Perhaps a general licence, for any news and commentary site commanding a large audience through any medium, would be a useful innovation.

The rest of the media are less blatant in their biases, but they still misrepresent the balance of scientific opinion on global warming, by insisting on giving sceptics nearly equal time, and thus creating the false impression that the climate science community is seriously divided.

The media's use of a simplistic notion of balance is quite inappropriate when technical subjects are being reported. The 'balance' conveyed should roughly reflect the balance of the weight of evidence, as interpreted by specialists. Anyone is free to disagree with specialists, but the interpretations of the specialists should not be misrepresented, as they routinely are when the media treat them as just another group demanding attention.

Even in reporting politics, the media should use a more sophisticated interpretation of balance, instead of just lazily serving up the views of the two major parties, which anyway are quite close together in their world view. The views of independents and minor parties are only sporadically represented. The media would serve us better if they went beyond the political fray and reflected the range of views in the community. Even better would be to convey some historical perspective, which could convey how the present range of political views is well to the right of where they were several decades ago.

'IT'S YOUR ABC' was the ABC's promotional slogan a few years ago. Technically the ABC belongs to all Australians, and we pay for it through our taxes. However it is no longer our ABC. It is the Liberal Party's ABC.

John Howard stacked the ABC board with extreme right wing partisans, people like historian Keith Windschuttle, whose scholarship has been found seriously wanting by his peers, and the acerbic far-right journalist Janet Albrechtsen. The recently-retired managing director, Mark Scott, had been a staffer for the NSW Liberal Party. Remarkably, the subsequent Labor governments of Kevin Rudd and Julia Gillard did little to reverse these ideological abuses, although there has been some turnover of membership of the ABC board. Perhaps they were afraid of offending the Murdoch press? Later Albrechtsen was appointed by the Abbott Government to a key post vetting ABC appointments.

A previous ABC Board Chair (and head of Prime Minister Tony Abbott's business advisory council), Maurice Newman, has self-identified a climate denier, claiming on the basis of absurdly cherry-picked data that we're actually on the brink of an ice age, according to Oliver Milman. Worse, Newman has claimed attempts to avoid global warming are a grand conspiracy, an attempt to impose 'a new world order under the control of the UN' according to Jeff Sparrow. This verges on the deranged.

The standard of editorial judgement at the ABC has been debased from informed commentary to mere partisan 'balance'. In fact, if the political entertainment show Q&A is a guide, the range of opinions balanced routinely extends beyond the Liberal Party to extreme right wing think tanks and inflammatory reactionaries.

Simply by pursuing a policy of balanced news and informed commentary, the ABC used to help to balance the routinely right-wing commercial media, and without having any explicit left-wing or socialist point of view. However that was not good enough for the radical Right, whose plans were impeded by the informed populace that followed the ABC. So John Howard set about dragging the ABC to the Right.

We need to restore the independence and funding of the ABC. The Greens have long had a proposal for a Board at arm's length from politics, comprising representatives from the community and with political hacks excluded. It is hard to tell how much the ABC's funding has been cut over the decades, as reporters usually only tell us how much it is been cut over the last year or two. A funding boost by at least 50% would seem in order. That way the ABC might be able to provide Australian programming to replace some of the endless parade of English murders, English renovations and English antiques. Paraphrasing Phillip Adams from decades ago, we need to hear our own voices, see our own stories and dream our own dreams.

THE COMMERCIAL MEDIA promote discord in our society, for profit. They do this in a number of ways. They routinely seek the most extreme views on controversial issues so as to inflame the controversy and promote sales and views. Shock jocks play the same role. Philosopher Eleanor Gordon-Smith quotes a series of revealing comments by Australian and US shock jocks: many do not believe what they're saying, they are only 'entertaining' to increase their ratings. They subvert the possibility of a sensible, well-informed discussion.

The commercial media promote fear for the same reason. Currently there is a big scare campaign concerning the possibility of isolated extremist youths becoming terrorists. This is a serious concern, but it needs to be kept in perspective. For example no more than a few people so far have died from terrorism in Australia, whereas around 300 die every year from domestic violence.

The hysteria promoted by the tabloids, and by a prime minister desperate to stay in office, advances police state powers out of all proportion to the threat. They already go well beyond what is wise for a notionally democratic society. Meanwhile the real source of the problem, our meddling in other societies' affairs which we'll look at later, will remain obscured and unaddressed.

The worst aspect of this irresponsible behaviour is that it induces us to be suspicious of each other. To be sure, the suspicion falls most heavily on certain ethnic groups, but fear is indiscriminate, and it divides us all against each other. Our society is more fractured, we are less willing to help each other, and our lives are more base and unfulfilling.

There are always fearful people in any society, and there will be those who try to spread the fear. Pauline Hanson is one of those. Her fear mongering would have fallen on less fertile ground in the mid-1990s had many people's livelihoods not already been destabilised by neoliberal economic policies. Still, her xenophobic tribe would have remained a minority had not John Howard taken over her policies and fear mongering in 2001, in a desperate attempt to avoid a landslide electoral defeat. It was obvious at the time that Howard had set our society on a slippery slope in which the Government would have to become more and more authoritarian to retain power, until we lived in a police state.

Of course Hanson and Howard were not acting alone. They were ably abetted by the commercial media, who happily propagated the myths that Australia was about to be overwhelmed by hordes of alien and illegal refugees, many of whom were probably terrorists.

Foreign Minister Julie Bishop gave the latter myth a bit more oxygen in 2016. She told journalists that unnamed officials in Europe had told her that some 'people smugglers' operating in the Mediterranean were supplying funds to Middle Eastern groups of alleged terrorists. She was ever-so-careful to say she wasn't suggesting this was also true of Southeast Asian 'people smugglers'. But she got what she was fishing for. The headline in the Fairfax press read 'Smashing people smuggling the priority due to terrorism links'.

The replacement of Tony Abbott by Malcolm Turnbull somewhat muted the scare-mongering but did not eliminate it. One might hope the trend will continue, but the extremists in his party will be doing what they can to keep the hysteria bubbling.

NEOLIBERALS TRUMPET THEIR BELIEF in free speech. Yet when you look at what they do, you see that, like the Mad Hatter's words, 'free' means whatever they want it to mean. They would like their friendly media thugs, like Andrew Bolt, to be able to say whatever they want about anyone. They insist anyone has the right to be a bigot.

Yet not everyone seems to get the same licence. For example, animal rights activists attracted the Abbott Government's ire for exposing ill treatment of cattle exported to other countries. In response, the Government promoted so-called Ag-gag laws that, if passed, would involve media agencies receiving harsh penalties, including heavy fines and the possibility of gaol terms, should they choose to publish or broadcast footage or material exposed through covert operations or surveillance. The aim of these laws is not to enforce laws regarding animal welfare and cruelty, but rather to shut down the exposure of commercial operations committing criminal acts, as Peter Wicks has explained.

The Abbott Government also imposed unprecedented peacetime restrictions on reporting their dealings with asylum seekers. They banned reporting of what they choose to call 'on-water activities', in other words their interceptions of boats carrying asylum seekers. It is highly likely, based on their record, that the asylum seekers are not given a proper opportunity to make their case before they are summarily turned around. The Government also severely restricts information about overseas 'detention centres', although enough has emerged to make it clear there are serious and systematic abuses of human rights, including those of children, and including sexual abuse. It has even legislated to make it a crime for health professionals to fulfil their professional duty to report cases of abuse that come to their attention.

The point of these restrictions is to keep asylum seekers out of the headlines and to ensure their personal stories are not accessible. So long as they are just unidentified 'illegals', the public's empathy will be less likely to be triggered. The point of the policy was amply illustrated by the outpouring of sympathy triggered by a picture of a drowned little refugee boy on a Turkish beach. That one image, that connected people with a real person, may have significantly shifted the Australian debate on asylum seekers.

A BIG LIE HAS TAKEN OVER Australia. It is amazing that we are in the grip of fear of invading hordes, yet asylum-seeking refugees are such a relatively moderate challenge for Australia. Perhaps the media were just indulging their habit of seizing upon sensational and scary words and images. Yet the effect of their behaviour has been to magnify the politicians' scare mongering into a national obsession.

It seems a powerful synergy operated between politicians and media to turn a concern of fringe xenophobes into a destructive national obsession. Politicians must take responsibility for exploiting the fear of refugees in their quest for power. It would have been possible to limit and assuage the fear if politicians have chosen to be more responsible, and just a little bit courageous. This was demonstrated in the 1970s, when Malcolm Fraser and Labor cooperated to receive and peacefully settle refugees from Vietnam, not all of whom were very savoury as it turned out. However once John Howard let the genie out, the hysterical media coverage and the haranguing of shock jocks ensured that spineless politicians thereafter were afraid to speak the truth. So the Big Lie became established by endless repetition, echoing back and forth between politicians and media.

It would be unfortunate enough if the effect of the Big Lie was only to turn a formerly easy-going society into a divided and fearful society. However the lives of innocent people are being destroyed, emotionally and psychologically and sometimes physically, so as to deter a relatively small number of other desperate refugees from trying to reach Australia.

How many other myths circulate within Australia because the media are sensationalist, superficial, lazy, and/or pushing their proprietors' agenda? Climate scientists are divided about global warming, so we should wait until the science is more settled before taking serious action. Aborigines were simple wandering nomads before Europeans arrived. Modern aborigines get much greater welfare benefits than anybody else, and they are just too lazy to get off the grog and get a decent job. Most Moslems are extremists. Australian Government debt is a threat to the stability of the country, and the budget must be balanced at all costs. The government budget is just like a household budget. These are just a few of many examples of misinformation that the media could quickly dispel if they chose to present balanced news coverage and well-informed commentary instead of hysterical rubbish.

How can we run our affairs sensibly when we are burdened with so much mythical nonsense? How can anyone pretend there are any quality commercial media in Australia? Of course we're so used to this kind of media that we shrug and say that's just the way things are. How could it be any different? Media will always be sensationalist and they will always push their owners' agendas. We should be grateful there are any 'independent' media at all, otherwise we would live under tyranny.

So is that the choice? Either we live under government tyranny, or we live under Rupert's tyranny? No, we can be more imaginative than that.

HOW MIGHT WE IMPROVE the quality of our media? We could make some improvement through regulation, though regulation is a blunt instrument and its effect would be limited. A better approach is to look at ownership. There are many more options than ownership by government or rich people.

First, there could certainly be more effective regulation of the media. A licence for major media is an idea worth considering. Anyone who wants the right to broadcast (by any means) to large numbers of our citizens also ought to have responsibilities. Those responsibilities ought to include not being consistently misleading or factually incorrect, clearly distinguishing opinion from reporting, and not systematically promoting discord. Such requirements would not be simple to police, but even some modest restraint on the present excesses of irresponsibility could be a considerable improvement. There would certainly need to be care not to over-police and unduly restrict discussion. That of course is the difficulty of this approach. It is also why the ownership approach is more promising.

In the meantime a public internet campaign calling out the worst of the distortions and lies of the media could be useful. A campaign to boycott the Murdoch press might also have a role. It might not have a large overt effect, but the Murdoch press is already struggling financially so even a few percent of sales lost might get their attention. More importantly, both actions could create a little more room for politicians to advocate progressive policies with less fear of being isolated and attacked in a Murdoch vendetta.

One thing progressives can do anyway is to subscribe to those outlets, mostly online, that offer more balanced news and informed commentary.

Regarding ownership, at a minimum foreigners should be excluded from owning our media, and empires should be broken up. Our media are for our society to have its conversations, and we must be firmly in control. Media ownership is more concentrated in Australia than almost anywhere, and everyone agrees it is unhealthy, it is just no-one has the guts to do anything about it. There should, perhaps, be at least two major independent centres of editorial control in each major city. Of course that doesn't work for internet news, because it is available everywhere, so the limit would be on newspaper, radio and TV editorial control. Therefore a national minimum number of editorial centres above a certain size would also be needed. Of course such limits would not be simple to determine or enforce, but any fairly simple scheme would still be a big improvement on the present oligopoly that reigns over both print and internet, with broadcast forming a parallel oligopoly.

A quite different approach would be to require ownership to be distributed among large numbers of people. For newspaper and broadcast media, each outlet could be owned by the people it serves, with no-one permitted to own more than a small fraction of the business. In the big cities, one could require at least 10,000 or 100,000 owners, so no individual or small group could gain control, and there could be a residency requirement to ensure ownership is within the community served. Clear rules to ensure democratic control among owners would be required, unlike present corporate governance rules. For the internet, analogous limits, depending on size of audience, could apply, with no-one being able to hold shares in more than one news organisation.

I wrote about distributed ownership of the media over a decade ago (in *Economia*, 2004), and had never encountered any real-world interest. It is heartening to learn, therefore, the UK magazine *Positive News* has moved to become a cooperative. As they say, '*Positive News* will be owned by hundreds or thousands of people with an equal say on important matters, meaning it is a more democratic form of ownership. We will then be ultimately accountable to you, our readers, ensuring that we always report in your interests.'

The collective ownership approach would still allow some large organisations, required for comprehensive news gathering, to exist, but it would be much harder for individuals or groups to dominate or control them. Some charter limits could be mandated to ensure an appropriate kind of service was provided, so an organisation did not drift away from its purpose, such as news, commentary, analysis, with social and entertainment news.

Nothing is perfect in this world, and neither would such media avoid management and operational issues, but they would move us away from domination by big government or big money, and this would be a vast improvement. It would be so different it might perhaps be hard to imagine. Hopefully our grandchildren might find it hard to imagine why we allowed ourselves to be browbeaten and deceived for so long by a handful of the rich and powerful.

10
Markets: Taming the Wild Horses

Thanks to Dilbert and Scott Adams

The idea of free markets has been central to the neoliberal project. It is the most potent expression of the larger philosophical idea of maximising individual autonomy and minimising government. It is also, at its core, wrong, a flimsy construction, a paper tiger.

Debate about markets is both polarised and confused. Much of the confusion derives from a false dichotomy – we can either have capitalism or socialism, end of story. There are many possible forms of market economy, and many degrees of socialism, so we need to be open to a wider range of ideas.

In one polarised debate, some people advocate for markets and take it as given that free markets deliver wealth, that the wealth enriches everyone eventually, and that is the end of the matter. At the other pole, some people reject markets entirely and insist only big socialism, meaning government ownership of most enterprises, can be fair to everyone. But markets are not a natural phenomenon, they are created by people, and free markets are not the only possible kind of market. In fact there really are no free markets, because all markets operate within rules dictated by governments. The real question is what are the rules and who benefits?

Some people conflate markets with capitalism. If you criticise the way some markets operate at present you are presumed to be against capitalism and you may cop a lecture on the wickedness and failure of socialism. But markets existed before capitalism. A village produce market can operate without the presence of capitalists. Anyway it is often unclear what people might mean by 'capitalism', except that it is some kind of system that involves rich people and markets that may or may not be free or un-manipulated.

Mainstream economists, those of the neoclassical tradition, go further and claim free markets will automatically balance supply and demand and, best of all, the resulting state of *general equilibrium* is a blessed state because it is the most efficient of all conceivable states. That is not a small claim.

All of this heat and confusion makes it a bit difficult to have a calm and sensible discussion of markets and how they might operate. So committed neoliberals, capitalists, socialists and neoclassical economists may wish to stop reading at this point, because what follows might be offensive to you. It will be argued here that markets can operate in many ways, depending on the rules under which they operate, and historically they have operated in many ways. We can therefore look to see what determines the way markets behave, and see if we might adjust the rules so markets do things we want.

But, some may think, markets have never acted benignly before so it is not credible to claim they could. However markets have behaved sometimes better, sometimes worse. They were not so bad in the postwar years when they were more regulated, and they have been worse in the neoliberal years with less regulation. So clearly we can have an influence on how they behave. If we look carefully we might see how to make them much better than in the past. It is not really hard to see how, it is just that our vision has been obstructed and distorted by a century or so of misguided thinking.

We have already seen that less regulation of markets has resulted in inferior economic performance and has harmed the lives of many people. Here we will look at how some markets actually work, how they clearly are not following the claims of economic theory, and how they cause harm. Then we'll see the claim that free markets are best actually has no basis at all – not in practical experience, nor in any theory that can claim relevance to the real world.

The latter (counter-) claim may strike some as preposterous, but there it is. It is not hard to establish, as you will see. Nor does it require obscure jargon or difficult ideas, let alone mathematical equations.

MAINSTREAM ECONOMISTS' FAVOURITE METAPHOR is *the invisible hand*. Adam Smith is purported to have argued that each person, by following only his own self interest, is 'led by an invisible hand to promote an end which was no part of his intention'. Supposedly, the free market will gather all our self-interested actions and bring about an optimal balance of supplies and demands, with prices not too high, incomes not too low, products of good quality and so on. However Smith never gave it the universal significance modern economists claim. Smith did use the metaphor in discussing the domination of trade by merchants in collusion with tame governments (mercantilism), but he was not arguing for trade to be freed from government regulation, he was arguing for trade to be freed from distortion by *big business*.

Sometimes the invisible hand works, and our individual actions combine to produce a desirable result. At other times markets gather our individual actions to produce a perverse result: a crashing financial market, a credit boom and bust, contaminated food or a polluted atmosphere. Some wit said these problems reflect the action of *the invisible foot*. Experience would suggest the invisible foot acts about as often as the invisible hand.

In 2015 frozen berries were withdrawn from sale in Australia because they were contaminated with Hepatitis A. The berries came from China, where the disease is more common and apparently the hygiene of workers is not as good, nor as closely regulated and supervised as in Australia. But why were berries imported from China when we already grow berries in Australia? Evidently because it is cheaper to get them from China. That sounds strange, because there would be extra costs of storage and transport involved with bringing the berries from China. Evidently the final cost can only be lower because Chinese workers are paid a pittance.

Bringing berries from China denies a local market to Australian berry growers. It also increases greenhouse gas emissions, because of the power required to freeze, store and transport the berries. Nor will the berries be as fresh as the local product.

But the ultimate reason berries are brought from China is that Australia's two giant grocery retailers are competing for your custom. The only criterion in this competition is the final price of the goods on the shelf. In this world cheaper is always better. To force the price as low as possible, costs are ruthlessly cut.

Coles and Woolworths so dominate their market they can dictate the price they pay to suppliers. To stay in business producers have to cut their own costs to the bone, which means they cannot properly care for their land to sustain its fertility. Effectively, they are forced to mine the nutrients from the soil. As prices are pushed ever lower, even this short-term strategy fails and producers go out of business. It is at this point that the retailers look overseas for cheaper produce.

A healthy economic system produces wealth, and produces it in a way that can continue indefinitely. Coles and Woolworths are not producing wealth, or rather are not paying for wealth *production*, they are forcing the unsustainable *extraction* of wealth. Wealth is being *extracted* from our soils and from our rural communities and families.

This situation then begs the question of why Coles and Woolworths dominate our retail grocery market. The answer is that *competition eliminates competitors*. Once a firm becomes bigger than most of its rivals, it can undercut the prices of each smaller rival, eliminating them one by one. Of course the Australian Competition and Consumer Commission (ACCC) is supposed to see that this does not happen, but they don't seem to be doing a very good job.

Nor is this supposed to happen according to mainstream economic theory. The theory supposes that no firm can grow large enough to influence the market. This is rather blatantly untrue. Globally, many industries are dominated by only a handful of giant corporations. In Australia we have two dominant grocers, four dominant banks and two main airlines, one much bigger than the other. In the face of such obvious contradiction of their theory, mainstream economists make excuses, claiming that because Coles and Woolworths still compete, everything is fine, or claiming that the threat of *potential* competition will keep them on the straight and narrow. But everything is obviously not fine.

The case of the banks offers another example. When foreign banks were licensed to operate in Australia in the 1980s, the resulting competition led to excessive and reckless lending, a boom and subsequent recession according to George Megalogenis' *The Australian Moment* in 2012. Unrestrained competition can often have undesirable results.

The existence of the ACCC is a tacit admission that competitive markets don't work. If they did, we would not need a government watchdog to ensure prices are fair. This flagrant contradiction to the prevailing ideology has not slowed the flow of rhetoric in favour of free competitive markets.

So, competition eliminates competitors until the market is dominated by one or a few firms. Once this state is reached, the dominant firms heavily influence the market, controlling prices to customers and suppliers, and influencing legislation in their favour. So we have malfunctioning markets and corruption of our democracy.

THERE IS A POWERFUL PHENOMENON that keeps us charging along a doomed path, racing towards a precipice. In 2016 the Senate had hearings on tax avoidance by transnational companies like Apple and Google. The company representatives conceded little. They allowed they shift millions of dollars to tax havens to avoid paying Australian tax, but that's no secret. They did not concede there was any reason they should pay more Australian tax. It is legal so they do it. As far as they're concerned, they're in business to make profits for their shareholders and to out-compete their competitors. That means they minimise costs (including taxes) and maximise profits.

This attitude is completely amoral, but that's not my point here. My point is that they are exactly right, within the narrow frame in which they operate. They operate within competitive markets. They are only doing what they must do to survive. Corporations are required to make profits for their shareholders. If a CEO had an epiphany and tried to run his company to maximise quality of life instead of profits, his company would risk lagging in the rat race. The CEO might soon be removed.

So it is not just the greed of corporate managers that keeps the rapacious corporate behaviour going. It is also the *system* within which they operate. The *system* locks them in. There is no other way for them to behave, if they are to survive in this system.

How else can we explain myopic coal companies creating ever-bigger mines whose production, within the next decade, would almost certainly push the Earth's climate over tipping points and into irreversible, extreme global warming that will collapse the global industrial system they are feeding? If we want to change things, we have to understand the *system* we operate within, and how it can be changed to give us more of what we want and need.

THERE IS MORE TO BE LEARNED from the Colesworth (Coles and Woolworths) juggernaut. Malcolm Knox, in his 2015 book *Supermarket Monsters,* has compiled a sobering account of the place Coles and Woolworths have assumed in Australian society. They do not just drive farmers to bankruptcy, and they are not just supermarket retailers.

Between them, and Woolworths' parent Wesfarmers, they dominate or are major players in groceries (1000 supermarkets), petrol (700 Shell and Caltex stations), liquor (BWS, Dan Murphy, 1000 pubs and bottle shops, many with pokies), hardware (Bunnings and Masters, the latter now terminated), clothing and 'variety' (Target, Big W, Kmart; 500 stores including hardware), and they are making major pushes into small convenience stores (like Seven-Eleven) and even *finance*. New stores are being opened all the time. About $100 per week per man, woman and child is spent in their stores.

They conducted a milk war, starting in 2011. The result, combined with the deregulation of the milk industry in 2001, was the elimination of 30,000 dairy farms, 75% family-owned, replaced with 7500 farms mostly owned by foreign companies. Is there anything our politicians will *not* allow to be sold out from under us?

Their scorched-earth tactics are repeated in every industry they touch, where they squeeze suppliers until only a few large and dependent ones are left standing, and if those suppliers fall over then they look for suppliers overseas.

Competition is supposed to be good. The German retailer ALDI has moved into Australia and is perceived by Colesworth as their most threatening competitor. Will this extra competition restore our farmers and wholesale suppliers to health? As Liza Doolittle put it so delicately in *Pygmalion,* not bloody likely. ALDI is even more ruthless, and it already gets most of its supplies from overseas.

Colesworth also squeeze small retailers who are not even in direct competition. This comes about because so much of our retail trade occurs in shopping malls. Every mall needs one or more *anchor* stores, and they are almost always a supermarket, and commonly a Coles or Woolies. Because of their market dominance, Colesworth demand and get heavy discounts on the rents they pay the mall owners. The mall owners then have to make up the shortfall by charging very high rents to the other retailers in their mall. That is why there is a rapid turnover of small retailers in your local mall. Increasingly it is only the *chains* of smaller retailers that can survive in such a punishing environment. So much for small business, which politicians are fond of saying are the engines of employment.

It is astonishing Coles and Woolworths have been allowed to reached such dominance of our retail sector. They get away with it because they always pitch their moves in terms of lower prices for customers. Very few politicians have the wit, let alone the guts, to challenge that simplistic and misleading line, independent Senator Nick Xenophon being a notable exception. Even so, they are moving through our whole economy. At this rate they could end up running almost everything, including the banks.

And of course it is all totally against the neoclassical economic religion, which requires that no competitor should be large enough to influence the market they operate in. The mainstream economists have learnt to look the other way, or to make feeble noises claiming that someone *could* enter the market if they chose. Politicians no doubt will also be adept at using their blind eye to examine the problem.

However the damage is not just to our industries and jobs, as if that's not bad enough. Knox cites studies that alcohol problems are well-documented to rise in proportion to the number of alcohol outlets in a neighbourhood. The Colesworth strategy is to saturate areas with BWS and Dan Murphy outlets, so they drive out other competitors and so neither of the biggies gets the advantage over the other. In other words they are drug pushers.

They loudly claim to sell 'fresh food'. (The ABC TV series *Checkout* explained to us that the meaning of 'fresh' must be understood 'in a retail context'.) However their fastest growing lines are junk, like tobacco, cigarettes, soft drinks, confectionary, chips, ice cream, and medicinal goods. Knox quotes Professor of Health Services Heather Yeatman: it is 'very depressing ... It is in keeping with all the data and research we are seeing, which shows Australians have rising obesity and declining health driven by poor diet and eating habits.'

The spin doctors will always claim your health and well-being are your personal responsibility, but Colesworth compete fiercely to put temptation in the way of everyone, even as the whole consumer-neoliberal project makes everyone more stressed and manipulates us to be more self-indulgent.

The invisible foot has been busily at work in our retail markets. Colesworth is laying waste to small retailers, our primary industry and other wholesale suppliers, depressing wages, exporting jobs, threatening to take over more and more of the total economy, and harming our health and social fabric. *Politics as usual* fails even to notice a problem.

THE MODERN FORM OF MARKET ECONOMY is globalised consumer capitalism. Consumer capitalism manipulates us to buy ever more stuff, so as to continually increase its flow of profits and so as to 'keep the economy growing'. Through the operation of this system we have become obsessively materialistic. We also tend, I'm afraid, to become progressively more infantile in our appetites. Homer Simpson, on being told his microwaved food would be ready in forty seconds, whined 'Forty seconds? I want it now!'.

The beauty of consumer capitalism, from the point of view of capitalists, is that it is *addictive*. It pushes our insecurity buttons, so we feel inadequate. It then offers us a never-ending stream of things that will supposedly make us feel better about ourselves, but the emotional effect of which soon wears off, so we keep coming back for more. And they have just the dope for us.

It is a fool-proof recipe for ever-increasing profits – until physical limits interfere. At some stage we will have to come to grips with consumerism and its driver, marketing, so we can return to having what we need rather than what we are manipulated to want.

WHY DO MARKETS NOT FUNCTION the way they are claimed to function? It is because real-world markets are very different from the abstract markets imagined in the *neoclassical theory*. That's the theory, dating from the 19th century, that claims free markets give you the most efficient economy conceivable. To get that result the theory requires a few conditions.

The theory completely excludes social interaction from its considerations. It thus excludes the possibilities that we are motivated by fashion, crowds, altruism, compassion, sexual attraction or love. These things are excluded so as to make the mathematics of the theory easier. At least that was the original reason. The other reason is that if you don't exclude social interaction then the theory doesn't lead you to the conclusion that free markets are best. Never mind that fashion in clothing is a multibillion dollar business, nor that fashion has a great deal of influence on other things we buy, such as cars and houses. Never mind also that many traders in financial markets follow the crowd, thus pushing rising markets higher and falling markets lower.

The theory is based on a robotic caricature of people called *rational economic man* or *homo economicus*. This creature is supposed to be completely rational, totally informed about nearly everything, able to predict the

Markets: Taming the Wild Horses

probabilities of future events, and unaffected by what other people think or feel. He (clearly *he*) spends his life calculating his optimal combination of choices so as to maximise the satisfaction of his wants. Should he buy an ice cream now, or put the money in savings so he will be able to buy a bigger house later?

To leave out fashion, compassion, peer pressure and other manifestations of our social nature clearly makes him inhuman. In fact all mammals are social in nature, so he does not even resemble mammals. This is why I have called him a *calculating reptile*. The dominant economic theory presumes we're all calculating reptiles.

Rather than admitting the reptile is inhuman, many people argue instead that we should be like him. This is why I opened the book with the claim our governments want us to be more like reptiles. One of the clearest expressions of this attitude was in the movie *Wall Street* in which the main character, Gordon Gekko, made a speech arguing that greed is good. Perhaps it is not a coincidence that Gordon's name sounds like a lizard.

It would be a big joke if we had not been dragged so far down this path for the past several decades, and if this were not an accurate description of how *corporations* actually do function. Is it any wonder our social needs and the natural environment are simply ignored by the most powerful in our society?

Obviously the neoliberal lauding of extreme individualism and rational economic man is completely at odds with what we know about ourselves, both from common observation and from modern psychology and other fields. As Joshua Greene has recounted in *Moral Tribes*, we are highly social beings, innately cooperative and compassionate, and we can be altruistic when it is called for.

We haven't even mentioned some other silly neoclassical assumptions. There must be no economies of scale, beyond an ill-defined point of diminishing returns. That would be a surprise to Henry Ford, Bill Gates, Google and Colesworth. Most bizarrely, the flow of time should be suspended. There is more silliness that you could read about in my book *Sack the Economists*, or more technically in Steve Keen's *Debunking Economics*, but that will do for now.

IF INSTEAD YOU USE MORE REASONABLE propositions as the basis of your theory of markets you get a very different answer. If you allow that social interactions and fashion are important, that we do not know everything, that we cannot predict the future and that we are not particularly rational, in the formal sense, then you predict that the market system will be full of instabilities: its behaviour will be rather erratic and it will be a long way from balance most of the time. It may follow a fairly steady pattern for a time, but it is prone to suddenly shifting into a different kind of behaviour. Small shifts happen often, and occasionally there is a very large shift. A stock market crash is an example of a large shift.

Just to name it, this kind of system is called a *far-from-equilibrium self-organising system*. It can also be called a *complex system*, where *complex* has a technical meaning narrower than the common meaning. There's a lot known about such systems from modern work in other fields. The fact that such knowledge is little-known among mainstream economists reflects an amazing degree of intellectual isolation that has persisted for a century.

Mainstream economists claim their silly assumptions don't matter very much. They say no theory fully represents the real world, it merely approximates the real world. There's a little bit of truth there, but unfortunately in this case if you make the assumptions more realistic then the predicted behaviour of the economy *changes radically*.

The neoclassical theory says the economy is like a rocking horse. If you push it, it will rock predictably, and soon return to its balance position. Real economies are more like wild horses. They are powerful, but their behaviour is complicated and subtle. A wild horse can be tamed and subjected to a trainer's will, but she is not so foolish as just to leap on a freshly caught wild horse and expect it will carry her sedately around. That, in effect, is what mainstream economists do. Then they are surprised when things don't proceed in quite the way they expected. *Then* they assure us everything's fine and climb on another wild horse.

The mainstream neoclassical theory has nothing useful to tell us about real modern market economies. It is not just that it is only a rough approximation to real economies, it is that the theoretical behaviour is *nothing like* real economies. The theory is quite misleading.

How could such an obviously unrealistic and misleading theory allow economists to gain so much power over our lives? A large part of the answer seems to be that rich people love what economists say. Economists say the best thing you can do for the world is to make as much money as you can as fast as you can. Rich people say thank you very much, and we'll pay you to keep saying that, and to convince the politicians it is true.

SOME QUITE FUNDAMENTAL IMPLICATIONS flow from this new conception of an economy. They reach to the core of the neoliberal regime. They open the way to living sensibly together, with the natural world thriving around us.

There is no reason to believe free markets will yield an optimally efficient society. Our more sensible theory can say nothing general about free markets. An unfettered market might be efficient, or not, and it might yield results we like, or not. You have to look at each market and see if it is working well or not. Common experience might suggest that's not a bad description of our real modern economy. This means *we can dispense with the whole neoliberal ideology* that dominates the world at present. It also means we can, if we are smart enough and emulate our horse trainer, guide markets so they deliver what we do want.

There is not just one way to organise an economy. The neoclassical view is that free markets are the best of all conceivable ways to organise an economy, so that's what we all must do. However real economies have many possible states, and they are continually changing, so it is not possible to decide which is the 'best' state. It is not really a meaningful question to ask what is the 'best' state when we can't hope to know much about the multitude of ever-changing alternatives.

We therefore need to use a different criterion. We can endeavour, more pragmatically, to manage our economies to yield more of the kind of results we prefer. The results we prefer will depend on our situation and our culture, so each society and each culture may tailor its economy to support the kind of society it chooses to be. Thus we are not condemned to a global economic monoculture, nor to its consequent political and social monoculture. Human cultural diversity might thrive once again.

There is no fundamental reason why an economy can't be compatible with the living world. Living systems are also complex self-organising systems. In fact they are far and away the most sophisticated exemplars. If an economy is a complex self-organising system, like living systems, then it might be brought into compatibility with living systems. Our present economy violates the biosphere's basic operating principles, such as by not recycling waste. It is therefore highly incompatible with living systems, which is why so many living things, including people, are dying. With sensible management and careful exploration, we ought to be able to stabilise our economies and return them to being good biospheric citizens, so people and other living things may thrive within them and around them. That is our challenge. It is also necessary, if our civilisation is to continue.

Together, these conclusions imply the economy can be restored to its proper place, which is within the biosphere and subordinate to and supportive of the kind of societies we choose to live in. There need not be any conflict between the economy and social needs, nor between the economy and the environment. The economy should be supporting both.

BUT WHAT DO WE DO WITH MARKETS, if they are erratic and not very predictable? Markets are certainly powerful, they provide strong incentives for firms to improve their product, to innovate, and to run more efficiently. Unfortunately modern markets, as currently mismanaged, also provide strong incentives to increase production without limit, and strong incentives to avoid costs, which means shifting costs onto others and onto the natural world. Furthermore unfettered competition tends to eliminate competitors and to yield monopoly, as we've seen. The invisible foot is as likely to operate as the invisible hand.

So, do we have to give up on markets and all become socialists? I don't think so. The problem is not markets *per se*, the problem is *unfettered* markets. The lesson is that markets should not be left to themselves. Rather, we should *treat markets like wild horses*: they are powerful, but they need to be tamed and guided if we want them to take us where we would like to go.

Guiding markets is not a new idea, we have been doing it for a long time, just not with coherent intention. There are two main traditional tools: rules and incentives. A third tool, reconnecting feedback pathways, is not so well known and will be illustrated later.

Incentives affect what is profitable and what is not. Where the profit is, markets will follow. So long as it is profitable to exploit people and trash the Earth, we can expect people to be exploited and the Earth to be trashed. If we want that to change we must find ways to make it profitable to treat people and the Earth well. There is a long history of applying subsidies and taxes to influence what is profitable. Subsidies are positive incentives, whereas taxes are negative incentives.

Market operation can also be changed through rules, usually referred to as regulation. This is a blunter instrument, but it also has a long history. We use rules to outlaw immediately harmful things, like dumping poison in the creek.

To get a bit technical for a minute, incentives affect the feedbacks that operate within the economy, and feedbacks are what determine the character and behaviour of a complex self-organising system. When a market functions according to the neoclassical claim, our individual actions are collected through a stabilising (negative) feedback and the collective result is a benign outcome – the invisible hand does its work and prices come to an equilibrium. However in some situations, as in an unregulated common or a falling stock market, our individual actions are collected through a destabilising (positive) feedback and the result is not benign – the commons are eaten out, or the market crashes. The invisible foot takes over and there is a dramatic instability.

Economists do allow that markets don't always work. They say that sometimes there are *imperfections*. They know about the example of the commons being eaten out, and understand that some kind of intervention, like regulation, is needed. But most economists think most markets work well most of the time. Our earlier review of Coles and Woolworths indicates, rather, that market malfunctions are commonplace: the invisible foot is as likely as the invisible hand.

Pollution is another case of market failure. Sir Nicholas Stern, reporting in early 2007 on the likely costs of avoiding global warming, called the pollution of Earth's atmosphere with carbon dioxide emissions 'the greatest market failure in history'. Really though, it is part of an even larger failure – the failure to care for the natural environment as a whole. Rather than pretending that bad outcomes are the exception, an 'imperfection' in an otherwise orderly system, we must recognise that bad outcomes are common.

The incentives relating to carbon dioxide emissions can be changed. A carbon tax or other carbon pricing scheme is intended to discourage the burning of fossil fuels *and* to encourage the development of clean energy sources (the positive side of it is often overlooked). So far this approach has not been used very effectively. The European Union introduced a carbon trading scheme, but it was designed by a committee of nations and ended up weak and full of loopholes, so it was quite ineffectual. Australia also introduced a scheme, but it was rather weak because the price was set very low. Even so, it had some positive effect and had the potential to develop into a more effective mechanism, but of course the Abbott Government abolished it.

A different kind of market adjustment would be to encourage employees to own the enterprise for which they work. Employee ownership modifies incentives in more dramatic ways than just changing the cost of something. The conflicting incentives of employees and owners are completely removed. Employees who also own have a direct incentive to ensure the long-term health of the enterprise and, simultaneously, to ensure that working conditions are healthy and the local creek is not poisoned.

The latter approach would be an example of redirecting the connections within the economic system so feedbacks flowed differently. We will encounter other such examples later in the book, when we look at how to encourage better business practices, and they can be quite powerful. Believe it or not, it is possible to run a business that is both Earth-friendly and highly profitable.

IN PRACTICAL TERMS changes like those just discussed are not so radical. The big changes are in the recognition of the beast we are dealing with, and in the overall intention of our management. We need to run our economies without the fundamental misconception that markets can be left to run themselves. We need to free the whole subject from the messianic ideologies with which it has been plagued for the past couple of centuries. Indeed the existence of those messianic movements is symptomatic of the lack of firm grounding of the discipline of mainstream economics, which is pre-scientific. We can manage markets to ensure a fair go and to enhance general wellbeing, not just to produce more and more stuff.

This has been a rather terse introduction and sampling of how markets malfunction, why they malfunction and what we can do about it. It gives an indication of how we can manage our economy rather differently, and potentially with more benign results. There is of course much more to how an economy works and to managing it. More about the real behaviour of markets can be found in Steve Keen's *Debunking Economics* and Eric Beinhocker's *The Origin of Wealth*. Some more specific ideas for guiding markets are given in my books *Sack the Economists*, or at greater length in *The Nature of the Beast*.

Anyway, the implication of the failure of the neoliberal paradigm is not that we need radically new kinds of policies. Rather it is to remove a persistent objection to the kind of market intervention we have been doing anyway, but fitfully, incoherently and often counter-productively. With a clearer justification for 'intervention', meaning sensible management, and with a clear intention and a clearer political will, we are likely to manage much more coherently and therefore much more effectively. We might be surprised how well we do.

11

Finance: Corralling the Feral Extractors

The Global Financial Crisis of 2008 was not the first such financial collapse. The collapse of the stock market in 1929 triggered the Great Depression. Almost as severe in Australia was a land price collapse, focused in Melbourne, in the 1890s. Before the GFC there was the collapse of the dot-com boom in 2001, a global currency crisis in 1998, and a stock market crash in 1987, and so on back through history. Dozens of collapses occurred in the 19th century reaching all the way back to an infamous speculative frenzy over tulips in the Netherlands in the 17th century.

Are these collapses just a fact of life, as inevitable as the weather? Perhaps not. The GFC was triggered by the collapse of the mortgage market in the United States. A mortgage is a debt: if you get a mortgage from the bank, the bank gives you money to pay for a house but you owe the money, plus interest, to the bank. Mortgages were given to people who did not have enough income to repay the money. The banks counted on the price of houses and land continuing to increase, so that if the mortgagee defaulted they could sell the property and recover the money.

The trouble started when they ran out of people to push mortgages onto.

It was aggravated because many of the mortgages had very low interest rates for the first two years, so-called teaser rates, but then the interest rate jumped much higher and many people could no longer maintain the payments. With some people defaulting and fewer buyers coming into the market, prices start to drop. The banks were no longer able to recover all of the money. Banks operate with only small reserves of capital, so as losses mounted there was a danger they would become insolvent. Some banks and insurance companies did fail and many others were likely to fail. That's when the global financial system virtually froze up and governments came in to bail them out.

That was the core of the story, but it was more complicated and much worse because of the games played in financial markets. Michael Lewis' 2011 book *The Big Short* gives a fairly readable account. The 2015 movie of the same name gives an entertaining and digestible account that conveys the essence of the problems, even if you don't keep up with all the fast-paced dialogue. Sometimes the action stops while they explain some technicality with graphic metaphor, such as when a foul-mouthed movie starlet explains mortgage bonds from her bubble bath. The story is based around the small number of traders who realised the whole junk mortgage business was rotten and bound to collapse, so they placed bets that it *would* collapse, and made a lot of money, eventually.

It is worth digging into this a bit because it reveals how the financial markets have become feral, parasitic, destructive and often illegal. Financial collapses are not just a fact of life, they happen because a lot of people play a lot of very dodgy games to siphon wealth into their own pockets. Financial markets *could* be much smaller and more stable, and they *could* just provide a valuable service to the real, productive economy.

THE FINANCIAL GAME PLAYING greatly magnified the amount of money at stake and the risks involved. The first layer of complication was that banks bundled packages of mortgages into bonds and sold them to other investors who would then in effect collect the mortgage repayments. However this act broke a fundamental requirement for a healthy market, because it separated the risk from the profit. The banks took the profit but offloaded the risk. This was such a good deal that of course they kept doing it.

The mortgage bonds bundled very risky mortgages with much safer mortgages. Computer geeks in the big banks convinced themselves the whole package was very safe, and they gave their computer software to ratings companies who used it to stamp the bonds AAA. However almost no one went through the complicated internal details of the bonds. The few independent players who did realised the bad mortgages could ruin the whole package.

Why did the bank geeks think that bundling risky mortgages into bond packages made them safer bets? Three reasons. First, many people just think mortgages are safe investments: bricks and mortar after all, and most people repay their mortgages. Second, in normal times mortgages don't all go bad together. Third, it is a human quirk to underestimate the risk of an event that's not very likely. The central flaw in this thinking is that if the economy or the housing market go down then a lot of mortgages do go bad at the same time.

The mortgage bonds should not have been rated AAA. The ratings companies were remiss in using the banks' software instead of doing their own independent checks. They did this because they were operating under a conflict of interest. If they gave a bond a bad rating the bank would go to one of their rivals who would then make the profit. The invisible foot was at work: the incentive was to give the bank the rating it wanted for its bond rather than to give an honest rating. This would also be illegal, but perhaps hard to prove. By the way these big rating companies are commonly called 'ratings *agencies*' but that is also false labelling: they are private-sector companies, not government regulators. You may have heard of them: Moody's, Standard and Poor's and so on.

Many innocent investors bought these falsely rated bonds, which were supposed to yield a small, reliable return on the investment: retirement funds, local governments, even charities. They were all cheated out of a great deal of money.

But there were more layers of game playing. The banks did not sell all of the mortgage bonds they created, and they bought insurance on the ones they retained. This also shifted risk off themselves and out into the financial system. At first this was reasonably sensible, but the level of risk was disguised. American Insurance Group issued much of the insurance with a very low premium.

A few people saw the risks were much higher than claimed and looked for a way to bet that the market would fall. They came up with something called a credit default swap (CDS). It is like an insurance policy, but you don't have to own the thing you're insuring. It was like getting an insurance contract on a slum district with a history of house fires, without having to own any of the real estate. It was also like a side bet at a blackjack table, a wager made between spectators.

Meanwhile the banks had come up with a second layer of clever complication. They made packages of lower-rated *bonds* and claimed, by the same flawed logic, that the risk was reduced. So they had packages of packages of mortgages, called CDOs for short.

Then they made *synthetic* CDOs, which were packages of CDSs. A CDS is much easier to create than an actual mortgage, so they encouraged those few betting against the market, and even did a lot of their own betting, so they could package the CDSs into synthetic CDOs. These synthetic CDOs did not even have shonky mortgages at their base, just side bets. Confused yet? By the way, they were betting against their own management of other people's money, which is unethical if not illegal.

All these clever 'derivatives' were sold throughout the global financial system. In total, something like $600 trillion of debt was created through multiple layers of bets upon bets. That is why, when the house of cards finally gave way, the entire global financial system was at risk.

THE POINT OF TELLING YOU THIS is not so you'll absorb all the gory detail, but so you'll get some feel for the kinds of crazy games that are played in our financial markets, and for the magnitude of the money they throw around, or promise to throw around. It is what happens when you deregulate financial markets.

Internationally, through the 1970s and early 1980s, restrictions on finance were rapidly broken down. The US dollar was removed from the gold standard, major currencies were 'floated', so their exchange rates were determined in financial markets instead of being fixed by governments, and restrictions on cross-border movements of money were removed.

After deregulation the rate of transactions in financial markets jumped by around a factor of 50. The rate is also around 50 times greater than the rate at which you would need to adjust your share portfolio, as some firms prosper and others fall back. In the postwar decades regulations were deliberately tight to keep the financial markets focused on investing in productive enterprises. It means that these days only around one in 50 financial trades serves the productive economy. The other 49 are gambling.

In other words the financial markets are completely dominated by gambling. However, unlike a casino, the odds are not stacked in favour of the house. Rather the odds are stacked in favour of the gamblers, who have much more inside knowledge than most of us. The objective is to siphon wealth into their own pockets. Where is that wealth coming from? It can only come, ultimately, from the productive economy. It means the productive economy is being hollowed out by a parasitic financial system.

But that's not the end of it. The frenetic rate of trading, combined with the common strategy of betting on trends, means the market speculation greatly magnifies market fluctuations. Rises are driven too high, then the following falls are driven too low. Long-term 'bubbles' are inflated, and when they burst they turn into a crash.

Thus not only are the unregulated financial markets parasitic, they destabilise the whole economy. The rapid fluctuations in share prices makes it harder for managers of actual productive activity to optimise their operations, so the efficiency of the whole economy is degraded. Then, if the financial markets crash, they bring the whole economy down with them, visiting great tribulation on the world.

Even that is not the end of it. Financiers have amassed so much wealth they have bought the US Congress. Despite grossly negligent and allegedly criminal behaviour on a grand scale, in bringing about the Global Financial Crisis and the ensuing Great Recession, Congress has fought to prevent even moderate regulation of the finance industry. Allegations of similar criminality and pliability of our own politicians go uninvestigated, according to Philip Soos (2014) and Ian Verrender (2015).

Then, just to add insult to all that injury, some of these Wall Street gamblers (think Donald Trump) stand up and claim they contribute great wealth to the nation. The word *hubris* doesn't really capture the gall of this claim. One definition of *chutzpah* I have heard is the man, convicted of murdering his parents, who pleads for mercy because he is an orphan.

NEOCLASSICAL THEORISTS CLAIM the financial markets' role is to allocate 'capital' (investment funds) to their most efficient uses in the productive economy. They have a theory, called The Efficient Markets Hypothesis, that says markets always reflect the underlying values of the firms being traded. Essentially, they allow that no one actually has complete information, but that the traders as a group will have a good enough sample of information so that the average price will accurately reflect the underlying value. Some people have done elaborate statistical analyses or computer models that show that in fact market prices often drift far from underlying values for quite long periods.

However we don't really need fancy models to expose this claim as nonsense. If it were true, there would be no market crashes. It is a variation on the neoclassical obsession that markets will always bring things into balance. If that were true, there would be no bubbles and busts, there would be no booms and recessions and depressions.

And then there are the stories like those told in *The Big Short*, the stories of what people actually do in the financial markets. They build towering houses of debt cards, deceiving themselves and many others that their gambling systems are sound, and legal. Sure, financial markets efficiently allocate investment, and I have here an amazing financial product I'd like to interest you in.

WE DON'T HAVE TO PUT UP with these crazy parasitic financial markets. A key regulation in the postwar era prohibited deposit-taking institutions from also being investment banks. In simple terms, they could not gamble with other people's money, unless that money was explicitly intended for that purpose by its owner. Remember, the underlying purpose of a commercial bank is to make a profit, and if gambling with your money and mine increases their profit they will do it if they can get away with it. There were other regulations, such as stricter limits on insider trading, that also should be brought back.

But there is a simpler and more direct remedy for the gambling. It is to impose a small tax on every financial transaction, made just large enough to take most of the profit out of the gambling. Speculators commonly operate on very small margins, so a fraction of a percent might be enough to stop most of it. Legitimate trading would be hardly affected by such a small charge, because legitimate trades do not need to happen very often. Such a charge is known as a Tobin tax, after the economist who proposed it many decades ago.

There are current proposals for this form of tax, but their sponsors seem to miss the main point. They call them 'Robin Hood' taxes, because they want to transfer some of the wealth from rich financiers to the rest of us. But much the biggest benefit of such a tax would be to eliminate the 98% of trades that are parasitic and destabilising, so the financial markets would be much more stable and investment would flow into productive enterprise. If it worked properly, such a tax might not maximise revenue, because the frequency of financial trading would be much lower than at present. However the economy would function much more efficiently and profitably, and one of the main causes of gross inequality of wealth would be removed, so we would all be much better off.

THE MENTALITY OF THE FINANCIAL MARKETS is hollowing out productive enterprises in a more direct way as well. The managers of big corporations have been learning they can make quicker profits, especially for themselves, by playing financial games than by actually making stuff. Many of their lurks are spelt out in depressing detail by Rana Foroohar in her 2016 book *Makers and Takers*. Foroohar is a business journalist, and she's no slouch, having worked for *Time* magazine, CNN, MSNBC and others.

Some of these practices have been around for decades. Corporate raiders buy struggling companies, strip them of assets, including employee pension funds, break them up and sell them for a tidy profit. Or they run them for a short while with costs cut to the bone and then sell them before their growing dysfunction becomes obvious. Tax avoidance, using offshore tax havens and so-called transfer pricing has become routine.

It was argued a while back that managers should be paid in company shares so as to align the managers' incentives with the company's incentives. However managers soon found ways to temporarily jack up the company's share price so they could cash out at a tidy profit.

A popular practice now is the share buyback. Until the 1980s this was considered illegitimate manipulation of the market and was outlawed. However the ban was lifted and buybacks are now commonplace. The demand for shares goes up as the number of shares on the market goes down, so the share price rises, shareholders are happy, and the managers are happy. Of course it is only a temporary flush, and it uses funds that could have been invested productively in the company business. So it is just another parasitic way of manipulating money instead of doing something productive.

The hyperactive financial markets had already shifted the focus of business from medium-term productivity to next quarter's bottom line. If the quarterly report is not as positive as shareholders like, they can bail out and put their money somewhere else. The productive economy was already being greatly harmed by this short-term focus of financial markets. Now that managers also have a greater personal stake in the quarterly bottom line the problem is worse. Regulations should ensure corporate managers' incentives are less conflicted.

The financial markets' short-term focus on quarterly bottom line instead of longer-term productivity could be ameliorated by a transaction tax on share trades, to give share-holders an incentive to actually invest in a company and its future, rather than to just play for quick arbitrage or capital gains. Shares should not need to be traded more than perhaps once every few years, and a transaction tax could make it unprofitable to trade more often than that.

Foroohar recounts the story of General Electric, the iconic company founded by Thomas Edison and the only company to remain in the Dow Jones Industrial Average since the Dow began 120 years ago. In the 1980s under Jack Welsh GE turned to financial manipulation. Its financial arm, GE Capital, became its biggest earner and eventually America's biggest non-bank financial institution. It was a taker, not a maker. It crashed and burned in the GFC and had to be bailed out with $139 billion of taxpayer-backed loan guarantees. Unusually, GE seems to have learnt a lesson. In 2015 GE announced it was getting completely out of finance and henceforth would return to focusing just on being a maker.

For three years in the 1970s I lived in Rochester, New York, home of Kodak. Kodak was the globally iconic name in photographic film, the biggest employer in town, and the employer of choice. It looked after its employees with secure employment, good wages and generous benefits. It fell victim to the finance mentality in which 'corporations were nothing more than portfolios, bundles of assets to be managed like stocks,' as Foroohar puts it. Infamously, its own development of digital image technology was shut down, leaving the field to Japanese competitors. In 1990 Kodak had 145,000 employees and $19 billion in revenue. Today, having come out of bankruptcy, it employs 8,000 people and makes $2 billion a year.

Foroohar begins her book with the words 'It wasn't the way Steve Jobs would have done it'. She then recounts how in 2013 Apple, under new CEO Tim Cook, borrowed $17 billion for a share buyback. It did this even though it had $145 billion sitting in offshore tax havens and $3 billion in profits flowing in every month. Interest rates were at record lows, and blue-chip companies can issue bonds at very low rates, so it can borrow cheaply, jack up its own share price, reap some unearned profit for managers and shareholders, and look very good on paper.

Foroohar asserts, plausibly, that Steve Jobs never worried about the share price. Rather, he focused relentlessly on creating the next amazing product, and figured the share price would look after itself. Certainly Apple would never have become the world's most valuable company if he had focused on playing money games instead of creating the iPod, the iPad, the iPhone and so on.

These words are being written using Apple software. The latest version has annoying bugs, and it lacks some simple things, like a Save icon, that make for convenience and efficiency. Does that reflect a short-term focus on cost-cutting to maximise share dividends? The Outline function that used to be there, and was immensely helpful for organising large manuscripts, disappeared in the latest version. The reason put about is that Apple wanted its software to be identical on desktop and mobile devices. Not just compatible, but identical. So they *dumbed* the desktop software *down*. That sounds like a decision of marketers to me, and I wonder if Steve Jobs would ever have allowed it. Will they force me back to Microsoft? Apple products used to be renowned for their reliability and ease of use. They are declining. It is all too plausible to associate that decline with the passing of Steve Jobs.

Will Apple continue to be a world leader, or will it be content to make incremental improvements and eventually lose its leading place? Apple is another iconic company, both as the world's biggest and as a measure of the state of the US economy. The United States has been in decline for decades now. Managements' fascination with financial manipulation instead of production, with taking instead of making, is another major reason for that.

12

Banks: Seeing Behind the Curtain

Money is perhaps the least understood yet most powerful component of our economies. Perhaps you never thought much about where money comes from, and even less about what rules might apply to it, but how money is created, what rules govern it and what costs are involved have a profound effect on the economy, particularly in concentrating wealth and in promoting booms and busts. Yet the modern system of banks and money is complex and opaque. As a result discussions of it are confused and confusing. You would think mainstream economists ought to be the experts, but it turns out they have a very limited understanding of the roles of money and debt, because of fundamental ignorance and misconceptions about how banks work.

There is confusion about even the most basic aspects of money. What is it, and where does it come from?

I'll skip all the history and just talk about the modern money we use every day. If you have a $10 note, it is a token of a debt owed to you. To get it, you had to spend some time and effort, such as working for a wage or running a business. In return for your effort you get… a piece of paper? Or a number in a computer? You can't eat the paper, much less a bit of computer memory. A debt is still owed to you. On its own the note or the number is useless. It is useful, or valuable, only because you can exchange it for something of immediate value, like a bag of flour. To end up with a fair deal you have to be able to exchange the money for something of value, in return for the effort you put out to get the money.

So your $10 note is a token of a debt owed to you. Who owes you? In our modern world, it is Australian society that owes you. Anyone offering goods or services for sale is required by law to accept your $10 note in payment for their goods or services, and thus to redeem the promise implied by the note. How did Australian society come to have this obligation to you? It is because there is an implicit agreement in our society that these $10 notes will be honoured as tokens for some goods or services.

You didn't sign any agreement to that effect, it was done on your behalf by the government, and your implicit agreement is one of the obligations of living here. You might have worked for a farmer, and he might have paid you at harvest time with a bag of wheat. But we agree it is usually far more convenient to be paid with token money that's easy to carry and can be spent anywhere to buy anything.

This little discussion reveals three key features of our money: it is a token, it represents an implicit agreement, and it involves a debt. First, it is a *token*, a piece of paper of little value in itself. Rather, it carries potential value: it carries a *promise* that it can be exchanged for some goods or services. Thus it represents *an agreement*. The agreement, implicitly, is between the holder of the money and the rest of Australian society. Because the agreement is a promise involving the future, there is a *debt*. You are owed a debt because of the effort you expended to get the token money.

You could print your own $10 note, or hack a bank's computer and add $10 to your account balance, but that is regarded as counterfeiting. It is cheating. Why? Because there is no agreement. We have not agreed to honour any old piece of paper you print. We have only agreed to honour notes designated as *legal tender*, because to get legal tender you have to contribute to our society in some way.

I have walked us slowly through some detail here because we need to get basic ideas clear if we are to find our way through all the confusions about money and banks. To reiterate, money is a token of an agreement, a promise, and the promise implies a debt.

The fact that money involves a debt makes it *powerful* and *risky*. It is powerful because it allows us to defer fulfilling an agreement: I'll be compensated for my effort, but not just yet. This gives token money great versatility. However the ability to defer brings in risk, because we don't know what the future will bring. If you work for the farmer, but his wheat crop is destroyed by a fire or a hail storm, then he is unable to pay you with a bag of wheat. The implicit agreement, your work in return for a bag of wheat, cannot be fulfilled. You took a risk in allowing payment to be deferred and you lost.

Many times in past centuries money changers would issue more paper notes than they could redeem in gold or coins, according to Michael Rowbotham. If their deceit were found out the bench (*banco*) from which they operated was broken (ruptured) – in other words they would be *bankrupt*. Their necks might also be in danger. Even in the nineteenth century a run on a bank was not uncommon. If your notes were issued by that bank, they could suddenly become worthless. Our modern money is more reliable because it is backed by a system of laws overseen by the government. Even so the Australian dollar can devalue relative to other currencies, so if you are an importer you lose.

We create debt in many other ways, apart from issuing token money. The previous chapter recounted how great amounts of debt were created within the financial system. Our society creates copious amounts of debt. This means we accumulate huge risks. It is the central reason why our economies collapse with such painful inevitability.

WHERE DOES OUR MONEY COME FROM? Most of it comes from private banks, who create it out of nothing with a few strokes of a keypad. A small fraction of our money – notes, coins and deposits with the Reserve Bank – are created by the government.

Perhaps you did not know that private banks create most of our money. Does it mean the banks can just go and buy anything they want with the money they create? Can the bank manager create $10 and go and buy ice cream with it? No, the banks are not allowed to directly spend the money. Their job is to issue it into circulation, not to use it themselves. However there is a kicker. They charge *interest* on the money they issue.

When you get a loan from a bank you are not borrowing someone else's hard-earned cash. Rather, the bank creates new money out of nothing, with a few computer keystrokes, and puts it in your account. A small fraction of what appears in your account may be pre-existing money, and thus a genuine loan, but most of it is new money. Mainstream economists mostly ignore or deny that money is created this way, but it was recently affirmed by no lesser authorities than the Bank of England's Michael McLeay and others. Several important things flow from this.

Banks drive investment bubbles. Most of the profits a bank makes come from issuing 'loans', so they're quite keen to do so. If you can get a slightly larger mortgage loan from them, you can bid up the price of property. Next time around, the market value of that property will count as equity for another loan, which can be a little larger again. In this way a land-price spiral can take off, creating a housing bubble (though it is really a land bubble, because the cost of building of a house changes only slowly). In the 1980s their profligate lending promoted a business investment bubble, the bursting of which caused the severe early 1990s recession.

If a property bubble takes off, then no-one wants to be left behind, and many want to buy low and sell high, so they keep driving prices up. Nothing in the real world may be changing, just the price of the land that's available. It is really a pyramid scheme. Economists call it a Ponzi scheme, after a shark who took 'investment' money from more and more people and paid off the earlier people with the new money, without actually investing in anything. It works so long as the scheme is expanding, but at some point it will collapse, for want of more mugs to invest or because mortgage payments are too high. Then the whole thing crashes down, as we saw in the previous chapter.

Another result of letting private banks create money is that banks profit by misrepresenting their issuance of new money as a 'loan', and charging interest on it. Now it might be proper for banks to charge a fee, because they are providing a service. The service is the provision of the money we need to go about our daily lives and to keep the economy functioning. However the amount of interest charged is not related to the service. It is determined by a remote authority, the Central Bank, in an ineffectual attempt to regulate the amount of money in circulation.

The amount of interest we pay is much greater than it needs to be, not so much because interest rates are high, although sometimes they are, but because the banks' incentives in our system are to issue a great deal of money. Because banks are competitive profit-making businesses, and loans are a main source of income, their incentive is to induce us to take on lots of loans, so we'll pay lots of interest to them.

Charging interest on new money is one of the important mechanisms driving inequality. There don't seem to be many studies of this, but a study in Germany in the 1980s was reported by Margrit Kennedy. It showed that median households paid out an average of 5000 Deutschmarks per year in interest, whereas households in the top 10% received an average of 34,000 DM in the form or interest.

Interest payments also greatly increase the cost of many items, and flow on through the economy. This is especially true of housing, for which mortgage interest can easily double the cost. Interest charged on new money is like a private tax on the entire economy, charged by bank shareholders.

If issuing money was done as a public service under government supervision, there could be much less money and therefore much less debt. There was a short-lived experiment in Austria during the Depression, recounted by Greco in 1994 and in my 2013 book. A local government issued a local currency that carried a significant monthly fee for holding it. This money circulated much more rapidly than the national currency. There were many things to be done in the town, and many people able to do them, but a shortage of national currency restricted the local economy. When the local currency was issued, many of those things began to be done and people found employment doing them. It performed the primary role of money: to facilitate what we already want to do. It actually lifted the town out of depression.

This attracted a lot of attention across Austria and Germany, but the local currency was outlawed by the government because it infringed the monopoly of the national currency. The town sank back into depression and despair, along with much of Europe. Hitler rose to power on that despair.

Abraham Lincoln conducted another experiment, recounted by Michael Rowbotham. Having difficulty raising funds to fight the Civil War, he had the government itself issue money, which he used for wartime procurement. The notes were called greenbacks. At the end of the war he issued a statement indicating his intention for the government to keep issuing money, free of any interest or service charge, as a service to society. Shortly after that he was assassinated. Then the greenbacks were withdrawn from circulation, causing a savage recession.

Lincoln's logic was that a sound money system was a foundational requirement of a healthy society, and it was a service the government could readily provide for free. On the other hand he was proposing to go against the fact that many of the biggest fortunes in history have been made in private banking.

The purpose of money is to facilitate exchange, and thereby to facilitate the real, productive economy. It is to facilitate the things we want to make and do, and then exchange with each other. Money has been so manipulated and perverted and its role so obscured that we lose sight of this basic fact.

The point of money is not to *drive* the things we do. The point of money is to *facilitate* the things we want to do.

We've got it the wrong way round. Many projects don't happen because, it is said, there is not enough money. However if we have the will and the resources, meaning the people and materials we need, then it should be easy to create the money that will facilitate a project.

IF WE HAD ASKED THE DEVIL to design a mischievous monetary system, he might be hard put to improve on what we have. Issuing new money in the form of 'loans' entangles the fate of the entire economy with the machinations of the financial markets, whose craziness we looked at in the previous chapter. This connection seems to be much overlooked, but it's not so hard to understand.

Because new money is issued in bank loans, as a bubble inflates the amount of money in circulation goes up. People have more to spend, the economy cooks along and may boom. Unfortunately if the bubble pops the amount of money suddenly decreases, because loans are terminated and written off. Then people have less money to spend. As well, those who still have money may focus on paying off debt rather than buying more stuff. The economy may go into recession. This was the main mechanism behind the Global Financial Crisis, as also averred by Steve Keen in *Debunking Economics*.

Many other countries suffered a crash of property prices, but in Australia the level of private debt, which is mostly mortgage debt, paused but did not come down (remember Figure 5.2). Property prices did not fall and we did not have a recession. However household debt is still around three times greater, relative to income, than it was in 1990: equivalent to 18 months' income now versus 6 months' in 1990, as reported by Kathryn Diss.

The last two paragraphs address a quite fundamental question that seems hardly ever to be asked. To set the context, if I borrow money, build a factory and the factory goes bust, then I and anyone connected with the factory will be worse off, but the rest of the world should be able to go about its usual business. So, if the stock market is about investing, and the stock market crashes, then all those involved in investments will be worse off, but why would the rest of the world be affected, except marginally? Most businesses are going concerns, not new investments, so they should be able to carry on, should they not? Why would an investment failure interfere with business as usual? To put it in colloquial US terms, why would a Wall Street crash bring Main Street down with it?

The answer to that question is that new money is created in the course of making *investments*: it is because money is issued in the form of a 'loan'. The increased money supply stimulates the economy. Then, if the investments go bad the money supply shrinks, which slows the whole economy.

If we had followed Abraham Lincoln's advice, the supply of money would not depend on the success or failure of investments, nor on whether the current state of financial money games was booming or had reached its inevitable fate of crashing. We would have a much better chance of keeping Main Street cruising.

MONEY AND DEBT ARE EXCLUDED from mainstream economists' models of the economy, on the basis of a quite elementary misconception of how modern banks work. This is the central reason mainstream economists failed to foresee the Global Financial Crisis, though others clearly warned of it.

Economists claim private banks do not create new money, they merely take deposits from some people and loan that money to other people. Thus banks would just be neutral intermediaries. Perhaps you thought that too, it is a common but incorrect story of what banks do. If it were true, then a new loan would merely shift existing money from one person's account to another. The total amount of money in the economy would not change. In economists' jargon, total *demand*, meaning the money people are able and willing to spend, would not change.

I cannot really enlighten you as to why economists think this. One thing they say is 'one person's debt is another person's asset'. Perhaps they are confused by double-entry bookkeeping. If you get a loan from a bank, it is entered in your loan account and represents your debt to the bank. It is also entered in the bank's accounts as an asset, because money is owed to them. Thus it is true that there is a debt and a corresponding asset, but both the debt and the asset are new, and the purchasing power available in the economy, the demand, has increased.

Perhaps economists know in their hearts that if they admit banks create new money, that would be another reason why there is no general equilibrium and the neoclassical theory would not apply. It is another fundamental deficiency of mainstream economics, one that makes it blind to the role of debt in causing booms and crashes. It is a fairly important oversight.

GOVERNMENT 'BORROWING' DOES NOT 'CROWD OUT' private borrowing, as is commonly asserted by the commentariat. Rather, when the government borrows, the Central Bank issues new money. This increases the amount of money in circulation. It can also increase the 'reserve' funds facilitating the private banking system. This is a very simplified account of the sometimes Byzantine complexities of how central banks, commercial banks and governments work, but it is the essence distilled out by Randall Wray in *Modern Money Theory*. Several fundamentally important things follow from this system.

Mainstream understanding has things exactly backwards. Whereas government debt is supposed to be a dire threat, the dangers of excessive private debt are ignored. Supposedly, if the government borrows a lot, then there is less money available for the private sector to borrow.

However if a government with money-issuing authority runs a deficit it actually *increases* the amount of money circulating in the economy. A deficit does not crowd out private borrowing and does not slow the economy. Rather a deficit makes more money available to the private sector and stimulates the economy. The effect is as Keynes proposed, and as most countries experienced in the postwar decades.

The other big threat from government borrowing is supposedly that it will bring on ruinous inflation. There has in fact been serious inflation, but it doesn't show clearly in official figures. The inflation has been in the housing market, which of course has a big effect on many household budgets. However in another of those inexplicable quirks of mainstream economics, the cost of housing (rent and mortgage payments) is not counted in official inflation figures.

So debt *is* driving inflation, but it is *private* debt, not government debt. Private borrowing from banks increases the money in circulation.

In principle, inflation should only be a concern if the economy is running at full capacity. Then the supply of goods cannot quickly be increased to match the supply of money, so prices are bid up. Throughout the neoliberal era economies have been running below capacity, as indicated by unemployment rates of 5% or more. It should be possible to increase the money supply so as to lift activity, reduce unemployment and bring the economy up to full speed. That seems to have been the situation in the postwar decades, when unemployment averaged 1.3% and inflation was only 3.3%.

These days, however, economic managers keep unemployment around 5% because otherwise, they fear, inflation will take off. Why is that? Perhaps it is because banks are free to issue a lot more money these days. It is as though the private banks have their feet on the accelerator and the Reserve Bank has its foot on the brake. It is not the best way to drive a car.

Anyway, the solution to the fear of inflation is judicious government budgeting. Nothing new or radical has been proposed here, I have simply been describing the current system. The government's ability to print money in this way has existed for decades, and doom by automatic government excess has not come to pass.

The implications of these insights into money are fundamental to the economy and its management. The current obsession with balancing the Federal budget is quite misplaced. Spending could be adjusted to keep the economy near full capacity, with minimal unemployment. Taxes, which withdraw money from the economy, can be adjusted to prevent the economy overheating and going into inflation.

On the other hand, private banks can create money virtually at will and they do create inflation. Private banks need to be better regulated, so they do not loan excessively in pursuit of shareholder profit, and thus generate dangerous levels of private debt. How to do this can be debated, but private credit was directly regulated by the Government only a few decades ago (it was called a 'credit squeeze') so as to dampen an overheated economy.

THERE ARE OTHER WAYS MONEY could be supplied that avoid these fundamental problems. Money could be made available by the government, as Lincoln proposed. It could be supplied by private banks, under different rules, or by credit unions. There ought not to be any interest charged on issued money, because it is not actually a loan.

If you use your credit card, the bank creates new money for you to use, but it charges a very high interest rate. A more sensible system would work, for you and me, rather like a credit card or a line of credit, but without the exorbitant fee. You would have an agreed credit limit, and you could draw money as you needed it up to that amount. There might be a fee for this service, but it would be regulated and in direct relation to the service provided, rather than an extraneous charge like interest.

There are more creative systems, analogous to the 1930s Austrian system, in which positive balances would also be charged, to encourage the money to keep circulating and performing its role of facilitating exchange. Savings would be accomplished in separate accounts. Such systems are counter-intuitive at first. You can see more about them in the books by Kennedy,

Greco and my *Nature of the Beast*. The key ideas were developed by Silvio Gesell nearly a century ago.

Another option is for government to issue money with no interest due. Actually it already does. The money that comes in the form of *notes and coins* is issued by the Commonwealth Government with no interest due, in the same manner as Lincoln's greenbacks. There's no real reason the Government can't issue computer money as well. Much of Australia's funding of its effort in World War I was done through the newly-created Commonwealth Bank for much less than the private banks would have charged, as was recounted by D. J. Amos in 1940. When I say government, the functions of issuing and managing the money supply can be delegated to the Reserve Bank, but with rather different rules from those it currently operates under.

This could ensure, among other things, that the supply of money is not mis-labelled *government debt*. This distinction would do much to bring sense to our affairs even under the current regime, as the Modern Money Theorists have been at pains to stress. If government 'debt' were reduced strictly to zero, there would be *no money*. There would be no notes and coins, and no reserves to enable the private banks to function. Remember, money intrinsically involves debt. If we want money, we will have debt. The useful question is how to keep the debt from getting out of hand.

The government might issue *all* the money. It could then more readily manage the amount of money in circulation, so inflation was not a threat. Already it can increase the money in circulation by spending, and decrease it using taxes, but its management would be more effective if all money originated with the government. Private banks could be required to draw money from accounts with the government instead of just creating it at will.

If we really want to stabilise the economy we ought to consider a more substantial change. We could completely separate the supply of money from the investment process. This would require investment to be funded from existing savings rather than by printing new money. It sounds radical, but once established it would not function much differently. There would be a revolving fund of savings that would cycle into new investment as old loans were paid off. Perhaps you thought that's how the system works already? Bank loans would be actual loans, rather than new money disguised as loans.

Debt brings in risk, and too much debt is what brings Wall Street crashing down, which brings down the money supply, which brings down Main Street. Instead of burdening our children by borrowing, effectively, from the (unknown and risky) *future*, we could invest from the fruits saved from our own *past* efforts. And if money was supplied independently of investment,

Main Street could continue operating even if Wall Street did crash. Of course we could also stabilise Wall Street, as indicated in the previous chapter.

Furthermore, just as we do not need to 'borrow' our money from private banks, private banks do not need to borrow money from overseas, as they do at present to fund some of their lending. If a bank borrows US dollars, it can't spend them in Australia. What happens is the US dollars sit in an account as collateral while an equivalent amount of Australian currency is issued. The Australian currency could be issued anyway, without the burden of interest payments to overseas banks in a foreign currency.

THIS HAS BEEN ANOTHER FAIRLY BRIEF SUMMARY of a big and confused subject, focused on identifying problems and sketching alternative possibilities. It cannot answer all the questions that will arise, nor deal with all the misconceptions. It is, however, summarising ideas that have been developing for some time outside of the mainstream echo chamber. This summary indicates what is possible. These possibilities deserve to be debated, and the detail of the ideas is out there to be scrutinised.

Of course these ideas are a direct threat to one of the most powerful sectors of our society. They would respond by warning that not only the sky but probably half the universe would fall on us if we tried any such radical nonsense. Banking has always been a secretive and immensely profitable business. We have been conned for centuries.

We have every right and responsibility to ensure our money system is sensibly structured and regulated. Just as the media are the main signalling mechanism in society, money is the main signalling mechanism in the economy. They are strategic components of our system that have a profound effect on the behaviour of society and the economy. They need to be elevated to a special status, as the courts are elevated to a special status.

Leaving money and banking in the hands of wealthy private interests is high folly. It regularly leads to instability and disaster, and also results in the perpetual burden of a private tax, in the form of interest. We can bring light and simplicity to banking and take charge of it ourselves.

Desperately Seeking the Fair Go

Thanks to Joel Pett (2009)

13

Not Back to the Caves: Smart Ideas, Proven Practices

Getting more done with less effort is supposed to be a distinguishing feature of human beings, a product of the intelligence we claim to have. Yet we don't seem to have been doing it very well lately. We are extremely wasteful of natural resources.

We've spent some time looking at big picture stuff – the economic system, financial markets, banks and money. Now let's bring it down to practical things. I said in Chapter 2 that people have been busy inventing clever ways of doing things that use less energy, recycle more materials and keep the Earth healthy. Doing things this way won't wreck the economy and send us back to living in caves. Rather, it will increase employment and have spin-offs that further improve our quality of life.

We'll look at a sampling of these ideas and practices, because they point to the potential for a better society, if we can organise ourselves to support them. We'll look at the potential for clean energy, because that is our most urgent need, but also at recycling materials, being more efficient, and especially at organising and designing things in such a way that we get more done with less effort.

US energy consultant Amory Lovins has argued for nearly forty years for clean, cheap energy, since he wrote *Soft Energy Paths* in 1977. In 2005 he wrote 'Increasing energy end-use efficiency ... is generally the largest, least expensive, most benign, most quickly deployable, least visible, least understood, and most neglected way to provide energy services.' In 2011 he published *Reinventing Fire*, a strategy to wean the US completely off fossil fuels by 2050.

Clean energy sources are developing rapidly and will go quite a long way towards reducing greenhouse gas emissions. However the other side of energy is to use it *efficiently*. Eliminating energy waste is just as large an opportunity, and it is the reason Lovins and some others think we can quickly and dramatically reduce greenhouse gas emissions, and be rid of them well before 2050.

Lovins has always been clear that his strategy is not just about energy *sources*. It is about efficient use and efficient design. It is also about avoiding danger by reducing our increasingly heavy footprint on the planet, and about improving our overall *quality of life*, not just our material 'standard of living'. By stressing the potential for *reducing waste*, by emphasising the large and multiplying benefits of *synergistic designs*, and by focusing on *providing services* rather than selling *things*, he has pioneered an approach that can be applied to much of our society and take us a long way towards the future we seek.

CLEAN ENERGY TECHNOLOGIES have been developing rapidly. The more credible estimated costs of reducing carbon emissions have always been small, a reduction by 0.1-0.2% in the GDP growth rate. A recent paper finds that estimated costs have been declining rapidly, to a quarter or a tenth of a comprehensive estimate made in 2008, according to Frank Jotzo and Luke Kemp in 2015. These authors cite several reasons for the rapid decline in cost.

- Technological progress in many low-emission technologies consistently exceeds projections.
- Costs are falling much faster than expected. Solar panels are the prime example: large-scale solar panel power stations are already only half the cost estimated for 2030 by Treasury's 2008 and 2011 modelling studies.
- The underlying drivers of emissions growth are weaker than expected, partly because of the end of the mining boom.
- Analysts and businesses are becoming aware of ever more ways in which emissions can be reduced, and that it is a good investment.

Both major Australian political parties resist serious action, but Australia's electricity market is changing rapidly because of rooftop photovoltaic installations, and will change more rapidly again as cheap battery storage becomes available. Myopic policy makers and energy companies are being caught out, and we will pay more for the lack of a coherent national strategy of the kind Germany has already implemented. But change is happening anyway. Lovins and others who have claimed we could eliminate fossil fuels by 2050 have been consistently ridiculed, but perhaps they will turn out to have been conservative.

To stay within even the official limit of 2°C of warming, developed nations must reduce their emissions by at least 5% per year and perhaps 8-10% per year, according to Kevin Anderson in 2012. This is incompatible with the present form of perpetual-growth, consumer capitalism, but it is still plausible if we rein in the excesses, remove the drivers of excess and waste and begin a transformation of our economic system and its motivating values.

According to Naomi Klein the *Great Energy Transition* might require something like $2 trillion per year globally. That's a lot, but it is only 3% of global GDP. Much of it could be redirected from dirty energy and other unproductive uses. That's why the *net* cost to the economy cited above is only 0.1-0.2% of GDP. So we spend more on clean energy, but less on, say, dirty energy and indulgent tax breaks for the rich.

Phasing out direct fossil fuel subsidies globally could yield at least $800 billion. A startling finding comes in a working paper published by the International Monetary Fund. Damian Carrington reports that the total direct and indirect subsidies of fossil fuels globally totals $US5.2 trillion. The vast sum is largely due to polluters not paying the costs imposed on governments and societies by the burning of coal, oil and gas. These include the harm caused to local populations by air pollution as well as to people across the globe affected by the floods, droughts and storms being driven by climate change.

We can also impose a carbon tax of around $50 per metric ton of carbon dioxide emitted in developed countries, close tax havens, impose a 1% billionaire's tax and a financial transactions tax. Just shifting subsidies from dirty energy to clean energy will get markets to do a lot of the work for us, because many sources of clean energy would immediately be the cheaper alternative.

Even better, clean energy creates many more jobs than fossil fuel energy. Research in Canada found that an investment of $1.3 billion could create around 20,000 jobs in renewable energy, public transit, or energy efficiency. This is 6 to 8 times as many jobs as that amount of money generates as subsidies to the oil and gas sector.

GERMANY PROVIDES AN INSTRUCTIVE MODEL, described by Osha Gray Davidson and Naomi Klein. It is in the midst of a remarkable energy transformation, to phase out nuclear and coal power and promote renewable energies. The transformation has been implemented with a well-designed national program including generous 'feed-in' tariffs and other incentives. These ensure that anyone who wants to get into renewable power generation can do so in a way that is simple, stable and profitable.

The most successful part of the German program has been the promotion of local ownership of energy, through farms, municipalities, and hundreds of newly formed cooperatives. That has decentralised not just electrical power but also political power and wealth. Roughly half of Germany's renewable energy facilities are in the hands of local groups.

Responding to the national incentives and to citizens' desire to move to clean energy, many local governments have set up enterprises or even re-acquired previously privatised utilities. A notable example is Hamburg, whose citizens in 2013 voted to buy back their electricity, gas and heating grids.

Some detractors have claimed that the phasing out of nuclear power has resulted in greater burning of coal. However that turns out to be because German power companies have been exporting electricity to make up for the reduced domestic market for their product. The lesson is that not only must clean energy be promoted, but dirty energy may need to be restrained.

The speed of the German transformation has surprised even its supporters. According to one, 'Virtually all expansion estimates have been surpassed. The speed of expansion is considerably higher than had been expected.'

Denmark pioneered this approach in the 1970s and 1980s, so that now it obtains more than 40% of its electricity from renewables, mostly wind. Roughly 85% of Danish wind turbines are owned by small players like farmers and co-ops.

The key to success in both Denmark and Germany has been the encouragement of local collective enterprises working in the context of a well-designed national framework. Some of the bodies are independent of governments, others are run by local governments. In Australia we take little interest in local governments, and they are commonly dominated by developers and other special interests, but they are still more accessible to an active citizenry than a national government. Local German enterprises, of whatever kind, have exceeded the performance both of big private corporations and of big government monopolies.

These successes are contrary to the both the neoliberal and the socialist approaches. They are a dramatic illustration of the potential of creatively managing markets by using alternative ownership models, especially more localised models. They illustrate the power of creative decentralisation, and of greater empowerment of local citizens.

MAINSTREAM AUSTRALIAN THINKING about public versus private enterprise, about sizes of firms, and about an appropriate role for government is far too simplistic. As a result our approach is incoherent and much less effective than it might be.

Despite all the neoliberal claims about innovative private enterprise, the private sector commonly defends its current market position rather than initiating a major change of approach or technology, let alone managing its own extinction. The larger the firm, the more this seems to be true. It does this because, typically, firms become heavily invested in their current business model, both intellectually and financially. It is facilitated by the ready access big firms have to our politicians. This is most obvious with the coal industry in Australia, which has our Parliaments in a vice-like grip and is heavily impeding the emergence of clean energy systems.

In the face of this juggernaut, Parliament's support for clean energy is so inadequate and fitful as to comprise only window dressing. Although many incentives and programs have been instituted over the years, they are frequently changed, especially if they are starting to make a difference, leaving clean energy industries in perpetual uncertainty. Recent victims have been the carbon price, the Renewable Energy Target, and a renewable energy investment fund. These were regarded as the most effective of several recent policies.

Despite these impediments rooftop photovoltaic panels have proliferated. This change is disrupting the business models of privatised electricity suppliers, because daytime demand has been dropping rapidly, and even overall demand has declined. Their response is to raise prices rather than to change strategy, and rising prices only exacerbate their downward spiral. On top of this, electricity distribution has suffered from highly skewed investment. Because of a poorly designed pseudo-market in the building of poles and wires, the infrastructure has been overbuilt, including an entire substation that may never be used.

What is needed is a coherent strategy for phasing out dirty energy and phasing in clean energy. A well designed and modern grid would be important for levelling out the fluctuations of wind and solar power. Were these assets still in public ownership it would be much easier to pursue a coherent transition strategy.

ENERGY STORAGE now looks even more feasible than it did a few years ago, because of two developments.

The better-known one is the emergence of relatively cheap batteries that can store several hours worth of electricity. These would help households to smooth the daily fluctuations in supply from photovoltaic panels, so for example energy generated during a sunny day can be saved for use in the evening. This would also help to smooth demand on electricity grids, which are not yet well adapted to the different patterns of fluctuation of wind and solar supply. However the batteries are not that cheap, and they still involve toxic materials such as lead. Unless requirements for recycling are quickly introduced we will create yet another pollution problem.

A more promising alternative is pumped hydro storage, or Short-Term Off-River Energy Storage (STORES), outlined by Andrew Blakers. The idea is to have two water reservoirs at different elevations. When solar or wind power are plentiful, water can be pumped from the lower to the higher. When power is needed, the water can be run back down, passing through a generator and supplying electricity. The process is about 80% efficient. This system has been used for a long time in big hydro-electric schemes to supplement other short-term sources.

A key realisation is that relatively small reservoirs away from major rivers are adequate and much cheaper than giant hydro dams. The cost is likely to be no greater than batteries, perhaps significantly less. There are no toxic materials, little disruption of river systems and all the technical components are mature. A study has shown many suitable sites around Australia, some along the coastline. Estimates for the small town where I live suggest a week's worth of energy could be stored for modest extra cost. That possibility would be a game changer. The alleged problem of wind and solar – fluctuating supply – would be resolved.

'GLORIFIED TENTS' is how environment campaigner Nick Roberts described Australian houses. There are more deaths from cold in Australia than in Sweden, because many older houses do such a poor job of keeping occupants warm in our relatively mild winters. It is cheaper for builders to leave out insulation, to not take the trouble to tightly seal the structure and to not worry about passive solar design features. Builders don't have to pay the heating bills, so they have a perverse incentive to build wasteful buildings. Regulations are required to overcome this market failure. We do have a star system to rate the energy efficiency of houses, and some requirements that new houses have to meet prescribed standards. As a result our heating and cooling bills are smaller, for only a modest extra investment. However much more is possible.

Back in the 1990s, Amory Lovins estimated that poor building design in the US had resulted in the installation of about *$1 trillion-worth* of unnecessary airconditioning equipment (in von Weizsäcker, 1997). This figure was based on the estimate that buildings could readily save 80-90% of their cooling costs for little or no extra capital cost, just by using design features that had been shown in practice to be effective. Lovins found that perverse incentives commonly apply to those who conceive, approve, finance, design, build, commission, operate, maintain, sell, lease and renovate buildings. Wasteful buildings are more profitable for them all. Regulation is a crude counter. A better solution is to write energy efficiency into the contract in the first place, with the professionals' fees dependent on the building's actual performance meeting agreed criteria. With that incentive, they might then begin to discover the many synergies available through good design.

Household appliances are more energy efficient than they used to be. Today we have an energy star rating system on fridges and washing machines, thanks to people who campaigned to improve the designs. In the bad old days American fridges were amazingly inefficient, because energy was supposedly cheap and marketing imperatives like inside space (requiring thin, leaky walls) prevailed. This was true even though Europeans were producing far more efficient models.

There is still considerably greater potential for household energy savings. A house in Davis, California, where summer temperatures reach 40-45°C, already in the 1990s saved about 80% of energy for space heating, 80% for water heating, 80% for refrigeration and 66% for lighting. More impressive, 100% of space cooling costs were saved, and over 90% of combined cooling and ventilation costs.

Such impressive savings are achieved through *carefully integrated designs*, where the effects of one change are considered in relation to other aspects of the building. For example, insulation in the California house eliminated the need for a furnace and its associated ducting and equipment. However this was not sufficient to eliminate the need for summer cooling until a collection of more efficient household appliances, lights, small appliances and other measures eliminated the release of waste heat into the interior, heat that otherwise would have required compensating cooling. Through such measures the need for airconditioning was also eliminated, with another substantial and offsetting saving. In this example, the more efficient appliances did not pay for themselves directly through electricity savings, but they were cost effective when considered in conjunction with space cooling.

Paul Hawken and others in 1999 found even greater benefits from thoughtfully integrated design can be achieved by considering the people who use a building. A lighting retrofit in a mail-sorting office not only saved energy, but improved employees' view of what they were doing and reduced distracting and fatiguing noise. Typically about 6 times as much is spent on the people occupying a building as is spent on the building itself, expressed as rental cost. Energy costs are even less, only about 1% of people costs. Energy savings are usually worthwhile investments by themselves. However improvements in the work environment have been found to improve employee productivity by 6-16%, which means that the financial benefit is at least ten times the direct savings in energy costs. A 1% improvement in employee productivity would cover the entire energy cost, and a 16% improvement would cover the rent.

Progress is being made in applying appropriate forms of energy to particular tasks. Energy comes in what may loosely be called high grade and low grade forms. Warm air or water are low grade. Pressurised steam is higher grade. Electricity is the highest grade, highly versatile and capable of being adapted to many uses. However electricity from power stations is quite inefficient for many uses because about two thirds of the fuel energy used is wasted, and only one third converted to electricity. More is lost in transmission.

Space heating and domestic water heating require only low-grade energy, much of which can be readily obtained from the sun using energy-efficient passive solar designs and solar-panel water heaters, which are already commonly available (not to be confused with photovoltaic solar electricity panels). It is very wasteful to use electricity, the Rolls-Royce form of energy, for such low-grade, horse-and-buggy uses as space heating.

Retrofitting old buildings has more benefits than may at first appear. When the life-cycle of a building is considered, a great deal of energy and greenhouse gas emissions can be saved by reusing old buildings that already 'embody' a lot of energy. Even though a new building may be more efficient than a retrofitted old building, the large initial energy cost of knocking the old one down and building a new one may not be made up for decades, anything from 10 to 80 years according to Greg Hanscom writing in *Grist*.

Zero-energy houses are being built for a cost comparable to a conventional Western house. One example is called Earthship. The concept is being extended so they require no water supply, process their own wastes and even grow food indoors through severe winters.

There has been a lot of progress over the past couple of decades in finding affordable ways to reduce household energy use, and there's a large literature out there. Daniela Ciancio provides just one example, using mud brick or rammed earth construction, which is usually cheap, uses local materials, is easy to build and can be made very energy-efficient.

Such houses may have a different aesthetic, but they can also be more attractive than your average tract house. A consistent theme of people who live in high-efficiency houses is that they are more pleasant to be in, because they have more even temperatures without hotspots and coldspots, and the well-directed natural lighting is more pleasant. The concepts are being adapted further to dramatically reduce the cost so they will be within reach of third-world people.

These are the pioneers. Let it not be said that we can't reduce our footprint on the Earth without suffering. We can save the Earth, save money and be more comfortable too.

WE USE PRODIGIOUS AMOUNTS OF MATERIALS. In our present industrial system, most materials are mined, used once, and dumped. About 2,000 tons of material is mined, extracted, shovelled, moved, pumped and dumped every year for each American family. Total annual wastage of materials in the US, excluding waste water, exceeds 20 billion tons. Such vast material flows not only disrupt and pollute the Earth, they involve a large proportion of our total energy usage.

Here is an example that shows what we can aspire to, and what is possible even within the present pathologically-structured market system. Interface Inc. is a billion-dollar carpet manufacturer. In 1994 the CEO of Interface, the late Ray Anderson, had an epiphany while reading Paul Hawken's book *The Ecology of Commerce*. Anderson in 2010 recounted how he decided he wanted to transform his company from an Earth degrader to an Earth restorer. His most far-reaching change was to switch from *selling a product* (carpet tiles) to *providing a service* (floor covering). In other words, rather than simply selling and installing office carpet, Interface undertakes to maintain attractive floor coverings as a continuing service.

In adopting this role, Interface *reversed its own incentives*. Before the change, its profit was proportional to the amount of carpet it sold. Not only that, there was an incentive to make the carpet as cheaply as possible so it would need replacing as often as possible. After the change, its incentive was to make the carpet as durable as possible because Interface, not the customer, was paying for the replacement of worn carpet.

Having placed on itself the requirement for its carpet to be durable, Interface developed new synthetic materials that were not only more durable but more readily recyclable, and redesigned its carpets' fabrication so its materials were more easily separable. It found it could then recycle its materials more cheaply than buying more petroleum products extracted from the Earth. It developed non-toxic dyes that also turned out to be cheaper, so a source of serious chemical pollution was eliminated.

How much did these planet-saving, warm-fuzzy-inducing good works cost? Less than nothing. Manufacturing costs were substantially reduced and margins increased. In fact Interface prospered. Four years after it began this quest in 1994, Interface's revenues had doubled, its employment had nearly doubled and its profits had tripled. In 1999 it was a billion-dollar company with manufacturing facilities in seven countries. By the early 2000s it was selling more than 40 percent of all the carpet tile used in commercial buildings.

Interface intends to go much further. It aspires to eliminate all waste, to use only the power of the sun, and even to mine old waste landfills for the millions of tons of carpet fibre previously dumped there.

By offering an end-use *service*, attractively covered floors, rather than a product, carpet, Interface took upon itself the imperative to improve durability and reduce the quantity of materials it processed. Our whole system at present is geared to maximise material throughput, in other words to maximise material wastes. Through creative shifts in incentives, of the kind Interface has demonstrated, our system can incorporate the imperative to minimise wastes and toxins.

We can, if we are smart, harness markets to help us to live healthy lives in a healthy society and a healthy biosphere. To quote Ray Anderson:

> We look forward to the day when our factories have no smokestacks and no effluents. If successful, we'll spend the rest of our days harvesting yesteryear's carpets, recycling old petrochemicals into new materials, and converting sunlight into energy. There will be zero scrap going into landfills

and zero emissions into the ecosystem. Literally, it is a company that will grow by cleaning up the world, not by polluting or degrading it.

VEHICLES HAVE BECOME considerably more fuel efficient since the bad old days of the 1970s, but there is still a lot of potential for improvement. Zero-carbon-emission vehicles are a serious possibility within a decade or so.

The improvements have come about through a combination of regulation and innovation. The US required its manufacturers to steadily improve their atrociously wasteful performances, an act that probably saved them from competition from Japanese and European manufacturers. Much of the savings came from reducing vehicle weight. Lovins in 2011 said there is potential for new materials and fabrication methods to dramatically reduce weight again, though that has not happened much yet.

The advent of hybrid-drive vehicles (a small petrol motor combined with battery-electric drive) doubled fuel efficiency, starting with the Toyota Prius. However they are still expensive and have not taken much of the market. In the meantime turbo-diesel motors have improved considerably, so they are nearly as efficient as hybrids, and they're cheaper.

So-called transitional fuels like natural gas power and biofuels are of only marginal help in reducing greenhouse emissions from vehicles. Biofuels are claimed to emit nearly as much as fossil fuels once the full lifecycle is accounted for, and emissions from natural gas, though less than from oil, are still substantial.

An important advance would be to replace internal combustion motors with fuel cells. Whereas conventional electric generators convert only about a third of fuel energy to electricity, fuel cells convert fuel energy to electricity with nearly 100% efficiency, so they would be a step beyond hybrid drive. They have been in development for some time and a few are emerging onto the market.

The ideal would be to use hydrogen as a fuel because its waste product is harmless – water. It can be generated by running solar electricity through water, so the lifecycle emissions are still low. It is challenging because it would need to be stored under pressure, though it should be no more dangerous than natural gas storage on vehicles. Pressure containers might be heavy, which has led some to claim it is unviable, but an ultralight vehicle built of modern composites would make the combination feasible.

There is at least as great a potential for transportation savings by reducing the *need* for transportation, which can be done by making our cities smarter.

AUSTRALIAN CITIES ARE VERY INEFFICIENT in every respect – greenhouse emissions, people's time, amenity, cost. Although the general principles for building a smart, pleasant, efficient city have been known for a good while and are being improved all the time, we make very little use of them. This seems to be due to a combination of ideology, lack of ambition, the resulting ignorance, lack of coordination among levels of government, and our combative political system, in which each side tries to dismantle what the other has been doing.

A key principle is to mix the main uses within neighbourhoods. As William McDonough put it in *Cradle to Cradle, transportation is a symptom of being in the wrong place*. Rather than doing long commutes across sprawling cities, we can arrange our lives so most of the time we don't have far to go.

If there are transport nodes, housing, shops, entertainment, offices and other businesses all close together, then people need to travel less and they can even walk to many of their activities. Housing can be fairly high density, but if it is interspersed with parks, shops and entertainment then residents can have much of the best of our current city and suburban duality. If there is a good public transport system, then longer journeys through the city can still be accomplished easily, comfortably and efficiently, especially as demand for longer journeys would be lower.

The inner parts of Melbourne still provide some of this amenity, with tramlines and suburban train stations within walking distance, plenty of park space and medium density housing, although much of the housing stock is old and not very efficient.

Melbourne was one of the few cities in Australia and North America to retain its tram system in the face of a deliberate campaign by the automotive industry to buy public transport systems, run them down and then close them down. This set in motion the leapfrogging process James Kunstler has called *suburban buildout*, in which people move progressively further away from a city centre in search of a pleasant hideaway. One might think that after a century of doing this we might have noticed it doesn't work. Instead we have the insanity of people driving for two hours or more every day through congested, inefficient and unhealthy traffic. As complaints rise, the reflexive response of authority is to bulldoze or tunnel more roads through the mess, but that only perpetuates the process.

Many cities in Europe have been showing us the way for a long time, but of course our politicians are oblivious to anything beyond our shores, and besides we're not like those funny foreigners. Perhaps some examples from

North America would resonate more here, because their cities are more like ours.

Portland, Oregon and Vancouver, Canada have been working to restore some sense to their structure and functioning. According to Carolyn Whitzman, both cities have been able to contain themselves within a boundary for more than 30 years, in part due to a governance structure that is based on local governments working together on a common vision, rather than having it imposed by their state government. This has the additional benefit of depoliticising planning. Rather than priorities being completely revised after each state election, metropolitan planning outlasts both state and local government election cycles.

Both cities also have political cultures that promote deliberative decision-making between the private sector, governments and civil society. For instance, both have task forces to end street homelessness, bringing together all levels of government with philanthropic and private sector contributions towards a shared goal. Both cities have a goal of 'complete communities', with all residents having easy walking access to public transport, schools and health care (which are all sources of local employment). Both cities map access to this infrastructure, and then prioritise infrastructure spending in poorly served areas, along with prioritising affordable housing provision in well-served areas.

The strategies are a little different in each city, but in each city the results are publicly monitored, with feedback from residents. Almost half of the residents of central Vancouver walk to work, which cuts down considerably on living costs and improves residents' physical and mental health. William McDonough would be pleased – the people are already in the right place, and don't need transportation.

There are plenty of examples from around the world, but one of the more striking comes from the regional Brazilian city of Curitiba. It is not a rich city by our standards. A carefully integrated city plan was implemented in the 1970s involving development along main axes with a bus system running on central dedicated roadways. Disruption of existing buildings along relatively narrow streets in the city centre was minimised by using three parallel pre-existing streets, the inner one as an express bus route and the outer ones for one-way private traffic. Both commercial and residential development was encouraged along the city axes.

The benefits of foresight were dramatic in Curitiba's case because the city's population tripled to 1.6 million (over 2 million counting surrounds) and ridership on the bus system grew from 50,000 in 1974 to 800,000 passengers per day by 1996. About 75% of the population used the system each day. Innovations in the bus system itself have been important contributors to its success. These include the dedicated roadways, enclosed 'tube stations' that function like train stations, simplifying ticketing and speeding loading and unloading, and the use of articulated and bi-articulated buses. The system has about four times the throughput of conventional bus systems. Express bus lanes carry peak loads of 20,000 passengers each per hour, similar to a subway.

The capital cost of Curitiba's bus system was more than 100-fold lower than an underground rail system would have been, and about 10 times lower than conventional surface rail. Fares are very low: a flat 20 pence-equivalent (about AUD0.55) over the whole city in 1996, but the system still paid for itself. The city provides the infrastructure and the buses are run by private companies. The private operators are paid per kilometre served rather than per passenger carried, which maximises coverage of the city and convenience for passengers.

Other benefits of Curitiba's bus system are the cleanest ambient air in any Brazilian city, 30% lower petrol consumption per capita and the lowest car drivership despite the highest car ownership in Brazil, and a large amount of open space (52 sq m per capita). The latter is also due to the broader integrated city plan, which involves zoning, flood control, welfare, education and an innovative combination of trash collection, recycling and nutritional assistance in poorer neighbourhoods.

A feature of Curitiba's planning, and a principal ingredient in its success, has been the major effort to involve the populace and gain their trust and support. There are major efforts to explain the benefits of integrated planning and of environmental compatibility, starting with school programs. The progress of programs is regularly monitored. Mistakes are identified and corrected. Information and government services are readily available through conveniently located 'shopfronts', hotlines and other services.

Curitiba shows how an imaginative approach to integrating city functions, that actively involves the populace, spreads benefits beyond those immediate affected and through the broader community, as described by Rabinovitch and Leitman in 1996. It all came about through the imagination and initiative of one man, Jaime Lerner, who got himself elected mayor back in 1971. If they can do it, we certainly can.

Not Back to the Caves: Smart Ideas, Proven Practices

WATER IS USED MORE SPARINGLY in Australian cities than it used to be, especially since the '10-year drought' in the first decade of this century. (Country people didn't need much education on the subject.) Despite improvements, huge quantities of drinking-quality water are flushed down toilets of 19th century design. That sewerage then goes through vast networks of pipes of 20th century construction, many of which leak into the groundwater.

Sewerage composting has been commercially available for some time, and it was installed in a terrace house by Michael Mobbs in Inner Sydney in the 1990s. This house was actually disconnected from the city's water and sewerage systems. Instead the household relies on rainwater and sewerage composting. There is no odour or other problem. Rainwater is used for cooking and personal use and in the hot water supply, while recycled water is used for clothes washing, toilet flushing and the small garden. Excess water is directed to a 'wetlands' pit, which acquired its own mini-ecology, including frogs that control such potential pests as mosquitoes. No water had been brought into or left the property for over a year when I visited. The water quality is excellent, and better than that of the city.

Efficiencies at the household scale certainly help, but when we look at such improvements in the context of a large city we see the much larger potential savings in city infrastructure costs and avoided environmental disruption. Sydney's water supply comes from a series of dams in nearby highlands. The dams disrupt the natural flow of rivers, causing environmental changes, species extinctions and concentration of agricultural pollutants. Water from the dams is piped hundreds of kilometres and then distributed through a vast urban network of underground pipes. This water is used once and discharged into an equally vast network of sewerage pipes. Plumbers say that the pipes in older areas are commonly cracked, so raw sewerage may be seeping into the underground all over the city. Sewerage is piped to huge and expensive treatment plants. 'Treated' freshwater sewerage is discharged into the sea, where it disrupts the coastal saltwater marine ecology. Malfunctions are not uncommon, and there has been a recurrent problem of raw sewerage washing onto Sydney's famous beaches. On top of all of this, most of the rainwater that actually falls on Sydney is not used. Instead it is turned into a drainage problem, and the problem is exacerbated by large, non-absorbent paved areas which cause rapid, high-volume runoff into another extensive system of stormwater drains, which overflow during large storms.

A thorough rethink of our water and sewerage systems could lead, over time, to great cost savings, more robust services and a large reduction of environmental impact.

CREATIVE, INTEGRATED DESIGN is the key to all of these examples. Over the past few decades there has been a proliferation of efficient designs for houses, buildings, cars, factories and household devices. These make it clear that we could considerably reduce our use of energy and *save money at the same time*. By now many studies, including those of Lovins in 2011 and McKinsey in 2007, have shown that for a modest investment, with a short pay-back time, we could further reduce energy use to half or less of present use. This means that reducing emissions of greenhouse gases need not be hugely expensive, and certainly will not wreck economies. We could also dramatically reduce our use of other resources.

Whether it is for a refrigerator, a house, a factory or a city, a well-integrated design can achieve much greater efficiency than a design in which efficiency was not a consideration from the beginning. Even today, for example, most house designs are controlled mainly by builders' standard operating procedure, fashion and block orientation. Having thereby lost many opportunities for efficiency (and comfort), builders add some insulation because they're required to, and try to make up the deficiencies with expensive heating and air conditioning. The result is wasteful because the various elements are working against each other. In contrast, in the cold winters of Germany or the hot summers of inland California and Australia there are houses that require 80-90% less energy than average houses. These houses would cost little more than present, inferior, designs if they became standard practice. They achieve such performance because their designs are well-integrated, so that the various elements work together.

In other words, the goal of good design is to achieve *synergies*. When this is achieved, the result is better than the sum of the parts. Then you have a *beautiful solution* – a solution that resolves more than one problem simultaneously. Many of our present attempted solutions are ugly – their negative side effects create more problems. More ideas can be found, for example, at the *Beautiful Solutions* web site.

14

An Economy to Support Society

Fear not, this chapter is not a lesson in obscure economics of the conventional kind. It is a contemplation of what an economy is, what determines how it functions, and how we can ensure its benefits flow equitably.

The previous chapter shows there are many things we could be doing right now to lessen our heavy assault on the Earth and, simultaneously, to improve our quality of life. However many of the best options are inhibited or obstructed by the way we are organised and managed. To allow the full flowering of this promising potential we need to reorganise ourselves to facilitate and promote them. This means not just changing some incentives and disincentives but also removing bottlenecks and blocks and promoting synergies. It means promoting the growth of an industrial and economic *ecosystem* that gets more done with less effort and promotes the quality of life of people and other living things.

Ecosystems are about connection, but the neoliberal ideology promotes separation. It tries to separate the economy from the rest of society, and it wants us to act separately from each other, as competitive little economic units. In the real world, however, virtually all of our economic activities are collaborative, explicitly or implicitly, and so require cooperation among various parties. We also have a huge common inheritance of ideas and culture that facilitate our lives, and it belongs to all of us.

We are an intensely social species. It is normal, healthy and necessary for us to cede some of our autonomy in return for the greater benefit of working together. It is also healthy and necessary that we all receive a reasonable reward for our contributions. Unfettered markets alone cannot ensure reasonable rewards because the division of wealth is more on the basis of power than merit. J. Persky has pointed out that even Adam Smith recognised this. Enormous disparities of power have been allowed to accumulate. We find ourselves in highly integrated and collaborative modern societies, many of which are very rich, so there cannot be any justification for large numbers of people being left poor.

Rather than allowing ourselves to be slaves to 'the economy' (meaning the rich), we saw in Chapter 10 how we might harness markets to serve us all. Serving us all would mean ensuring everyone has access to a reasonable livelihood, and gets a reasonably fair share of the wealth, in relation to their contribution. It would also mean supporting the fabric of the society we are all part of, so our collaborations are facilitated, and so we are enriched in all the other social and cultural ways that flow from a healthy society.

We are a wealthy society and we can afford to live well. We can easily afford, for example, to put our children and families ahead of excess working hours, to care for the unfortunate, and to fund cultural institutions that enrich our lives. We can easily afford a good education system, which is in any case an excellent investment in our society's future.

Politics at present treats the economy as an entity separate from and superior to society, rather than as *the material basis* of society. The economy does not have to be in conflict with society, nor with the environment. Rather, if we redefine the purpose of government policy to be the promotion of wellbeing for all, then the economy can directly support a healthy society and a healthy environment.

THE 'ECONOMY' IS THE WAY OUR SOCIETY makes its living. It is the collection of activities within our society that takes care of our material needs, and wants. It is not worth trying to define it too precisely. If there are fuzzy boundaries there, that's fine, because the economy is an aspect of society, and society is a highly inter-connected system of people, things, activities and so on. No part of it can be isolated.

An Economy to Support Society

Still less should the economy be thought to be dominant over society. Why ever would it be? We live together, we do what we do and, nominally, we are a democracy, so we decide the way we want our society to develop. We can tailor the economy, the more material parts of our society, *to support the society we choose to live in*.

The modern identification an economy (as a complex, self-organising, far from equilibrium system, Chapter 10) is entirely compatible with this vision of an economy. Market fundamentalists insist there is only one way to organise an economy, but the theory they base this claim on is an abstract fantasy. Rather, complex systems theory tells us a complex system can exist in many possible states, and its behaviour can't be predicted very reliably. We live in an uncertain world and the best-laid plans of mice and men gang oft awry. We make tentative plans, but often we just muddle along as best we can. So it is with our economy. We can organise it to suit us, as best we can judge at any given time.

The economy supplies our material needs and wants, I have said. But what exactly are our 'needs', and how many of our 'wants' is it reasonable to provide for? Can we just go on an ever-increasing binge of pandering to our whims and fads? Well, the Mayan leaders apparently *wanted* to go on building ever-greater pyramids. It seems they did this until they surpassed the carrying capacity of their land, which may have been declining anyway because of changes in the climate. Plausibly, their crops failed, their leaders lost authority, the society's organising principle failed and it fell into anarchy. Ditto the Easter Islanders.

Jared Diamond, in *Collapse*, points out it is characteristic of societies that blindly pursue a trajectory of ever-growing wealth and power that their greatest power and most glorious achievements occur just as they start to crash. 'My name is Ozymandias, king of kings: Look on my works, ye Mighty, and despair!', says Shelley's poem. Ozymandias' once-grand statue lay fallen in a desert: 'Nothing beside remains. Round the decay Of that colossal wreck, boundless and bare The lone and level sands stretch far away'. Our name is Lehman Brothers, masters of the universe: look on our works, ye mighty, and despair.

Clearly it matters what our economy is meant to accomplish. At present it is to provide ever-more stuff, without limit. The way we do things now, this requires extracting ever-more resources, and dumping ever-more waste and pollution, and we have already exceeded the planet's carrying capacity. We need a different purpose for our economy.

W̲HAT THEN SHOULD OUR ECONOMY be for? Well, what kind of society do we want? What are the goals of your life, and what are mine? Such questions quickly get us into deep and personal territory. To focus this line of thinking, I'll offer this: the purpose of the economy is *to promote quality of life for everyone*.

What is quality of life? Well that's for us to decide, collectively, as we go along. The merit of stating the purpose this way is that it gets away from just the material. It allows for life goals such as to have enough to live comfortably, to love and be loved, and to pursue our passions. It allows for the economy to be subordinate to larger purposes.

The past President of Uruguay, José Mujica, amazed people by donating most of his presidential salary to charities and continuing to live in his simple house in the country, with vegetable gardens and animals, rather than in the presidential palace. He said 'I'm called 'the poorest president', but I don't feel poor. Poor people are those who only work to try to keep an expensive lifestyle, and always want more and more.' He's right, those people never have *enough*. Of course some people really don't have enough for a basic, dignified life, and that's a different case. Those of us who are well off need to learn to say *enough*, and we need to change our system so it *provides enough*, and no more.

So now we'll look at how we might modify our economic mechanisms so they promote quality of life for everyone. We've already covered the principle. If we get the incentives right, the economy will take us where we want to go. It means quality of life has to be economically profitable, as well as socially, aesthetically and (for many) spiritually beneficial.

T̲HE STORY OF INTERFACE CARPET INC., from the previous chapter, shows how a shift from *selling a product* (carpet) to *providing a service* (attractive floor coverings) can reverse the incentive applying to material use. Instead of maximising profit by selling stuff, Interface maximised profit by using a durable, recyclable material to provide a service.

Paul Hawken, in *Natural Capitalism*, quotes Interface CEO Ray Anderson from 1997:

> At Interface, we are on a quest to become the first sustainable corporation in the world, and then we want to keep going and become the first *restorative* company. ... ultimately, I believe we have to learn to operate off current income the way a forest does, and, for that

matter, the way we do in our businesses, not off of capital – stored natural capital – but off current income; i.e., the sun.

In the early 1990s, before neoliberal insanity became established there, California revised its regulations of electric utilities so they would profit from helping customers to *save* energy, instead of just profiting from selling them more and more energy. The logic was that it is cheaper for society overall to not generate energy in the first place, so if some of those savings could be shared appropriately between suppliers and customers then everyone would be financially better off. Getting the regulations right was not simple, it took several goes, but eventually they got the response they were trying for, as recounted by von Weizsäcker and others.

The response of one utility company was to offer rebates to customers who installed compact fluorescent light bulbs, which are much more efficient than the old-style incandescent bulbs. But then the utility found it was more effective and more cost-effective to offer an incentive to stores to carry compact fluorescents, so they were readily available. Then it worked its way further back along the supply chain, offering incentives to distributors, then to manufacturers and designers, offering them subsidies for more efficient products. At each stage the leverage of the utility's rebates was increased, and the response was greater, with the result that compact fluorescents became widely available and their price dropped substantially because of the economies of large-scale manufacturing.

In both of these examples, Interface and the electric utilities were selling end-use services rather than just a product. As Amory Lovins puts it, people don't want electricity, they want cold beer and hot showers. The power company was helping them to get those amenities in a different way. Similarly, people don't need to own carpet, they only need attractive floor coverings.

So, with creative adjustments of incentives, businesses profited from *saving* resources. They were profiting from saving the Earth instead of trashing it. We can chalk these up as examples of *beautiful solutions* - saving money and saving the Earth at the same time.

Let's briefly get a bit technical again and look at the *feedbacks*, from customer to supplier. That was a good product, so I'll buy more - a positive feedback. That product broke, I want a refund - a negative feedback. Your price is too high, I'll buy the competitor's product - the invisible hand feedback. Stock prices are dropping, I'll sell mine too - the invisible foot feedback.

In the carpet and electricity examples, the nature of the feedbacks was changed. In the carpets example, the new feedback from customers promoted more durable, higher-quality carpets. In the electric utilities case, the new feedback promoted energy savings instead of energy generation (and waste). There was also a new feedback from the utility to light bulb suppliers - the more efficient your light bulbs the more we'll pay you. Then, the utility got more creative, and it connected its feedback further back along the supply chain, ultimately feeding back to design and manufacture, and its feedback thereby gained more leverage.

So, it is not inevitable that markets only reward greater and greater throughput. People are more creative than that. If we shift some overall incentives in the right ways, we can unleash that creativity in the cause of a more humane and durable economy.

ECONOMIC GROWTH IS THE MODERN HOLY GRAIL, but is it a good thing? To answer that, we have to ask: growth of *what*? Growth is commonly equated, in mainstream political discussion, with *growth of the GDP*, the Gross Domestic Product. However the GDP is a crude and unhelpful measure that mixes quite different things, such as creating new wealth *versus* extracting existing wealth. We'll get to that soon. So focusing the debate on GDP growth only propagates more confusion. A key confusion can be removed if we distinguish *quantity* from *quality*.

OUR PRESENT ECONOMIC SYSTEM IS BIG ON *QUANTITY*, and as a result it is highly inefficient in its use of resources. We waste a lot of energy, and we use prodigious amounts of materials. Our system is *linear*: we extract materials, use them once, then dump them.

The biggest and quickest way to reduce human impact on the world is to transition to a circular, *recycling* system. This means not just re-using a few things once, as recycling is commonly practiced at present. As exemplified by Interface Carpet, it means re-designing our products and systems so materials can be recovered nearly 100% at the end of a product's lifetime. The materials ought then be recyclable either through the industrial system (for example by recovering and re-using metals) or through the organic world (for example by using bio-degradable plastics made from living products, not fossil oil).

We will never recycle materials 100% because things wear out and disperse, but we could plausibly recycle well over 90%. It will take time to approach that goal, but the early gains are easy and could be quick, because we are so careless in our use at present.

It seems plausible that, with coordinated and serious attention, we could reduce material flows in the industrial nations (the main abusers) by, say, 15-20% per decade. That would reduce our material use by 50% within 3 or 4 decades, i.e. by mid-century. We are reported to be using resources equivalent to what can be supplied by about 1.4 Earths, so a cut by half could bring us back under the nominal maximum. However our Earth's systems are showing a great deal of stress, so it may well be desirable to reduce at a greater rate and ultimately to a lower level. Once we can see progress being made, that may turn out to be feasible.

The challenge of energy use is a little different. Energy can only be used once, and it then dissipates in unusable form. Well, high-grade energy (such as electricity or high-temperature steam) may emerge as medium-grade energy, still usable for some purposes. This is being done in some electric power generators, where some of the fuel energy is first converted to electricity and the 'waste' heat from that stage is used to heat water for industrial or space-heating use. So some energy may allow two cycles, but then it is dissipated.

The problem of our present energy use is that we waste a lot of it and we extract most of it from fossil fuels that threaten catastrophic global warming. We simply must eliminate fossil fuel use as fast as possible. We've already seen that is quite feasible, as photovoltaic and wind power are growing rapidly. Lower-carbon liquid fuels, for transport, are already in use and ultimately we can transition to non-carbon electricity or to hydrogen fuel generated from solar electricity.

Whereas new forms of clean liquid fuels are still a challenge, using energy much more efficiently for space heating and many industrial uses has been feasible for decades already, and it saves money. We are locked in to stupid, expensive, polluting systems by inertia, poor designs, ideology and the disparaging and disinformation of vested interests. As Amory Lovins said, energy efficiency is the quickest, cheapest, most neglected, … .

As we approach a system that recycles most material and uses clean energy sources, the present constraints on our industrial societies will relax. We will be living closer to the way the rest of the living world lives, and we can thrive indefinitely.

WHICH BRINGS US TO *QUALITY*. The debate about *growth*, to the extent there is one, focuses on growth *versus* non-growth. Some people, such as Herman Daly and Tim Jackson, advocate a steady state economy. However if we distinguish quantity from quality we don't even have to restrict ourselves in this way. We need to reduce the *quantity* of resources we use, and we can. That doesn't mean we can't keep doing new things.

We don't have to put our human ingenuity on the shelf and stop inventing. We can't anyway, our brains won't stop thinking. We can have our recyclable, toxin-free, clean-energy cars. We can have toxin-free smart phones and computers. *Progress* may continue.

We would be wise, however, to give up the automatic pursuit of something just because someone *calls* it progress, without examining it for potential problems. We may pursue progress with our eyes open, our brains in gear and our moral compasses at hand.

For example, nano-technologies and biotechnologies are extremely powerful double-edged swords. People already are seriously envisaging bio-engineered plagues, or swarms of self-replicating nano-devices accidentally proliferating into a toxic soup that pervades the ocean. People are seriously worrying about intelligent robots taking over the world. There are even people trying to turn off the ageing process. Not only is a plague of old farts the last thing the planet needs, but ageing is programmed into all multi-cellular, sexually-reproducing organisms, and has been from the beginning of their 600-million-year-plus history. We tamper with such fundamental parts of our physical and moral beings at our peril.

So, even if we clean up our act and survive the profound disruptions we are already visiting upon our solitary, beautiful, bountiful home, there are still plenty of ways our quirkily intelligent brains, unbridled, can visit misery and destruction upon ourselves in the name of progress. Progress is not the same as *quality*. Our goal ought to be *quality of life*. That includes all people, and all other life, not just our own.

WE NEED TO MEASURE WELLBEING, not stuff, and we need to do it sensibly. A government needs to monitor the effectiveness of its management. It therefore needs useful measures and sensible accounting. The main measure of economic success, a growing GDP, has fundamental problems: it is mainly focused on quantity of stuff, it is seriously muddled, and it doesn't really qualify as accounting.

If a chemical factory sells $3 million worth of chemicals in a year, but creates pollution that costs $1 million to clean up, then, in dollar terms, how much better off would you say we are? You would say, I expect, we are only $2 million better off. However economists and politicians say we are $4 million better off. Instead of *subtracting* the $1 million cleanup cost from the $3 million production, they *add* it.

Why do economists add a cost as though it is income? Because they rely on the Gross Domestic Product as a measure of wellbeing, and that is how you calculate a GDP. The GDP is essentially the sum of all those things we do that are bought and sold. It is the sum of all our activities that involve the exchange of money. There is no account taken of whether an activity is actually beneficial, or whether it is harmful, or merely useless, or fixing the harm from previous activities (like cleaning up pollution).

It is also true that the more the GDP goes up, the more stuff we produce, and throw away. That's not a law of nature, but it generally has been true since World War II.

Calculating a quantity like GDP would not necessarily be much of a problem if the GDP were just an obscure thing used by economists to measure total economic activity, so long as they were clear that's all it is. The problem is the GDP has become the dominant measure of wellbeing.

When the GDP increases, politicians and economists say 'the economy has grown', and this is universally acknowledged, within mainstream political discussion, to be a good thing. Earlier I posed the question 'What is the economy?' Evidently to mainstream politicians and economists 'the economy' often means just 'the GDP'.

It is claimed that a growing GDP means we are becoming materially richer. It is assumed that if we are materially richer then our wellbeing is improved. Neither claim is necessarily correct. Over the past half century or so the GDP and wellbeing have become less clearly related. It is quite possible that GDP could increase while both wealth and wellbeing were static, or declining. Some argue this is already true. For example over-harvesting forests will increase the GDP but decrease our overall wealth. Conversely, it is likely the GDP would decline if we focused seriously on improving our wellbeing, because then we might cease many activities that actually reduce our well-being, like spreading poisons that we then try, ineffectually, to clean up.

There are *several* quite fundamental problems with using GDP as a measure of overall wellbeing, as I have elaborated in *Sack the Economists*. One is that costs like pollution are added rather than being subtracted. Another is that many of our beneficial activities, like staying home with baby or growing backyard veggies, do not involve the exchange of money, so they are not taken into account. Another is that it is not a measure of wealth, it is a measure of income. Another is that it is a purely material measure, and no account is taken of the state of our communities and society as a whole, nor of the state of the Earth. Thus it is possible to trash a native forest and have that appear in the 'national accounts' as a pure benefit: people with jobs and a boost for the GDP, with nothing registering the loss of 'natural capital'.

It is quite possible to use more sensible measures of our state of wellbeing, or even just of our material net incomes and net wealth. Such measures have been developed and are being improved all the time. A sensible way to proceed is to set up a *balance sheet*, like a shop-keeper, with income on one side and costs on the other. You then add up both sides, *subtract* costs from gross income, and arrive at net income, or profit.

To calculate the GDP, you put everything in the credit column, income and costs both, and *add the lot up*. What shopkeeper would keep their accounts this way?

One sensible approach is called the Genuine Progress Indicator, described by Clive Hamilton and Richard Denniss in 2000. There are other measures, such as Triple Bottom Line that cover the economy, society and the environment. However the more sensible measures do not dominate the headlines the way 'growth' (of the GDP) dominates the headlines.

The heavy reliance on GDP severely distorts our priorities, and our view of ourselves. It counts extraction and destruction as production, and so facilitates exploitation of the world and ourselves. Anything that falls outside the materialist and very blinkered purview of mainstream economics is regarded as secondary, irrelevant, or an expensive luxury to be attended to only as and when we become richer. That dismisses a mother's love, healthy families, healthy communities, a tolerant and safe society, and the health of the Earth, our sole and irreplaceable life support system.

SO-CALLED GOVERNMENT ACCOUNTING has another basic deficiency. Somewhere along the way, governments stopped distinguishing capital funds from recurrent funds. When Ben Chifley and Bob Menzies borrowed to invest in national infrastructure, the spending did not show up as recurrent expenditure, and so did not push the recurrent balance sheet into deficit. However when major public assets were sold off through the 1980s and 90s, the proceeds were used to balance the budget. Hawke, Keating, Howard and Costello were less than honest about the state of recurrent income and expenditure. They were selling off the family silverware.

Conversely, no government now dares to borrow in order to invest for the benefit of the nation, because that would throw the budget into deficit.

The neoliberal agenda of privatisation has been served in both directions. Sales of public assets were used to disguise government deficits, and now the alleged threat of a government deficit is a deterrent to investing public money in public infrastructure. Both honesty and constructive management of the country require that we return to separating the capital account from the recurrent account, an elementary distinction in business.

THE LEGITIMATE ROLE OF GOVERNMENT needs to be rehabilitated. Markets cannot be left to run untended if we want them to benefit us: they must be managed. If markets need to be managed then obviously there needs to be a manager. As it is a government's role, in general, to implement the will of the people, then the government will oversee the management of markets. The government's role will be to monitor the results of markets, to monitor our collective opinion as to what kind of society we want, and to design and adjust policies so markets will yield results in accord with what we want. Such results will need to be judged much more broadly than at present, according to the quality of society and quality of life we achieve. The government will also need to continuously review its monitoring and management methods.

Most of this is ought not to be controversial in general terms. The government collects statistics on the performance of the economy and develops policies to manage it. It needs to expand the kinds of measures it uses, along lines just discussed, and its management needs to be more aligned with the will of the people, instead of in thrall to the neoliberal ideology and the demands of the wealthy. However government in general has been denigrated for decades now, especially any direct government involvement in the economy.

THERE ARE OTHER IMPORTANT CHANGES that would take us more efficiently to a better quality of life, with a fairer flow of wealth to those who contribute. I will just briefly note a few here, they have been developed further in my 2013 book and by Shann Turnbull in 2003 and 2007. Some of these possibilities are reasonably familiar, others less so.

There is great for potential for using different kinds of ownership, particularly local and group ownership. Ownership is already a flexible concept. It can be partial (as with partnerships and shares), time-limited, or limited, for example, to a building but not the land it occupies.

Firms can be owned by their employees. Well run cooperatives can actually be more efficient and progressive businesses than conventional autocratic firms. Suppliers and customers can be brought into governance structures. Local ownership of clean energy generation is benefitting both the locality and the nation in Germany.

Land speculation and property bubbles could be controlled by vesting land ownership in community land trusts, so the *emergent value* due to the proximity of activities can flow to the community rather than being captured as windfall by minority interests. Home ownership can be promoted through rent-and-buy arrangements in which ownership transfers progressively from developers, as is already done with some infrastructure projects.

Inequality of wealth could be greatly moderated just by eliminating mechanisms that at present unfairly pump wealth to the wealthy. We have covered financial market speculation and interest charged on new money. Ownership can be spread more widely, through arrangements such as those just noted, and emergent wealth captured for the community. Access to loans can be improved for low income people. Tax avoidance by the wealthy and overt corporate welfare could be eliminated.

THE NOTION OF AN INDUSTRIAL ECOSYSTEM is very poorly appreciated in Australian policy circles. Firms are not isolated, they are part of a dense network of suppliers, customers, banks and so on. Innovations depend on the conjunction of key products and ideas that may be very specific to a particular place and time. Policy should be to cultivate the ecosystem, instead of the present crude conception of isolated firms responding only to price signals. Such ideas were developed by Hawken and others in 1999.

Closely related is the potential for a recycling industrial system. Firms may recycle their own products, as does Interface Carpet, but the greater potential is to recycle each other's outputs, as occurs in natural ecosystems that recycle 100% of their materials. In *Cradle to Cradle*, McDonough and Braungart advocate moving to a near-100% industrial recycling system. A key facilitator is to design products so they can be readily reborn after their useful life.

HEALTHY LOCAL COMMUNITIES promote economic benefits, as well as the essential social benefits we noted earlier. The feedbacks central to the healthy working of an economy work best within small communities, and become increasingly attenuated at larger social scales. For example an economic system can only function in the presence of a minimum level of trust. Other critical feedbacks, such as suffering the consequences of economic decisions, as well as reaping their rewards, also function best within small communities. Local and community ownership can be an important way to revive this feedback.

Local money systems are being explored in the context of small communities, where they are viewed as an important way of strengthening social fabric as well as enhancing local economic fortunes, by recycling wealth into the local community instead of losing it to distant shareholders. Examples were described by Greco in 1994. This is particularly pertinent for communities that are being failed by the larger economic system. Such local monetary systems are a potent way to build or rebuild trusting communities, especially if they incorporate or promote a practise of giving gifts, which is the essential ingredient for a strong community fabric.

Our impact upon the Earth can also be reduced through the creation or re-creation of functioning neighbourhoods and local communities, within which work, recreation, social interaction and even food production are added to the mere residing that too many suburban 'bedroom communities' provide. Well-integrated communities of this type promise to be far less wasteful of energy and other resources than our present sprawling, car-dominated cities, as we've seen.

RUNNING AN ECONOMY WILL NEVER BE SIMPLE, just as living life is never simple. There are complications, and there are conflicting interests to resolve. The ideas that have been surveyed here are guides and starting points, not simplistic rules. It is the essence of complex systems that their behaviour cannot be simply predicted, and we must always be prepared to adjust our management as we go along, as a good horse trainer adjusts to the character of each horse.

For example, there will always be a tension between society's wish for business to improve the general good and an individual business's interest to maximise profit. It will often be more profitable to pollute than to neutralise or avoid pollution, it will always be profitable, in the short term, to underpay employees, and speculation will always tempt financial traders. Therefore a basic level of vigilance and protection against exploitive practices will always be required.

Over the past century or more the social democracies addressed such problems by imposing regulations, such as fines on polluters who get caught, requiring a minimum wage to be paid to employees, or (ineffectually) outlawing insider trading in financial markets. During the neoliberal era these protections have been substantially weakened.

Protections need to be restored and strengthened by the most effective means we can devise. Market mechanisms are preferable if they are effective and sufficient. However where market mechanisms are not sufficient there is no substitute for regulating abuses, and for adequately enforcing the rules. Difficulty is no excuse: neither is it easy to ensure that everyone pays their fare share of taxes, but we don't just give up and stop collecting taxes.

Some government ownership, for example of natural monopolies, is appropriate but more local forms of ownership offer promising alternatives. Social democracy was generally better than neoliberalism, but large organisations have their problems, whether they're public or private. It is pointless to be blind to the faults of one and not the other, as ideologues of both sides tend to be. We can move beyond both ideologies, and even beyond the 'mixed' public-private economies of social democracy.

Can we create so many *beautiful solutions* they end up forming a *beautiful economy*? That may seem like an oxymoron, but once you see past the limited, separatist thinking that dominates mainstream economics at present new vistas open.

We can now see the possibility of a far more stable and fulfilling economic system. We might make financial speculation unprofitable and remove the power of banks to issue new money in effectively unlimited quantities. We might harness markets so they directly improve social welfare and ensure the health of the living environment. Our societies might work to improve our quality of life and minimise our footprint on the planet. We might ensure that everyone who is able has access to a means of sufficient livelihood. We might ensure that we use some of our abundant wealth to help those less able. We might ensure that people can settle for material sufficiency so they can pursue other passions rather than working for the machine.

15

Not Wrecking Our Home: Working With the Land

Our most direct connection with the living environment is through agriculture. We need not only to reduce harmful emissions and other pollutants, and to stop bulldozing habitats for more sprawling suburbs. We need as well to get our food and fibre without harming the productivity of the land, and without degrading other living natural systems.

Ants are everywhere, but they do not routinely rampage through the land leaving a trail of degradation and destruction. To do so would sharply limit their time on Earth. Yet that is what is done in our name under the present regime. To every other species we are as a plague on the face of the planet.

On the other hand there are many examples of people cultivating abundance in sustainable or even restorative ways. It is clear we can feed ourselves without wrecking our home. Surviving indigenous cultures understand what it means to work with nature. Even most farmers up until about 1950, and many farmers still, understand they need to treat the land well if they are to pass it on to their children and grandchildren. Yet our mainly city-based political culture has only a dim understanding of the real world. The dominant regime continues to regard the Earth as something to be plundered as rapidly as possible. We had best relearn some fundamentals.

We are intimately connected with the natural world. Re-learning to work *with* nature is not just a nice idea, it is an imperative. Our neglect of connections with the natural world is understood and expressed in various ways. The need to reduce pollution of 'the environment' and the over-exploitation of natural resources is widely recognised. The reasons people cite range from short-term and practical, such as falling crop yields and rising respiratory illness, through such ideas as the 'ecosystem services' provided by the environment, to those who argue at the moral or spiritual level that all living beings deserve our respect and have a right to live. Each of these attitudes has validity.

However there is a more direct and basic reason to reconnect.

Essentially all of the food we eat comes from other living things.

All of the water we drink passes through other living things, and is purified by its passage.

All of the air we breathe passes through other living things, and is renewed by its passage.

In these ways each of us is intimately and intricately connected with every other living thing.

The biosphere's health is our health. If the biosphere dies, we die.

Our vaunted technologies have not changed these basic realities of our existence. Nor have our sophisticated lives in cities, nor our clever intellectual accomplishments. We are, every one of us, still intimately a part of the larger web of life that embraces this planet and couples with its mineral crust.

NON-INDUSTRIAL FORMS OF AGRICULTURE are often derisively dismissed as being incapable of 'feeding the world'. However agribusiness can't feed the world, because many people still can't afford the food, and it degrades Earth's productivity. There is ample but neglected evidence that non-industrial forms of agriculture can be at least as productive as the industrial form. They also meet the essential requirement that they can continue indefinitely into the future. And they can allow the world's people to *feed themselves.*

One of the longest trials comparing organic farming with conventional agriculture has run at the Rodale Institute in Pennsylvania for 30 years. They found organic yields were lower than conventional yields over the first few years, but then the build-up of soil organic matter and quality raised the organic yields to equal or exceed the conventional yields. On all significant criteria, organic did better over the longer term. Not only can organic yields match conventional yields, but they are better in years of drought. They build rather than deplete soil organic matter, and so are sustainable. Organic farming uses 45% less energy, is more efficient and produces 30% less greenhouse gas. Crucially, because their inputs are fewer and less expensive, organic farming systems are more profitable than conventional.

A study in Iowa comparing yields of corn and soybeans, two of the USA's principal crops, found results comparable to the Rodale study. K. Delate reported in 2007 that yields from organic methods equalled or exceeded yields from conventional methods. They found organic soils cycle nutrients more efficiently, making them available when and where the plants need them. Profitability was also greater, and soil quality improved steadily through the nine-year organic trials.

Another survey done at the University of Michigan by Badgley and others in 2007 showed that organic farming methods in developed countries consistently produce yields similar to conventional methods. A key input is to use 'green manures', meaning nitrogen-fixing cover plants that are ploughed under. The study found ample nitrogen was being supplied this way. A different study by Khan and others in 2007 showed that artificial nitrogen fertilisers are commonly applied excessively, and this actually depletes soil carbon and degrades soil fertility, as well as creating marine dead zones where rivers run out to sea.

Such results set a benchmark for industrial and non-industrial systems of farming, of which there are many variations. Rodale's 30-year report gives clear messages:

> The key to sustainable agriculture is healthy soil, since this is the foundation for present and future growth. Organic farming is far superior to conventional systems when it comes to building, maintaining and replenishing the health of the soil. For *soil health* alone, organic agriculture is more sustainable than conventional. When one also considers *yields, economic viability, energy usage, and human health*, it's clear that organic farming is sustainable, while current conventional practices are not.

THE BETTER TRADITIONAL FARMING PRACTICES in both rich and poor countries involve a rotating mixture of complementary crops and animals, so nutrients are recycled, fertility is restored and maintained and vulnerability to pests is reduced, compared with large monocultures.

The potential of non-industrial farming for third world countries is enormous. The Michigan study estimates that the productivity of third-world agriculture could be doubled or tripled by improved organic methods. This could be accomplished using local supplies and initiatives, without the need for the expensive fertilisers and pesticides of industrial agriculture, which poor people can't afford anyway. They would also avoid the environmental destruction induced by industrial agriculture and their soil quality would improve instead of degrading.

Perhaps they were too modest. In Ethiopia, composting has increased yields to 30% above those achieved with chemical fertilisers, and other trials indicate this result can be widely replicated, according to Mae-Wan Ho and others in 2008. Ethiopia has an image of being war-torn and poor, but it has a rich diversity of environments and a long tradition of agricultural productivity. Organic methods built on ancient traditional methods have boosted the lives of many small farmers and lifted national aggregate food production.

The potential of non-industrial farming has been dramatically demonstrated on a national scale in Cuba, as reported by Ho and others in 2008 and Bill McKibben in 2005. After the collapse of the Soviet Union, Soviet aid to Cuba dropped precipitously. Cuba had adopted the Soviet model of industrial agriculture, and it was also heavily dependent on trade with the Soviet Union, growing cash crops in return for oil, machinery, fertiliser and pesticides. When trade also dropped rapidly, Cuba found that it simply could not continue the old methods. A crash program to develop non-industrial and local food production was instituted. By necessity the methods were organic or semi-organic. The Government supported experimentation, and the dissemination of new (or rediscovered) knowledge as it was rapidly accumulated.

After several difficult years food production recovered almost to previous levels. Cubans are happy with the conversion. The food is of better quality, tastier and healthier. Substantial amounts are grown in and around cities, so fresher food is available. Chemical pesticides are actually banned within Havana, where up to one third of the city's food is now grown. There are more jobs and the work is more satisfying. Important ingredients in the success were the Government's willingness to make vacant urban land available to food production and to authorise farmers markets and deregulated prices, so that local urban growers could make two or three times as much money on their fresh, high-quality food.

More ecological and integrated practices were encouraged in rural farms, with greater diversity of crops and rotations, bio-fertilisers and bio-insecticides. Use of chemical fertilisers has been cut by over 90%, and use of chemical pesticides and herbicides by 97%. Large state farms were converted to private cooperatives, and smaller cooperatives were also formed spontaneously. Some of the small cooperatives have been among the most innovative and prosperous.

Clearly it is possible for people to feed themselves with revived and improved forms of traditional agriculture. Such agriculture might be summarised as *sophisticated mixed farming*, in which a variety of crops and animals is grown, each contributing to the productivity of others. For example food crops are rotated with nitrogen-fixing crops, and manure from food animals is used to fertilise crops. Agriculture using this more ecological conception can improve soil fertility, produce healthier food, reduce pollution, including greenhouse gas emissions, and support biodiversity. It can also adapt to the endless variations of local conditions, as it has for millennia.

Timothy LaSalle of the Rodale Institute in the US speaks of *regenerative farming*. This is a sobering phrase. What was farming supposed to be doing, if not tapping into the regenerative power of the Earth?

As well as its many direct benefits, regenerative farming will be vital in mitigating global warming, because it sequesters carbon in the soil. Currently our farming accounts for as much as 30% of greenhouse gas emissions. Farming with synthetic fertilisers and pesticides depletes soil carbon, because it kills or replaces the rich ecosystem of soil micro-organisms, fungi, small creatures and deep root systems. Soils in Illinois that once contained 20% carbon now have 1%. Regenerative farming can replace that carbon relatively quickly, and thus not only can it reduce carbon emissions but it can go further and help to get the carbon back out of the atmosphere. The carbon storage is long term, because *mycorrhizal* fungi create a protein encasement that has a thousand-year half life. Grassland protection and forest management can also contribute. Forest management tends to focus on the above-ground carbon, but the sub-surface carbon, including fungi, are as important, perhaps more.

Regenerated soil can also hold a great deal more water – 40 kilograms of water per kilogram of carbon. Organic crops do much better in drought years than industrial crops. This can help us to survive the worst effects of global warming. These benefits are on top of all the others – tastier and more nutritious food, yields equal to or better than those of industrial agriculture, thriving pollinators and general ecosystems, surviving biodiversity, no pollution from poisons and fertilisers, healthy rivers, no dead zones in the oceans, more jobs and greater life satisfaction.

A POLYCULTURAL FORM OF FOOD PRODUCTION is being pioneered by some enterprising individuals, who are going beyond the mixed monoculture approach of traditional agriculture. One of the best-known examples is the *permaculture* concept of Bill Mollison in Australia.

Permaculture and its variations endeavour to create a self-perpetuating and synergistic ecosystem that produces high yields of food, fibre and other materials for human use. The term *permaculture* is a contraction of *permanent agriculture*, but Mollison intends it also to carry the broader implication of *permanent culture*, because it also embraces attitudes, values and spiritual relationships. Mollison's description of permaculture is not only a concise statement of the approach, it is a concise and comprehensive statement of the kind of perennial economic system to which we can aspire.

> Permaculture is the conscious design and maintenance of agriculturally productive ecosystems which have the diversity, stability and resilience of natural ecosystems. It is the harmonious integration of landscape and people providing their food, energy, shelter and other material and non-material needs in a sustainable way. Permaculture design is a system of assembling conceptual, material, and strategic components in a pattern which functions to benefit life in all its forms. The philosophy behind permaculture is one of working with, rather than against, nature, of looking at systems in all their functions, rather than asking only one yield of them, and of allowing systems to demonstrate their own evolutions.

With a judicious mixture of trees, shrubs, bushes, herbs and so on, high yields can be attained with modest labour input, no fertilisers and no toxins. The low labour intensity of this approach is captured by Mollison in 1999: permaculture involves *'protracted and thoughtful observation rather than protracted and thoughtless labour'*.

A prairie equivalent of permaculture, focusing on grasses and grains, has been under development by Dr. Wes Jackson at The Land Institute in Salinas, Kansas for several decades, and described by him in 1994. Yields of conventional, vulnerable monoculture grain crops can be matched or exceeded by mixtures and hybrids of native perennial grasses and herbs that fix their own nitrogen, resist weeds and insects and require no tillage and little other labour. The inspiration for this *perennial polyculture* approach is the natural prairie, which already evolved over eons to maximise overall productivity.

Another version this kind of approach is agroecology (there's a website). Case studies were reported by the Oakland Institute in 2015. It is not necessarily fully organic, though it tends to evolve in that direction. The idea is to diversify crop plants into combinations that have the resilience and productivity of natural ecosystems. Because those combinations will be place-specific, agro-ecology will look different in different places. There are recent examples that approach the (short-term) productivity of industrial agriculture and that also increase resilience, store more carbon and avoid the release of carbon in the first place, according to Gimenez and Ponisio and others in 2014.

Polycultural agriculture is actually moving beyond ten thousand years of tradition. The agriculture that has been the basis of our civilisation is based on tillage and monocultures, the kind Richard Manning in 2004 called *catastrophe agriculture*. It uses plants that re-establish rapidly after some local catastrophe has disturbed the environment or the soil, what ecologists call pioneering species. Permaculture, on the other hand, aims to produce a mature ecosystem. Traditional methods typically use annual plants, whereas polycultural methods typically use perennials.

In their better forms, traditional agricultural methods have integrated a variety of crops and animals and been well adapted to local conditions. Nevertheless they involve breaking up the soil and growing one crop per plot. This puts the soil at risk of erosion and degradation and makes the crops more vulnerable to diseases and pests. In the polycultural approach the soil is left undisturbed to develop its ecology of micro-organisms to the fullest. The intermingling of species reduces the likelihood of pests reaching a critical mass. If the species are well chosen they help to fertilise each other and to protect each other from pests.

IN AUSTRALIA THE *LANDCARE AUSTRALIA* PROGRAM began locally in 1986 intending to reverse the degradation of farmland, public land and waterways. It has evolved to encourage integrated management of environmental assets, often based on a local water catchment. Actions may include planting tree lines as windbreaks and wildlife habitats and corridors, weed removal, erosion mitigation, sharing farming practices and education. The success of the Landcare model is due in part to its bottom up philosophy. It is community owned and driven. A Landcare group usually starts when community members with common objectives connect over their observations of a local environmental issue. There are over 6000 Landcare groups in Australia and it has been taken up in many other countries.

Many farmers are exploring better practices. State governments have recognised that water catchments are the natural units of land management, forming catchment management authorities or equivalent bodies. No-till farming as a method to retain and build soil quality may be of special value in Australia's dry climate and often limited soil quality. To mention just a few specifics of some who are innovating, Martin Royds of Braidwood, NSW, recognised from his own family history that the land had originally been extremely productive when his forebears moved onto it in the 1840s, but it degraded within a couple of decades. He is working to restore it. He has also won the Carbon Cocky of the Year award. Mulloon Creek Natural Farms is a diverse, sustainable working role model of profitable biodynamic farm production and landscape restoration. Its goal is to produce nutritionally dense food free of synthetic chemicals, while building natural capital in the environment and ensuring its animals live a natural and healthy life in the outdoors.

Peter Andrews offers a deeper understanding of our river systems, explaining that before they were degraded they flowed more slowly, spread more, recharged groundwater more, and were much more resilient in Australia's generally dry and erratic climate. Andrews also promotes what he calls natural sequence farming, in which vegetation regeneration proceeds in a natural way, and is a key part of restoring healthy hydration of the landscape.

THESE INNOVATORS WORK to develop an intimate knowledge of their local bit of land and its complex systems. They exemplify a more general need for stronger roots in place and community. Industrial systems fail to recognise the complexity and subtlety of the living systems they trample. Our physical survival requires people who know their local human and non-human communities intimately.

We need farmers who know how they must deal with their local patch of the biosphere in order for themselves and the living world around them to flourish together. Industrial agriculture uses homogenised means to grow monocultural crops, and it is destroying the fertility of the land and the diversity of life. Monocultures are prone to collapse from disease and plagues. Every locality is different and requires the intimate knowledge of those who have grown up with it. Few have expressed this more clearly than the American 'agrarian' Wendell Berry, who has written:

> I think good farming is a high and difficult art, that it is indispensable, and that it cannot be accomplished except under certain conditions. Manifestly, good farming cannot be fostered or maintained under the rule of the presently dominant economic and cultural assumptions of our political parties.
>
> ... I am a member, by choice, of a local community. I believe that healthy communities are indispensable, and I know that our communities are disintegrating under the influence of economic assumptions that are accepted without question by both our parties – despite their lip service to various noneconomic 'values.'

IN AUSTRALIAN ABORIGINAL CULTURE you belong to the place where you were born, and you are its custodian. When it is said that Aborigines have a spiritual connection with their Country, this is a large part of what is meant. This connection is of the kind advocated by Wendell Berry, but it is deeper and more comprehensive, one nurtured for hundreds or thousands of generations.

Our view of the nature of the Aboriginal lifestyle, indeed of their whole culture, has been transformed by recent work of historians, particularly of Bill Gammage and Bruce Pascoe, who have drawn on the records of early White explorers and settlers and on oral traditions of Aborigines. The landscape Europeans moved into was not a natural landscape, it was a comprehensively managed landscape, right across the continent. It was each family's responsibility to look after its patch.

The Aboriginal system of land management deserves to be called cultivation, though it was different from anywhere else in the world. Fire was used extensively, both to manage the kind of regrowth in each place, and also to limit the potential for wildfires in the flammable Australian bush. However there was much more involved than just 'firestick farming'. Crops of yams and grains were cultivated and harvested, and grains were stored. In some places kangaroos were herded into traps. Fish traps were widespread along the coast and in rivers. In at least one place eel farming was conducted in an extensively-engineered system of ponds, channels and traps.

Behind this management was an intimate knowledge of the landscape, including every species, their characteristics, their sensitivity to fire, their life cycle, and of course the many kinds of food. A similar template was used across the continent, with adaptations to the many kinds of climate and environment.

This management system, Gammage says, kept food sources 'abundant, convenient and predictable'. Europeans commonly were struck by the beauty of the landscape. Many times, coming across waving grasslands dotted with trees and small woodlands, they were moved to proclaim that it looked like a gentleman's estate. Hence Gammage's title, *The Biggest Estate on Earth*. A few Europeans were puzzled by what they saw. For example the best soil was supporting grass, and trees were confined to poorer and rockier locations, whereas in Europe trees occupied the best soil. Some realised it was not a natural arrangement, and must have been managed.

Unfortunately most Europeans did not recognise what they were seeing and assumed it was a wild, natural landscape. With the introduction of sheep and cattle many species were decimated or eliminated, not only because of their hard hooves but because sheep and cattle pull as they bite and uproot plants not adapted to them, whereas kangaroos bite cleanly. Yam daisies were an extensively cultivated staple, but they nearly disappeared, as did many arid-zone grasses. Between Europeans' ignorance, new animals, ploughing, and the elimination of the previous management system, the landscape quickly reverted to disordered regrowth. Soil fertility soon declined and the quality of the landscape degenerated.

The fact that the management system was used in Tasmania, which had been separated from the mainland for about 10,000 years, suggests that the system was at least that old. Australia's climate has been challenging and erratic for much of the 50,000 years or so of Aboriginal occupation. It is testimony to the remarkable adaptability and resilience of the people to have developed and maintained such a comprehensive, resilient and enduring way of life.

HUMANITY'S PRESENCE ON THE PLANET is now so pervasive and intrusive that we are, whether we realise or not, and whether we like it or not, necessarily custodians of the Earth. There are few places on Earth that are not significantly affected by our activities. Life is degrading almost everywhere. The planet's ability to support us is declining.

We need, quickly, to reduce our footprint, to learn to tread much more lightly on the Earth. We have permanently affected many parts of the Earth, so it will no longer be enough just to leave the landscape alone so it can return to what it was. It cannot return to what it was, because there have been too many extinctions and there are too many introduced exotic species. This is especially true in Australia. With care, each locality can return to health and resilience. However it will only happen if we consciously set about bringing it forth, and we will have to discover by trial and error what form each new landscape might take. There is no template for this because we have broken the old templates.

If our descendants fulfil this aspiration, we now know they will not have been the first. The example of the First Australians can inspire us, and perhaps it can also teach us many particular lessons in the modern search for another enduring way of being, in our very changed landscape.

This challenge goes far beyond what is often misleadingly called sustainable development. We cannot simply destroy the Earth more slowly. We must stop the destruction. Then we must *reverse* the destruction. We must aspire to have nature regenerate and thrive around us and with us.

16

Sovereignty

Australia has many involvements with the larger world. Some are stimulating and healthy, whereas others are debilitating. As with so many of our domestic affairs, our interactions with the rest of the world have been managed according to some very simplistic ideas. One is the promotion of so-called free trade. Another is a fearful conception that we are militarily vulnerable, or that displaced hordes are waiting to pour in and overwhelm us. We need a careful assessment of our real strengths and vulnerabilities, and a thorough questioning of some prevailing assumptions.

In the late 19th and early 20th centuries Australia's population was only a few million, scattered very unevenly across a large continent. It made sense that Australians wanted the protection of a powerful nation. That nation, of course, was Britain.

Things began to change in the 1930s. Britain was weakened by the First World War and the Depression. Japan began a brutal occupation of China and was an obvious threat to the region. This did not deter Bob Menzies from approving the sale of pig iron to Japan in 1938, earning him the derisive nickname Pig Iron Bob. In February 1942 Japan captured Singapore from the

British. Japan attacked ports across Northern Australia and even Sydney Harbour, and Australia seemed in imminent danger of invasion. British protection had evaporated, and Prime Minister John Curtin turned to the United States. Thus began an association that persists to this day.

The alliance with the US made complete sense in 1942, but things have changed a great deal since then. There has not been a substantial military threat to Australia since that time. There is no threat from Japan, China or Russia, and even if Indonesia were interested it would have difficulty mounting a successful large-scale attack. We have no land borders to defend. Our forces have modern weapons, and although the forces are relatively small they could be expanded quite rapidly if a threat seemed to be developing. Yet the relationship with the United States has come to dominate the way we relate with the rest of the world.

During the Cold War confrontation between the US and the Soviet Union, it was conceivable Australia might suffer a nuclear attack. It can be reasonably argued that we increased that possibility from remote to plausible by hosting key US intelligence bases and by maintaining a close association with the US. In other words our association with United States exposed us to danger more than it protected us. This is likely to repeat as the US responds aggressively to China's assertion of its rising power in its region. We would be wiser to step back from both, to avoid being caught up in their contest.

We have joined US foreign military adventures in Korea, Vietnam, Afghanistan and Iraq. These involvements have been justified as insurance, showing the US what a faithful little ally we are, so the US would be sure to defend us if the need arose. However we have never had a formal alliance with the US. The ANZUS treaty merely says we will consult, in the event of an emergency. It commits the US to nothing. We can be sure, based on its long-standing behaviour, that the US would weigh the balance of its interests before intervening on our behalf in any dispute. There is no assurance at all that it would not stand back, rather than offend another party it considered more important to its interests. That is how great powers normally behave.

Another justification for our involvement with the US was that we had to resist the spread of communism. But communism is an idea, not an army, and if people want it they may fight ferociously to have it, especially if they are also defending their homeland from invasion. The attempt to stop the spread of communism in Vietnam by force failed. More recently our so-called alliance has been justified by the need to fight an even more ill-defined war on terror. This has been completely counter-productive.

There is another reason, rarely acknowledged, that we have been aligned with the United States. It is to advance our commercial interests. Or rather, it is to advance the commercial interests of those our leaders choose to serve, some Australian, many not.

THERE ARE WELL-KNOWN ADAGES to *be careful what you wish for*, and to *know thine enemy*. Perhaps there should be one to *know thy friends*. We should know what, exactly, we associate ourselves with as we fawn before the power of the United States. Indeed, the world would benefit if US citizens themselves learnt more of what is done around the world in their name. Because our relationship with the US dominates everything we do in the world, we need to spend some time looking behind the rhetoric and clichés.

In one of its foreign military adventures, the US had vastly superior arms to those of the locals. The locals were small of stature and dark of complexion. They fought a bitter guerrilla resistance at great cost in lives and suffering. Nevertheless they resisted the invading US forces for several years. One of the US commanders said he was forced eventually to conclude that the resistance fighters had the support of the entire local population. A US soldier accused of massacring 11 defenceless locals said he was ordered by his general to kill and burn and to take no prisoners. He could kill anyone over the age of 10.

Referring to this and other foreign adventures of the time, a future US president said 'We want a foreign market for our surplus products'. A prominent senator said 'American factories are making more than the American people can use; American soil is producing more than they can consume. Fate has written our policy for us; the trade of the world must and shall be ours.' There was widespread agreement on this among prominent US figures.

The above description, following Howard Zinn, refers to the US invasion of the Philippines, 1898 to 1901. US behaviour in Vietnam, seventy years later, was nothing new. It is also instructive because the motivations are more clearly on display than usual, perhaps because it was a long time ago. It is usual when belated truth comes out for it to be dismissed – 'that was then, we're not like that now' is the offered pretence. The future president was William McKinley, and the senator was Albert Beveridge. Theodore Roosevelt confided to a friend in 1897 'In strict confidence … I should welcome almost any war, for I think this country needs one.' The invasion of the Philippines was only the largest in an already long series of US interventions in the affairs of other countries, 103 between 1798 and 1895. There have been many more since. So the US was acting like any other imperialist nation, all the while espousing the rhetoric of democracy and freedom.

The grim irony of this push for imperial expansion was that the markets the industrialists craved were right under their noses. If they had but paid a decent wage to their millions of impoverished employees, then those employees could have afforded to buy the goods they were producing.

There is another market failure here. The interest of each employer is to pay his employees low wages but to have other employers pay high wages, so his goods have a market. Left to themselves, short-sighted and self-interested employers drive wages down and end up hurting each other. The invisible foot operates. A legislated minimum wage can save them from themselves. This was a central difference between the prosperous years after World War II and the two gilded ages: the late 19th century and the present.

The dominance of commercial interests over US foreign policy was not an anomaly, it expressed the dominance of wealthy interests over every aspect of the US. This plutocracy, rule by wealth, was not of course what the US is claimed to be. A key ingredient in the United States' transformation from revolutionary democracy to plutocracy was the development of its corporations.

The American Revolution was not just a *rebellion* against the King's authority, it was a *revolution* to create the first modern democratic republic. The British still tend to refer to it as the American War of Independence, whereas in the US it is more accurately called the Revolutionary War. It was a rebellion against concentrations of wealth and power in general, not just British wealth and power. In the early decades of the Republic corporate charters were granted by the states, and they commonly carried specific limitations on such things as the life of the corporation or its maximum capitalisation. These limitations were intended to prevent corporations from becoming foci of wealth, and hence of power, that would intrude on the sovereignty of the people. Americans were alert to the fact that the lives of corporations have no natural limit, so they might continue indefinitely to acquire wealth and power without limit.

Corporations contested such restrictions from the beginning, and as their wealth and power grew, especially during the Civil War, they gained influence. One of their arguments was that they should be treated as 'natural persons', as distinct from their standing as individual entities or 'artificial persons' that could engage in commerce and legal agreements but could not claim the citizenship rights of a person. It is claimed that in 1886 the Supreme Court ruled that corporations have the rights of natural persons. However it seems no such decision was ever made, according to Thom Hartmann. Rather, in a nudge-wink conspiracy, a clerk of the court, a former lawyer for railroad interests, wrote that the Court had so decided, but the record of the case shows the question did not even enter the Court's discussion. Nevertheless thereafter an increasing number of judges acted as though the legal precedent had been set, and granted corporations rights of real people.

Recently the US Supreme Court has again ruled on the power of corporations, this time striking down most limitations on corporate financing of political candidates. Only the most blatant bribery of politicians is now considered illegal. This ruling was made on the basis that corporations are 'natural persons' protected by the Bill of Rights, including full rights to free speech. This is such a triumph of corporate power over the remnants of American democracy that it should perhaps be regarded as a judicial coup d'etat. Perhaps the 1886 'decision' should be regarded in the same way. The republic of the American Revolution has been twice struck down, leaving only an empty husk and hollow rhetoric.

Historian William Blum has documented that since 1945 the US has destroyed or subverted more than 50 governments, many of them democracies. It has supported mass murderers, like Suharto in Indonesia, Mobutu in the Congo and Pinochet in Chile, to dominate by proxy. In the Middle East, almost every dictatorship and pseudo-monarchy has been sustained by the US. Historian Alfred McCoy describes the US surrogates as autocrats, aristocrats, and uniformed thugs.

Those are harsh claims, and so contrary to the official lines we are fed that perhaps we need to hear it from the horse's mouth. In 2005, the US was annoyed with the rule of President Mubarak in Egypt, so it thought to threaten to promote democracy. This was done by Secretary of State Condoleezza Rice in a speech in Cairo: 'For 60 years, my country, the United States, pursued stability at the expense of democracy in this region here in the Middle East, and we achieved neither.'

Among the better-known examples of the US aiding the overthrow of democratic governments are Salvador Allende in Chile (1973), Patrice Lumumba in the Congo (1960) and President Sukarno in Indonesia (1965). Nearly forgotten now, apparently, is the overthrow of Prime Minister Mohammad Mossadegh in Iran in 1953, a collusion of the US and Britain, because Mossadegh proposed to nationalise Iran's oil industry. It was Iran's oil, one might have thought, but he threatened the profits of the precursor of British Petroleum and the flow of ultra-cheap oil to the West.

The overthrow of Mossadegh and his replacement by the Shah of Iran was a fateful action. The Shah ruled with an iron fist, became extremely rich, kept the masses poor, served his foreign masters well, and promoted the flow of Western culture into Iran. The resulting discontent was exploited by conservative Moslem clerics, who succeeded in overthrowing the Shah in 1980 and establishing a repressive Islamic theocracy. Iran is now considered to be perhaps the biggest threat to Western designs on the Middle East as it attempts to develop nuclear weapons and supports various insurgencies through the Middle East.

Among many comparable examples, Iraq also deserves mention. The US supported President Saddam Hussein through the 1980s, as a resistance and counter balance to the Iranian theocracy, overlooking brutish actions that including gassing ethnic Kurds in the north of the country. When Saddam apparently misinterpreted US wishes and invaded Kuwait, he incurred US displeasure. This resulted in Gulf War I in 1991, in which Saddam's forces were severely damaged and driven back into Iraq. The West imposed severe sanctions on Iraq that resulted in poverty, collapsed health and infrastructure systems and, reportedly, the deaths of many thousands of children from preventable diseases.

After the 2001 attacks on the New York World Trade Center, President Bush II determined to invade Iraq in 2003 for no evident good reason except to impose US power by force, at a time when the Bush II Administration still called themselves Masters of the Universe. It was also to gain more secure and more profitable access to Iraq's oil. Of course at the time it was claimed Iraq harboured elements of al Qaeda, who were blamed for the New York attacks, and maintained a stock of weapons of mass destruction. Both claims were flimsy at the time and both have been shown to be false. Gulf War II resulted in at least a hundred thousand deaths within the first year or so, and nearly twice as many since, as the country has descended further into anarchy.

Afghanistan is also significant to the story. A socialist government was established by a coup in 1978. It began a progressive social reform program that included the abolition of feudalism, freedom for all religions, equal rights for women and social justice for the ethnic minorities, and a mass literacy program. For women, the gains were unheard of. Unfortunately these reforms were bitterly opposed by much of the conservative, mostly-Moslem population, particularly in rural areas. The Government appealed to the Soviet Union for help, which led to the Soviet occupation of Afghanistan from 1979 to 1989. The rebels, known as the Mujahideen, were given aid and training by several countries including the US, even though there were severe tribal rivalries among them and opium smuggling was a mainstay of their economy.

This program of backing rebels was expanded and repeated in other conflicts. Recruits have been trained by the CIA and by the UK, and among their number have been Osama bin Laden. He and other recruits fed into the formation of al Qaeda, the Taliban and later Islamic State. The program thus fed into the 2001 attack on New York's twin towers, and thence to the so-called war on terror, which continues to exacerbate animosities. At every stage the US and its collaborators were warned they would only enhance the radicalisation and recruitment of Islamic extremists, and so it has transpired.

The US and Britain have been indirectly supporting Islamic jihadists through their support for states like Qatar, Kuwait and especially Saudi Arabia, as much of the funding of jihadists in Syria comes from these states. The most fundamentalist Moslem sect, Wahhabism, is aggressively exported by Saudi Arabia, and inspires most of the calls for the imposition of Sharia law and the persecutions of other Moslems and other religions.

The use of drones by the US to kill alleged terrorists is itself a form of terrorism, because it is inaccurate and evidently not uncommonly based on flawed intelligence. Even if the intelligence is accurate, drones have hit family compounds and wedding parties, killing many innocent people. The British human rights group Reprieve calculates that for every alleged terrorist killed, 28 innocent people are murdered, according to Tim Robertson. These people live with the possibility of death falling out of the sky without warning at any moment: that cannot be anything but terrorism. And of course there are no court proceedings verifying the accuracy of claims that targets are terrorists.

Islamic State reportedly makes sophisticated use of social media, and has apparently inspired or partially inspired a number of terror attacks in Western countries, including Canada, France, Belgium and Australia. Some claim the Sydney siege of December 2014 can be attributed to IS, though the perpetrator was an already unbalanced individual and it can be argued he merely invoked IS to attract more attention. That leaves a question of whether he would have acted, had not IS been advocating attacks, so the case is unclear. The more recent murder of a police worker in Parramatta seems to be a clearer case of Islamist terror, perhaps Australia's first.

The record of foreign invention, of which the above examples are only a small selection, shows a pattern in which the elites in a country, including senior military officers, are cultivated and supported in return for favours to the US. The strategy has often backfired over the longer term. Attempts to subvert governments through support for extremist rebels has backfired even more strongly, and we are now suffering direct consequences in Australia.

WHAT IS THE ATTITUDE TO DEMOCRACY revealed by US foreign policy? Everything done by US governments is clothed in the rhetoric of freedom and democracy, but what do its actions tell us? Does the US, in its actions, favour democracy? Is it indifferent to democracy? Is it even, perhaps, hostile to democracy?

Even the most cursory acquaintance with the news shows the US does not go out of its way to promote democracy. There is a longish list of democracies undermined, along with authoritarian regimes, and of authoritarian regimes supported. So for many years I have been inclined to believe that democracy was simply irrelevant to US foreign policy. What counted was US 'interests', meaning the wealth and power of the country's richest and most powerful.

However there may be reason to question this, and to think the US is actively hostile to democracy. One of the architects of the strategy of supporting extremists was Zbigniew Brzezinski, former National Security Advisor to President Jimmy Carter. He wrote in a book called, tellingly, *The Grand Chessboard* that if America is to control Eurasia and dominate the world, it cannot sustain a popular democracy, because:

'... the pursuit of power is not a goal that commands popular passion ... Democracy is inimical to imperial mobilisation.'

'Imperial mobilisation' means, simply, the building of empire. This was not something the US founding fathers had in mind.

The US and other Western powers were disturbed by the breakup of the old empires after World War II and the emergence of many new countries, many of them fiercely nationalist after their colonial subjection. The US developed a two-pronged strategy. One was the cultivation of powerful elites in the new countries, so as to seduce them to support US interests, as described by John Perkins. The other was to cultivate rebels where governments were not cooperative, or just as a hedge in case cooperative governments misbehaved.

In this context, for example, Brzezinski decided that if Afghanistan were to succeed under its socialist government, its independence and progress would offer the 'threat of a promising example'. Subsequently, in August 1979, the US embassy in Kabul reported:

'... the United States' larger interests ... would be served by the demise of [the socialist government], *despite whatever setbacks this might mean for future social and economic reforms in Afghanistan*' [emphasis added].

Admittedly the Afghan Government of the time was not particularly democratic, but they were implementing policies that many in the West would regard as very progressive. That is also true of other governments that are or were socialist to varying degrees, such as the Sandinistas in Nicaragua and the Chávez Government in Venezuela. The trouble is socialism and communism explicitly challenge the power of concentrated wealth. That is why most 'free-market' governments are viscerally hostile to them.

No government is perfect, and we should be prepared to grant some latitude in our judgements of them. If a government is authoritarian, it may nevertheless be better for its people then alternatives on offer. So was it wrong for the United States to support Saddam Hussein during the 1980s? Perhaps not, but it may well not have needed to had it left democracy alone in Iran thirty years earlier. Later Saddam made the mistake of crossing other US interests and was judged dispensable. For all Saddam's brutality, Iraqis would almost certainly be better off overall had he been left in power, rather than suffering hundreds of thousands of casualties in the illegal US invasion, and the subsequent descent into the present lethal anarchy.

How does the rule of the late Hugo Chávez in Venezuela compare with that of Saddam, for example? Chávez had himself installed indefinitely as president, so he did dispense with some democratic process. On the other hand he did not make war on any of his own people, and he spent a great deal of the country's oil revenue on facilities and education for the poor, who had been kept in grinding poverty for centuries by the ruling wealthy elite. Chávez' problem was that he explicitly interfered with the power of the wealthy elite, and thereby drew their enmity, and that of the United States elite, whose interests the local elite also served.

Allende, the Sandinistas and the Afghan socialist government also favoured the poor and oppressed over the elite, and had Marxists in their governments. The US elite can be pragmatically tolerant of authoritarian governments, but if such a government has socialist tendencies then it draws visceral hostility from the US, because the US elite perceives that socialism always explicitly challenges its power.

So it seems to come back to power. The United States acts, often brutally, to protect and extend its power. Democracy is at best irrelevant to its power plays, but seems to be regarded as generally unreliable as a basis for maintaining US power, except in the cases of the long-established democracies where the local elite has firmly established itself.

This conclusion is supported by Australian analyst Scott Burchill, who presents the evidence that 'The US is not primarily concerned about ideologies or religious convictions *per se*. Fundamentally, it is concerned about control and disobedience. Independence amongst the vassals has always been its biggest worry.'

OUR DEPENDENCE ON FOREIGN MONEY and corporations has been getting worse, not better, because of relentless pressure for so-called free trade agreements, the purpose of which is to give foreign corporations virtually unhindered access to and control over our economy. The latest of these proposed agreements is called the Transpacific Partnership, or TPP, involving major countries around the Pacific rim. The Abbott/Turnbull Government recently signed up to it, but it needs to be ratified by Parliament, here and in the dozen or so other countries involved, so it is still not a done deal. However there is very little concern about it among mainstream politicians and commentators.

Especially odious is the enforcement system used in such agreements. Essentially, they want the right to object to any domestic law or regulation that might plausibly reduce their profit. Such disputes would not be decided in any kind of law court, but in a closed and secret proceeding before a panel of technocrats, who would of course believe in the virtue of this so-called free trade.

Here are a few examples of how these enforcement mechanisms are used.

- A foreign-owned energy company filed a $250 million lawsuit against the Canadian Government, when Quebec placed a ban on dangerous fracking processes in a local river.
- In El Salvador, a Canadian company is suing the government for $315 million in 'loss of future profits' because local citizens won a hard-fought campaign against a gold mine that threatened to contaminate their water supplies.
- An international utilities company sued the Argentinean Government, for imposing a freeze on water and energy bills during the global financial crisis.
- In Canada, US pharmaceutical company Eli Lilly is suing the government for $500 million in compensation, because the courts revoked two of the company's patents citing lack of evidence around the drugs' supposed benefits.
- Similar provisions in an Australian-Hong Kong treaty are being used by US global cigarette and tobacco company, Phillip Morris, to sue the Australian Government over the introduction of plain-packaging laws.

- A plan by the Indian Government for a massive rollout of photovoltaic power has been blocked on the grounds that they did not provide equal access for any supplier in the world.

The goal, rather obviously, is the subversion of all protections for the environment, for employees and for our health and safety.

To add insult to these potential injuries, our own politicians and bureaucrats happily engage in secret negotiations on the details of these agreements. We only know about them because occasionally some draft documents are leaked. The documents frankly admit that the negotiations must be done in secret because the public would never agree if they knew what was being discussed.

There is no other way to describe these agreements than as attempts to destroy our sovereignty. We would not have the right to make laws protecting employees or our environment, nor to ensure the safety of products sold here, nor to prevent monopolistic gouging. Their advocates strenuously object to our subsidies of many drugs, or regulation of their prices, so people can have affordable access to them. In the US context, Joe Firestone foresees the end not only of national sovereignty but of State powers, separation of powers (among President, Congress and Courts) and democracy.

Such an agreement should not be entertained for a second. Politicians who really performed their sworn duty to serve their electors and the nation would simply laugh and tell the corporate minions to piss off, and that would be the end of it. There can be no clearer demonstration that the loyalties of our major parties are not to our nation. As for so much of our brief history, they are in thrall to powerful foreigners. They are, in a word, traitors.

It is doubly ironic that the same politicians, from both sides, who blithely or with utter stupidity entertain such proposals are the same ones working themselves into a lather because innocent refugees show up legally on our shores requesting asylum. For these interlopers, suddenly, our borders are sacrosanct, defended with billions of dollars of 'border security' and by perpetrating abuse amounting to crimes against humanity.

IF WE ARE TO SERIOUSLY REDUCE THE DAMAGE of global warming we must act quickly. This will require, at the very least, active government management of market incentives, along the lines convincingly demonstrated by Germany (Chapter 13). It will probably also require some direct government involvement in emission reductions.

Naomi Klein tells how the Canadian province of Ontario began an ambitious program in 2009 to eliminate coal from its energy sources by 2014. The program was very successful and became an icon around the world. An Italian company set up a photovoltaic factory in Toronto because of the generous incentives provided. However the Ontario government was sued by Japan and the European Union for preferring local labour and components. The World Trade Organisation ruled that the local content provisions violated free trade rules, which require suppliers from anywhere in the world to have equal access to local markets. The local content provisions were quickly rescinded and the photovoltaic factory was facing closure, even though it could produce panels that were more efficient and cheaper than any others in the world.

Established industries have great advantages that make it difficult for new firms to gain a foothold. Economic theorists pretend this is not so, but all nations that have successfully industrialised have protected their early industries from foreign competition. Japan showed the way last century and many other nations have followed suit. However even in the 19th century protections of infant industries were common.

Most policy makers understand this, and offer various kinds of incentives to new industries to help them get established. Politicians understand that if they spend taxpayers' money subsidising an industry they need to justify it, and their favourite justification is jobs. Thus it is also common to include incentives for the creation of local jobs. Local production will also be an essential part of reducing greenhouse emissions, by reducing transportation requirements.

Free trade agreements are all about giving foreign corporations access to local markets. They routinely restrict arrangements that favour local suppliers over foreign suppliers. Klein quotes an anonymous WTO official who claimed that the organisation enables challenges against 'almost any measure to reduce greenhouse gas emissions'.

This situation is no accident. The current free trade regime was negotiated in parallel to the international negotiations on reducing greenhouse gas emissions. Not only have the trade negotiations progressed much further, but it is explicitly written into both that in case of conflict trade takes precedence over reducing emissions.

Australian taxpayers subsidise fossil fuels by about $10 billion per year, and globally fossil fuels are subsidised by hundreds of billions of dollars per year. These subsidies are, of course, much larger than any subsidies of clean energy. Strangely enough this does not seem to violate free trade rules, or at least no-one has seen fit to sue the governments that do the subsidising, using our money.

Such free trade rules must be quickly jettisoned if we're to have any hope of limiting the worst effects of global warming. In fact it will be essential to creating a decent society that we manage our local markets and industries to phase out the destructive ones and develop clean and beneficial products. So if we are to create the decent, enduring society this book advocates, then we must exercise our sovereignty over our own affairs and resist these ridiculous attempts by giant corporations basically to take over the world.

CAN WE BE A MORE INDEPENDENT NATION? There is much more to Australia's foreign involvements than our relationship with the United States, but that relationship has dominated everything else we do in the world. It is a relationship of unhealthy dependence. We would benefit from being more autonomous and self assured. We can certainly maintain a relationship with the United States, but it can be a mature relationship within which we can disagree.

We would be more secure if we distanced ourselves from the counter-productive attempts to dominate that comprise much of US foreign policy. We would cease to become a target of Islamic extremists. The United States is developing a belligerent attitude towards China, whose power is rapidly growing. We would be well served to step away from that confrontation and maintain functioning independent relationships with both nations, a policy advocated by the late Malcolm Fraser in 2014.

Through history, some cities and nations have been traders rather than fighters. Venice, the Netherlands and Singapore are good examples. With our secure location, lack of land borders, abundant resources and skilled population, we're well placed to step into that role. Some nations might covet our raw materials, but if we trade fairly with them they would have little reason to try to take them from us.

We're close to Asia but not Asian. Through our immigrant communities we have many connections with our neighbours. We can be enriched by their cultures. They are anxious to learn more of Western ways, but still to retain their cultural identity. If we are independent and respectful we can enrich each other's cultures.

In 1983 I returned to Australia after 15 years in the US. I came home to some dramatic changes, such as the metric system and an invigorated culture. Especially noticeable to me was a developing fusion of popular music with

Asian and Aboriginal music. There was a great deal of experimentation and exploration going on and it was exciting to come back to.

At present our foreign relationships are dominated by economic considerations, as is our domestic society. We would be more secure if we developed more holistic and respectful relationships with other countries. It is possible to trade in a way that makes both parties better off. That is the ideal, but too often our attitude has been closer to making a fast buck without regard for either a fair deal or the integrity of their culture, or our own. So it is possible to trade fairly in goods. Trading culture in a sense is more straightforward: if we learn from each other we're both enriched. If we each share an idea, we each end up with two ideas.

Our relationship with foreign corporations is also one of unhealthy dependence. Much of the profit made from our mining industry flows overseas. Many of our services, such manufacturing as we have, and an increasing proportion of our agriculture are controlled from overseas. We are still too much like a colony. Our 'leaders' continue the old colonial mentality.

A fundamental flaw in the argument for foreign investment emerged in our discussion of banking and money (Chapter 12). It puts money before people and resources. What we can do is limited by our people and our resources, not by money. If we have the means and the will to do something, the money to facilitate it can be readily created. If the project is a sound investment, it will not provoke inflation.

It is entirely possible for us to insist on more equitable deals with foreign miners and other corporations. We can maintain majority Australian ownership in companies if we so choose. We can restrict or prevent the sale of our land and properties to foreigners; other countries do. We can regulate the flow of money across our borders, as we used to do routinely a few decades ago. The flows of money are now much greater and much faster, but this is not an obstacle because the banks and financial companies of course keep track of every cent. If they wish to continue to do business in Australia they will comply with our rules.

In 1998 Malaysia saved itself from the worst effects of the Asian currency meltdown by prohibiting the draining of foreign money through its borders until the panic was over. For this it earned the derision of local neoliberals, who apparently would have preferred to see its economy crash like its neighbours'.

Anyone who makes suggestions such as these is likely to be accused of being isolationist or 'nationalist' by the lazy defenders of the dominant ideology. That is rubbish. These proposals are about managing our interactions with the world, not stopping them. As one commentator has put it, we have a perfect right to place speed bumps at our borders. On the other hand, if we do step in that direction we will need to be mindful of the likely reaction of the US and its corporate proxies. On past form that would involve visceral and vitriolic opposition, delivered with moral indignation and injured innocence. We need to be mindful that in fact we need the US less than it gains from us in strategic bases and quick profits. There are few threats from other nations, and plenty of markets available to us.

In addition to simply asserting our own interests, we can adopt less reactive attitudes to other nations, even those with which we disagree. Europe has settled down to peaceful relationships, despite centuries of bitter enmity, and despite some of the most monstrous conflicts being in the recent past. It is possible to overcome reflexive, fearful impulses and to cultivate respectful relationships among nations.

17

The Strength to Offer Hope

Scapegoating happens when people feel threatened. It can be countered by encouraging people to keep the perceived threat in proportion, to identify the real threat, and to manage their anxiety. It can also be countered by attending to the real threats, which for many people currently are insecurity of income and a lurking sense of doom approaching, however unacknowledged. We thus need to encourage more responsible public rhetoric that soothes and informs rather than propagating ignorance and alarm. We also need to provide people with more secure livelihoods and to make serious efforts to stop degrading the planet. We need, individually and collectively, to have the strength to transcend our fearful reactions, to assert our better natures and to get on and actually do what needs to be done.

The real story of the White settlement of Australia is only lately being told, and beginning to be more widely acknowledged. It was a violent, often lethal dispossession of Australia's original inhabitants. Many of them, perhaps most, are still suffering severe inherited trauma from the dispossession, and the severe and prolonged marginalisation that followed. We need to face up to the fact that our country's present good fortune rests on that foundation of violence and abuse. Every non-indigenous Australian is diminished by the failure to fully acknowledge our history. If we can't face up to our past then we tend to lash out at those who seek to remind us, and we blame the victims rather than admitting our complicity. In this way racist behaviour is perpetuated in our society.

We need to release that stunted part of our national soul so we can face ourselves and the future with full and open hearts. It is also emerging that there is a great deal of knowledge and wisdom still surviving in indigenous cultures, and it would be greatly to our mutual benefit to share our futures together.

A clear symptom of our lack of resolution of our inner conflict is that we are still inflicting traumas on innocent people – people who came to us looking for help and hope. Many of them fled from wars that we have helped to provoke or prolong, for no good reason.

THE MAGNITUDE OF THE CHALLENGE of receiving asylum seekers in Australia has been grossly exaggerated by irresponsible media and politicians, whose distortions and outright lies have played on the fears of a segment of our society and spread those fears to much of the population. We need first to establish some of the basic facts.

- It is quite legal for anyone to seek asylum in Australia, regardless of how they arrive and whether or not they have identification papers, as McAdam and Chong make clear. This is established by the United Nations Refugee Convention, to which Australia is a signatory.
- The number of asylum seekers has always been a small fraction of the number of immigrants in any given year.
- About as many asylum seekers arrive in Australia by plane as by boat, but there is no fuss made of them and they are not removed to overseas detention centres.
- Many other countries receive far more refugees then does Australia.
- Australia is not easy to reach and it is unlikely we would be flooded with refugees.
- The vast majority of asylum seekers are found to be genuine refugees.
- The number of terrorists so far found among the boat people is zero.
- Most asylum seekers, like most other immigrants, quickly established themselves as productive members of our society, if we give them the opportunity.

It is widely regarded as a violation of basic morality to punish one group of innocent people in order to deter another group. It is one of the worst examples of the end supposedly justifying the means. Since 2001 Australian governments have 'detained' asylum seekers for years at a time in remote detention centres both onshore and offshore. The detention centres are punitive and dehumanising, and can just as well be called concentration camps. Abuse of detainees has been steadily reported for years. The abuse includes all kinds: mental, emotional, physical and sexual. The detainees are innocent men, women and children, but they are treated much worse than most criminals. Self harm and suicide attempts are frequent. Their treatment commonly induces serious to severe psychological disorders. Some people have died by their own hand or through violence or abuse. The lives of most of these innocent people are being ruined and sometimes ended.

Lately governments have claimed they must 'Stop the boats' so as to save people from drowning *en route* to Australia. No such concern was expressed in earlier years. In fact Australian authorities were conspicuously elsewhere in 2001 as a heavily overloaded boat left Indonesia and subsequently capsized with the loss of 353 men, women and children. Authorities were subsequently evasive about what they knew and why no aid could be offered, and it was true that the sinking seemed to deter further boats for some time after that, according to Tony Kevin in 2004. Politicians' recent professions of concern for the safety of asylum seekers have little credibility. As cartoonist David Pope expressed it, through a Cronulla yobbo character bearing a sign saying 'F**k off, we're full *deeply concerned about your safety at sea*'.

In recent years several Australian governments have made formal apologies to people who were mistreated through official policies of the past. Apologies have been made to the stolen generations, the indigenous children removed from their families over many decades, and to other children who were placed in abusive institutions. There is currently a major inquiry into sexual abuse of children in church schools and other institutions. Our current treatment of asylum seekers equals or exceeds anything in those episodes. It is clear that some future government, should it possess any shred of decency, will be similarly apologising for the treatment of the asylum seekers. Government officials may well be open to charges of crimes against humanity.

Asylum seekers pose only a moderate challenge to a wealthy country like Australia. Their numbers have ranged from a few thousand to a peak around 17,000 per year, compared with over 200,000 immigrants and tens of thousands of people who overstay their visas. We can absorb such numbers without great disruption. The safety of boat people is certainly a concern. It would be best addressed by a more serious and systematic program to process them in neighbouring countries, in cooperation with the governments of those countries. Such arrangements were made to deal with the many refugees fleeing Vietnam in the 1970s. They are not simple, but they are the only humane approach available. The simplistic 'Stop the boats' approach is worse than lazy, it is the lowest kind of exploitation of vulnerable people for political advantage.

WE HAVE IN AUSTRALIA A REMARKABLE, ancient and very different culture from the mainstream. It is remarkable for its resilience, diversity, artistic and spiritual sensibilities, perspective on life and the world, humour in the face of great difficulties, and for the ancient collective memory it carries. After two centuries of repression it is now resurgent. Australia is already the richer for it, and we all have much more to gain from a respectful and constructive interaction. Aboriginal culture is also struggling to emerge from deep traumas experienced since European settlement, and it will require understanding and patience on both sides to heal those wounds.

Just to cover some basics, Aborigines were not 'simple nomads', they have deep attachments to locations and sophisticated cultures; there are hundreds of Aboriginal languages, not just one; and they cultivated the landscape quite systematically, though in ways not so familiar to Europeans.

I sometimes still use the shorthand Black and White instead of indigenous and non-indigenous. However another important lesson for me has been that people who identify as Aboriginal come in all shades, from very dark to very light. Many light-skinned people were raised in Aboriginal families and culture, so skin colour is not important. On the other hand many people were taken from their families and raised in White families or institutions. This raises some sensitive issues, because they have not been taught and initiated or inducted into Aboriginal culture. If they can trace family connections then they can be accepted as Aboriginal by both cultures. However not all can find their family. On the other hand some who know they are related choose not to identify. There are probably also many of us who carry Aboriginal blood without knowing it. This cultural confusion is an important part of the destructive legacy of the White invasion. We all need to be tolerant and patient, and let people find their own identity and destiny. Shock-jock ranting is needless and destructive.

Aborigines had highly developed ethics and diplomacy that seem to have preserved territories for 10,000 years or more, as evidenced by the diversity of languages that could not have developed without long periods without invasions. Their arrangements still allowed for sharing during times of abundance or scarcity. We've already looked at their sophisticated cultivation and preservation of the landscape. There is much we might learn from them regarding their broad approaches, strategies and ethics.

The depth of their history is hard to grasp. There are stories that clearly refer to land now submerged by the ocean, so the stories must reach back at least 11,000 years to when the oceans rose at the end of the last ice age. There are also stories of that encroachment of the ocean, and of its eventual stabilisation. It must have been a scary time because they would not have known if the sea would ever stop rising. We are beginning to have a similar experience.

It is conceivable that some stories of ancestral beings refer to the giant marsupials and other creatures that became extinct about 50,000 years ago. There is at least one rock art depiction of the giant bird *genyornis* from that time. There are many rock art sites dating back tens of thousands of years. The ABC documentary *First Footprints* gives an excellent, no, stunning account of what we now know about this ancient history.

The resurgence of Aboriginal cultures is perhaps most widely known through such musical performers as Yothu Yindi and Gurrumul Yunupingu, the dance group Bangarra, and many artists whose work is known nationally and internationally. These are only some of the best known of a widespread and rapidly growing creative surge.

At the same time many of the people struggle with social difficulties ranging from serious to near-total dysfunction, and with paternalistic White policies borne of deep ignorance and narrow perspective, if not covert hostility. Recent proposals to close many remote communities in Western Australia, and the so-called Intervention in the Northern Territory in 2007, amount to little more than attempts at land clearance and pressure to assimilate into White society. This would break the deep connections people have with their own Country and destroy a lot of what remains of Aboriginal culture. The dispossession would merely shift the social problems to the fringes of towns, repeating sorry historical episodes yet again.

Like poor and traumatised people anywhere, Aborigines suffer the substance abuse, violence, sexual abuse and so on that typically accompanies such conditions, and the failure to deal with the problems allows them to pass on to new generations. Although some of the stories are horrifying, we need to bear clearly in mind that the dispossession and extreme marginalisation has been going on for over two centuries. The problems will not be resolved in one year or one generation. Some communities do manage to pull themselves up, but all too often they do not receive consistent support to consolidate their gains. Our role cannot be to fix them, the will must come first from them. However we must be ever ready to support their efforts, and willing to be patient with inevitable relapses and failures. Any experienced counsellor will confirm that this is the difficult path to healing.

Aborigines are among those hardest hit by our combative political and media culture. Cheap slogans, political posturing, bureaucratised policy development, narrow police perspectives on symptoms, sensationalism, and any top-down program developed without close and patient consultation, none of these things is helpful, they are all harmful.

It is possible to conceive, in our so-called multicultural society, of the Aboriginal culture or cultures living in tandem with the settler culture. This would require patience, knowledge, tolerance and goodwill, but there is no reason why it cannot come to pass. It is not very likely for as long as the present extractivist settler mentality persists, but that mentality has no future and its replacement is a major theme of this book. As a more durable culture of the settler population grows, there would be an obvious synergy between it and the indigenous culture, a synergy from which we can all benefit greatly.

For the settler population to be able to move forward with a full heart, and for the indigenous population to be able fully to move on from two centuries of severe trauma, the settler population needs to fully acknowledge the way it came into possession or occupation of this land.

It is by now well documented that there was prolonged and often lethal conflict at the frontiers of European settlement. It is pointless to debate the semantics of whether this could be called war. There were lives lost on both sides, but the losses fell very heavily on the indigenous side, and after all they were defending their Country. It is also clear enough that there were many incidents amounting to massacres of Black men, women and children. To be sure disease, and hunger resulting from displacement and from loss of food sources, would have accounted for many more deaths, but that does not erase the fact that Aborigines were often hunted down and killed like the wild animals many settlers regarded them as.

As the natives were subdued in each district a heavy silence descended, a great forgetting, a pretence of an easy, inevitable and largely peaceful displacement of one group by another. That silence is now being broken, and the truth emerging is not comfortable. However continued denial will diminish our society. Just as with individual healing, we will remain emotionally stuck and stunted until we face and honestly acknowledge the past, however emotionally painful that may be.

It seems there is no basis in English law for the occupation of Australia. There are or were three possible justifications for occupation: the land was empty, there was a treaty in which the natives ceded possession, or the land was won through an officially declared war. None of these conditions was met. The legal fiction of *terra nullius*, or an empty land, was overturned by our High Court in the Mabo decision in the 1990s.

There has been a government-endorsed process called *Reconciliation* that purports to reconcile the indigenous and settler populations. However that is the wrong application of the term, as quite a few Aboriginal people understand. Reconciliation implies acknowledging and forgiving past conflict between parties. However *we* overran *them*. They were defending their Country. They have little to acknowledge. We have little to forgive.

There *is* a reconciliation required. *We* need to reconcile *ourselves* with *our history*. We need to frankly acknowledge the deeds of our forebears.

One reaction to this proposal is to say it wasn't us, it was our ancestors, so why should we feel guilty? This is to misunderstand the process. It is not about us admitting personal guilt. It is about us acknowledging that our present fortunate circumstance is built on a foundation of violent and unjust acts by our forebears. This applies just as much to recent immigrants as to long-established settler families. All non-indigenous residents benefit from the European occupation of this continent.

I have observed that many Aboriginal people are remarkably generous in their willingness to share the land and their willingness to forgive the past. However they are wise enough to understand that their forgiveness without our acknowledgement would be an empty gesture. Only when we fully acknowledge the deeds of the past can we forgive ourselves, and be forgiven by them.

Then, and only then, can we move on. Then our different cultures can join in mutual respect and constructive engagement.

There is a rock, a public work of art, recently placed in my home town. On one side it carries an inscription from the settler population:

This rock stands as an acknowledgement that the land in the Braidwood region was occupied and cared for by the people of the Dhurga language group for tens of thousands of years before European settlement.

Their dispossession and displacement and the resulting suffering and loss of sacred culture are deeply regretted.

We aspire to a shared future in which Aboriginal wisdom is valued and all people and the land are respected and cared for.

On the other side, in symbolic response, a local indigenous artist has carved totemic animal and plant images. That is a settler acknowledgement, and an indigenous welcome. One of the more moving moments of my life was seeing local Aboriginal men and women smoking the rock and dancing around it, welcoming it in their Country, consecrating it, and acknowledging and receiving our gesture of reconciliation – with ourselves.

There are some things we Whitefellas can do that could help enormously. One is to teach the local indigenous language in our schools. Of course many languages have been lost or partly lost. We can still look for the nearest speakers of a surviving language, preferably from the Country we live in, and employ them to share and teach. This is being done sporadically, but it could and should be treated as an essential part of all our kids' education in the Australian culture. It can be powerful. A program ran in Dubbo for a while, until funds were cut. The teachers experienced respect and appreciation they had never known. The kids learnt about local culture. One little girl said 'I wish I was Aboriginal'. Those kids will carry that experience with them through life.

These days many schools teach an Asian language, and that's good, but actually we have plenty of native speakers of those languages already. Aboriginal languages are hardly known by Whites, and are rapidly dying out. Their preservation needs to be a high priority.

Of course language is not separate from culture, and culture for Blacks is all-embracing, their whole way of life and world view. Language is a door into that, as are dancing, singing and art. A local Aboriginal friend has been received into our local schools to teach some local culture, and the response has been enthusiastic on all sides. The schools and the kids want more, and we must find ways to support that.

18
Retrieving the Fair Go

The vast majority of us don't like our current direction. 93% of us prefer 'a greener, more stable society, where the emphasis is on cooperation, community and family, more equal distribution of wealth, and greater economic self-sufficiency', according to Richard Eckersley's 2016 study.

This means we need to express, collectively, *what we really want*, rather than timidly limiting ourselves to what we think is acceptable within politics-as-usual. The political indicators are beginning to register our discontent, but without defining a clear direction. Yet if we go deeper there *is* a clear direction. It conforms rather closely with the potential outlined here.

THERE ARE FUNDAMENTAL PROBLEMS with our present arrangements. The neoliberal ideology is misguided – we are not just individualists, we are also highly social, and we must balance those two opposed tendencies; free markets are not automatically good; the roles of money and debt cannot be ignored; and the GDP should not be misused as a measure of wellbeing.

Older attitudes also hinder us. Too many Australians are content to play second fiddle, to remain in the shade, or to serve other masters. The taker mentality is very old and quite counterproductive.

The ultimate logic of the neoliberal program, we need to recognise, is the dismantling of much of government. The effect of the program is to create economic anarchy. Anarchy does not promote freedom. It allows the strongest to prevail. Everyone else is then oppressed. Consistent with this result, neoliberals want to retain and enhance government force, and they want to control what is said and by whom. Neoliberals may imagine they are promoting freedom and the general welfare, but their conception is flawed at the core and the results of the program are contrary to their claims.

The result we can see forming rather rapidly around us. Its main components are economic anarchy and a social police state. The further consequences of staying on this course will be a declining economy, an increasingly fragmented and nasty society, a degrading land and an increasingly hostile climate.

The economy will be tied to failing extractive industries, we will have missed most of the new, clean technologies, there will be little manufacturing, we will struggle to offer services more cheaply than low-wage countries, and much of the economy and increasing amounts of the land will be foreign-owned. We will regress to being full-fledged colonials, poor tenants and servants in our own land.

As our economy lags and our control over our own affairs slips, we will turn more strongly against each other. At the same time the climate will certainly become more hostile for at least the next two or three decades, that much is locked in already by the inertia of the physics of the system. If the rest of the world behaves as we do, even just for another decade, then the climate will quite likely progress through severe and on to catastrophic warming.

All of these trends are more advanced in the United States. The economy that was once the powerhouse of the world is being hollowed out. Big American corporations have uprooted themselves and become effectively stateless, and they have moved American jobs to many other countries. The rich play shell games with their money and do not invest in a productive future. The rhetoric of the American Revolution is used to misdirect people's anger against the government rather than against the plutocrats who now control the government.

The *can-do* nation of the postwar years has become the *won't-do* nation. No-one wants to pay taxes, especially the rich. Infrastructure is declining and disintegrating. The education and health systems are inefficient, discriminatory and getting worse. The people are divided against each other. Civil strife is increasing. The United States is moving towards the South American condition: wealthy gated communities surrounded by poverty and despair.

The Liberal-National Coalition is the overt proponent of this vision for Australia. The Labor Party, by following a me-too strategy, not only fails to stop this strategy but actively colludes in it. By occupying the place in our political space where a progressive party should be, the Labor Party is a massive obstacle to a better future.

Most Australians would pull back from this future if they seriously thought it was likely. The regime continues only because the media pervasively misrepresent what is really happening. Whether they do so from selfishness, malevolence or stupidity makes little difference. Even so, many people are seeing through the facade and resistance is rising.

TO GET BACK ON TRACK to the decent society most of us thought we were striving for we need better governance, which means responsive and responsible political parties and media, much better information, clearer and more diverse policy options, and more positive and respectful attitudes. With such improvements it will become conceivable to restructure or replace political parties and media so they are less combative and divisive and more focused on constructive discussions and positive policies. Some other countries, such as The Netherlands and the Scandinavian countries, already manage to be rather more constructive than we are.

We can then promote the many practical things waiting to be done, to improve our quality of life and our future prospects. If we promote them rather than subverting them, we are likely to make rapid progress.

Serious change begins with attitude. We must *be* the change we wish to see. If we want a decent society then we can treat each other with decency. If we want our children to have a good future, we can act as if a good future matters to us, and we believe it is possible. If we want our daily lives to be less conflicted, then we can have the courage to make choices that move us in that direction.

There will of course be fierce resistance from the presently powerful. Over the centuries every move to extend democracy has been condemned as wicked and subversive by those in power. We should expect nothing less today.

WE CONCEDE A GREAT DEAL OF OUR AUTONOMY without seeming to realise. Change is driven not just by politicians and nations, but by processes we have unleashed. Globalisation and technology are commonly presented as inevitable, but they are created by people and can therefore be controlled by people.

There is at present a lot of handwringing about whether robots will take over our jobs. The automatic presumption, apparently, is that as robots become more capable then people are made redundant and unemployed. Thus a new development becomes a great problem. However a simple reframing transforms it into a benefit. It depends on our overall purpose. If it is simply for businesses to cut costs, then people may be displaced. However if the purpose is to benefit people and our society, then it means we don't have to work as much. We will need to structure the incentives so they support that purpose.

When I was a kid we were told that by the year 2000 we might be working only 15 or 20 hours a week. Until the 1980s the trend was indeed to shorter working hours. However the neoliberal regime changed the goal to greater output by working longer as well as (allegedly) smarter. Automation is nothing new. Neoliberals claim of course that displaced people will just find a different and more productive job, but that is simplistic, and not what has been happening. Automation can be of general benefit if we choose, but we have to be sure the incentives are properly structured to bring that about. At present they are not.

We seem to think it is the natural order that new technologies will spring up and we simply must adapt to them. Well if you create entities whose sole purpose is to profit in a competitive environment, then you might well get nasty surprises as they search out the means to gain advantage over other entities, other calculating reptiles. But corporations are created by people. The rules under which they and other businesses operate are written by people. The rules can be changed.

In the early American Republic corporate charters were granted by States and commonly contained explicit limitations, because those who created the American Revolution were alert to the problem of concentrations of wealth that accumulate without limit. I said earlier that our goal should not simply be progress, but rather we should undertake new developments with our eyes open, our brains in gear and our moral compasses at hand. An important part of our coming challenge is to implement that intention so we improve our quality of life, rather than unleashing destructive new technologies.

The subversion of our autonomy advances by other insidious means. So-called free-trade deals are negotiated in secret. Foreign ownership and foreign investment proceed apace with little public awareness. We blindly follow US foreign policy with very little mainstream debate, so most people are unaware of the cost and folly of being so obsequious.

Many of our politicians seem to imagine there is little we Australians can do for ourselves, and we must rely on foreign investment to further 'develop' the country. In fact we only need foreign currency to buy foreign things, and it is far better to earn that currency from our own exports. The notion that we need to solicit or borrow foreign currency is quite misguided. Borrowed foreign currency simply sits in a bank account, while local currency is issued to advance domestic projects. The misconception is that the foreign currency 'backs' the local currency, but it cannot because it is not legal tender within Australia. The local currency can be issued anyway, without incurring any debt to be paid in a foreign currency.

The whole notion of foreign investment and foreign borrowing is misguided. Whatever we are capable of doing we can facilitate with our own currency, and we can teach ourselves how to do things, as we taught ourselves in the 19th century. We may hire foreign experts and we may lease foreign patents, but we can still be in charge. The Chinese do it.

IF WE REALLY WANT TO SEE CHANGE, and see it soon, then we must be willing to consider voting and acting in new ways. Many people still are not willing to vote for new people or parties because, they say, we need experienced hands to run the economy. Well, people change when the pain of staying the same overcomes the fear of stepping into the unknown. So our old friend fear plays a big role in keeping us trapped.

Look again at what those 'experienced' people are doing to our society and the world. Consider whether the sky really might fall if we vote for someone new. The sky is falling now anyway. Besides, governments comprise not just elected representatives, but public servants whose job it is to implement policy. The public service has a great deal of experience and can ensure that most things will continue to run reasonably sensibly. That is why they are there. They are not perfect, but they deserve more credit than they get in this age of government bashing.

We don't all need to join the barricades, and it is better if we do a variety of things, depending on what we're good at. It seems one of the most potent agents of change is talking with other people. This was the method of the Purple Sage Project, which was then carried into political campaigning, via the kitchen table conversation.

The full power of the message of the *beautiful solutions* is that they do not just help, they are *transformative*. They change the way we think. They change our perception of where the problems are. Things we thought were problems may be opportunities. Things we thought were not worth considering, or that seemed quite inconceivable, suddenly seem within reach. Not only do they seem within reach, but they are highly desirable. They transform the dark present into a potential we dreamt of but dared not hope for.

AUSTRALIA IS NOT A POOR COUNTRY. We are so used to being told there is no money, we are so used to thinking everything is too complicated and too hard, that we don't often stop and count our blessings.

We can easily afford to see that little children are well cared for, along with their parents, regardless of their parents' situation. We can afford to help all those in need. We can afford to see everyone gets a decent income. We can all then afford to pay our farmers fairly so they can grow all our own food, grow it healthy, and ensure our farmland is well cared for. We can afford good schools and hospitals. We can afford to give Aborigines consistent, appropriate, respectful support for as long as it takes for them to be restored to dignity and functioning. We can afford good infrastructure. We can afford modern transportation and communication. We can afford a manufacturing industry. We can afford a thriving culture, and an ABC restored to full vigour and independence. We can afford a government that will see these things are done.

We will more easily afford these things if we remove the market distortions that unfairly pump wealth to the wealthy from the rest of us. For example, we can stop paying billions to the fossil fuel industry and other top-end leaners, we can remove tax breaks and negative gearing for the well-off, and we can reduce the haemorrhaging of wealth to overseas corporations.

We are not a threatened country. There is no prospect of serious aggression against us (unless we are foolish enough to get entangled in US provocations of China). The terrorist threat is still minor, and it would largely dissipate if we stopped needlessly provoking them. Asylum seekers are not a threat, they are a moderate challenge and they are good prospective citizens. We can dismantle the elaborate domestic surveillance system and accompanying police presence. We can restore civil liberties and legal protection. We can dismantle the so-called border protection forces. We can demand and expect our governments to abandon excessive secrecy and hostility, and to conduct *our* public affairs in public.

We can take up the challenges of global warming, the degradation of nature, and the global displacement of people. We can assume our place and contribute our fair share. If we should find ourselves at the forefront then we can have the national self assurance to carry on, leading the way. We can shift rapidly to clean energy for modest cost, and we can, over time, make our buildings and cities much more efficient and pleasant. We can pursue the beautiful solutions that are waiting for us, and create more as we go along.

We have many blessings. Australia has large land and sea areas with ample resources. With a range of climate zones we can grow almost anything, and we can comfortably feed ourselves. We have an educated population and clear records of innovation and resilience. We have the potential to create wealth and health, rather than degrading both. We manage our politics without violence. We have people who speak most major languages in the world. We have no international land borders and our geo-strategic position would be the envy of most other countries. Though much of our land is semi-arid and our weather is challenging at times, we still have large habitable and productive areas.

Can we complete our half formed nation? Can we return to the quest for a fair go for everyone? Certainly. We spend so much energy fretting and bickering about what we think we *can't* do we lose sight of our abundant blessings. It is time to focus on what we *can* do.

A fair go is central. It is a psychological, social and economic imperative. Our wealth is produced collectively, and we must ensure a fairer flow of wealth according to contribution. We would then find our wealth compounds more, because ordinary people don't play speculative games with their money, they spend it back into the productive economy. Our communities and social supports would strengthen. With most people feeling more secure, resentment would decline. Extremists would find less fertile ground and would fade back to the background.

We are indeed a lucky country, but we don't need to keep living on our luck.

Appendix: New Anthem Words

If we are to finish growing up, as a nation, then we need to move on from the old words of the national anthem, *Advance Australia Fair*, which were borne of the attitudes of the British Empire in the 1870s. Some people have modified those words to remove some of the more dated and inappropriate expressions, but the chauvinist sentiment of the original still comes through.

I think it is better just to start again, taking a more modern, more inclusive view of ourselves. We can also move beyond the need to trumpet our worth, or superiority, because that just perpetuates the old inferiority complex.

So I have written some words to celebrate who we are, what we are and what we might aspire to. They may or may not appeal to others, but at least they can demonstrate a different perspective and approach. If they help to stimulate others to have a go, then good. I think the old tune serves well as an anthem. It is not so hard for the average punter to sing and it tarts up well for grand occasions.

Australia We Share

An ancient land from Rock to sand
A Dreaming old and wise
White, brown and black from other lands
New ways from old arise.
From whips and chains through gold and fleece
Invention, sweat and care
A new refrain to grace the world:
A fair go and fair share.
To Dream together, old and new,
Australia we share.

A wilful land of flood and fire
Of forests lush and tall
Of rivers slow and jewel reef
And creatures fit for all
This land abounds in nature's gifts
Of beauty rich and rare
From aeons past a heritage
For us to take due care.
We all are now custodians
Australia, we care.

(Geoff Davies, 30 April 2013;
https://betternature.wordpress.com/new-anthem-words/)

Bibliography

Agroecology *Agroecology*, edited, http://www.agroecology.org, http://www.agroecology.org.

Alliance, N. R. H. (2009), Suicide in Rural Australia; Fact Sheet 14, *National Rural Health Alliance*, http://ruralhealth.org.au/sites/default/files/fact-sheets/fact-sheet-14-suicide%20in%20rural%20australia_0.pdf.

Alperovitz, G. (2013), What Then Must We Do?: Straight Talk about the Next American Revolution, Chelsea Green Publishing.

Amos, D. J. (1940), The Story of the Commonwealth Bank, http://www.alor.org/Library/Amos%20DJ%20-%20Commonwealth%20Bank.pdf.

Anderson, K. (2012), Climate change going beyond dangerous - brutal numbers and tenuous hope, *Development Dialogue*, 61(September), 16-40.

Anderson, R. C. (2010), Business Lessons from a Radical Industrialist, St. Martins Press, New York.

Andrews, P. (2006), Back from the Brink: How Australia's Landscape Can Be Saved, 244 pp., ABC Books.

Badgley, C., J. Moghtadera, E. Quinteroa, E. Zakema, J. Chappella, K. Avilés-Vázqueza, A. Samulona, and I. Perfecto (2007), Organic agriculture and the global food supply, *Renewable Agriculture and Food Systems*, 22, 86-108.

Barlow, T. (2006), The Australian Miracle, an innovative nation revisited, 278 pp., Pan Macmillan Australia, Sydney.

Bastian, P. (2009), *Andrew Fisher, an underestimated man*, 419 pp., University of New South Wales Press, Sydney.

Beinhocker, E. D. (2006), *The Origin of Wealth*, Harvard Business School Press, Boston.

Bell, S. (1997), *Ungoverning the Economy*, 324 pp., Oxford University Press, Melbourne.

Berry, W. (1995), *Another Turn of the Crank*, Counterpoint, Washington, D.C.

Blakers, A. (2015), *A Renewable Solution to the Problem of Peak Power*, in *Australasian Science*, edited, Control Publications, Melbourne, http://www.australasianscience.com.au/article/issue-december-2015/renewable-solution-problem-peak-power.html.

Blum, W. (2004), Killing Hope: U.S. Military and CIA Interventions Since World War II, 471 pp., Common Courage Press.

Bornstein, D. (1996), *The Price of a Dream*, 370 pp., The University Press, Dhaka, Bangladesh.

Burchill, S. (2015), Radical Islam and the West: the moral panic behind the threat, *The Conversation*, https://theconversation.com/radical-islam-and-the-west-the-moral-panic-behind-the-threat-43113.

Carrington, D. (2015), Fossil fuels subsidised by $10m a minute, says IMF, http://www.theguardian.com/environment/2015/may/18/fossil-fuel-companies-getting-10m-a-minute-in-subsidies-says-imf.

Ciancio, D. (2015), Cheap, tough and green: why aren't more buildings made of rammed earth?, *The Conversation*, https://theconversation.com/cheap-tough-and-green-why-arent-more-buildings-made-of-rammed-earth-38040.

Coady, D., I. W. H. Parry, L. Sears, and B. Shang (2015), How Large Are Global Energy Subsidies?, http://www.imf.org/external/pubs/cat/longres.aspx?sk=42940.0.

Bibliography

Comitatus, P. (2011), Australian Exceptionalism, http://blogs.crikey.com.au/pollytics/2011/12/08/australian-exceptionalism/.

Daly, H. E., and J. B. Cobb Jr. (1994), *For the Common Good*, 2nd ed., Beacon, Boston.

Davidson, O. G. (2012), Clean Break: The Story of Germany's Energy Transformation and What Americans Can Learn from It, http://www.amazon.com/Clean-Break-Germanys-Transformation-Americans-ebook/dp/B00A4IEJ5K.

Davies, G. F. (2004), *Economia: New Economic Systems to Empower People and Support the Living World*, ABC Books. Electronic copy available at http://betternature.wordpress.com/, Sydney.

Davies, G. F. (2012), The Nature of the Beast: how economists mistook wild horses for a rocking chair, 233 pp., Electronic copy available from http://betternature.wordpress.com/.

Davies, G. F. (2013), *Sack the Economists, http://sacktheeconomists.com*, 238 pp., BWM Books, http://www.bwmbooks.com, Canberra, ACT, Australia.

Davis, J. (2015), *Will NSW reclaim #ValuesInPolitics this Saturday?*, in *Voices for Indi*, edited, http://www.voicesforindi.com/will_nsw_reclaim_valuesinpolitics_this_saturday, http://www.voicesforindi.com/will_nsw_reclaim_valuesinpolitics_this_saturday.

Delate, K. (2007), Organic practices outpace conventional in long-term research*Rep.*, www.leopold.iastate.edu/news/newsreleases/2007/organic_111307.htm pp, Leopold Center for Sustainable Agriculture, Ames, IA, USA.

Diamond, J. (2005), Collapse: How Societies Choose to Fail or Succeed, Viking, New York.

Diss, K. (2015), Australian household debt has tripled in 25 years, new study finds, *ABC*, http://www.abc.net.au/news/2015-06-17/australian-household-debt-triples/6551352.

Dyrenfurth, N. (2011), Heroes and Villains: The rise and fall of the early Australian Labor Party, 281 pp., Australian Scholarly Publishing, North Melbourne.

Dyrenfurth, N., and F. Bongiorno (2011), *A Little History of the Australian Labor Party*, 217 pp., University of New South Wales Press, Sydney.

Earthship (2014), Radically Sustainable Buildings, http://earthship.com.

Eckersley, R. (2012), *Whatever happened to Western Civilization?*, in *The Futurist*, edited, pp. 16-22, World Future Society, www.wfs.org, Bethesda, MD, USA,

Eckersley, R. (2016), Is the West really the best? Modernisation and the psychosocial dynamics of human progress and development, *Oxford Development Studies*, 44(3), 349-365.

Egan, P. D., and P. Soos (2014), Bubble Economics: Australian Land Speculation 1830 - 2013, World Economics Association, UK.

Emissions, B. Z. (2010), Zero Carbon Australia 2020, http://bze.org.au/zerocarbonplanhttp://bze.org.au/zerocarbonplan.

Essential (2011), Reversing Past Government Decisions, *Essential Report*, http://essentialvision.com.au/reversing-past-government-decisions.

Fear, J., and R. Denniss (2009), Something for nothing: unpaid overtime in AustraliaRep., Policy Brief 7 pp, Australia Institute, Policy Brief 7.

Firestone, J. (2015), Fast/Track/TPP: The Death of National Sovereignty, State Sovereignty, Separation of Powers, and Democracy, *New Economic Perspectives*, http://neweconomicperspectives.org/2015/05/fasttracktpp-the-death-of-national-sovereignty-state-sovereignty-separation-of-powers-and-democracy.html.

Foroohar, R. (2016), Makers and Takers: the rise of finance and the fall of American business, 388 pp., Crown Business, New York.

Fraser, M., and C. Roberts (2014), *Dangerous Allies*, Melbourne University Press.

Gammage, B. (2011), The Biggest Estate on Earth: How Aborigines made Australia, 434 pp., Allen & Unwin.

Gates, J. R. (1998), *The Ownership Solution*, Addison-Wesley, Reading, MA.

George, H., and B. Drake (1879/2006), *Progress and Poverty*, Robert Schalkenbach Foundation.

Gessell, S. (1934), *The Natural Economic Order*, The Free Economy Publishing Co. (Translated from the sixth German edition of Die Natürliche Wirtschaftsordnung, Rudolf Zitzmann Verlag, Berlin, 1904.), San Antonio, TX.

Gimenez, E. H. (2014), Agroecology and the Disappearing Yield Gap, *Huffington Post*, http://www.huffingtonpost.com/eric-holt-gimenez/agroecology-and-the-disappearing-yield-gap_b_6290982.html.

Goodall, J. (2012), Havel's Legacy, *Inside Story*, http://insidestory.org.au/havels-legacyhttp://insidestory.org.au/havels-legacy.

Gordon-Smith, E. (2015), Should freedom of speech apply to the outrage industry?, *ABC*, http://www.abc.net.au/radionational/programs/philosopherszone/should-freedom-of-speech-apply-to-the-outrage-industry/6398072http://www.abc.net.au/radionational/programs/philosopherszone/should-freedom-of-speech-apply-to-the-outrage-industry/6398072.

Greco, T. H., Jr. (1994), *New Money for Healthy Communities*, Thomas H. Greco, Jr., P.O. Box 42663, Tucson AZ 85733, Tucson, AZ.

Greco, T. H., Jr. (2009), The End of Money and the Future of Civilization, Chelsea Green, White River Junction, VT.

Greene, J. (2013), Moral Tribes: Emotion, Reason, and the Gap Between Us and Them, 432 pp., The Penguin Press HC.

Ham, P. (2016), A half-formed nation, *Griffith Review*, 51, 174-188.

Hamilton, C. (2007), Scorcher: the dirty politics of climate change, 266 pp., Black Inc. Agenda, Melbourne.

Hamilton, C., and R. Denniss (2000), Tracking well-being in Australia - the Genuine Progress Indicator 2000, *Discussion Paper Rep. 35*, 70 pp, The Australia Institute, www.tai.org.au, Canberra.

Hanscom, G. (2012), This old house: Why fixing up old homes is greener than building new ones, http://grist.org/cities/this-old-house-why-fixing-up-old-homes-is-greener-than-building-new-ones/.

Hartmann, T. (2002), Unequal Protection: the rise of corporate dominance and the theft of human rights, Rodale Books.

Hawken, P. (1993), *The Ecology of Commerce*, HarperBusiness, New York.

Hawken, P., A. Lovins, and L. H. Lovins (1999), *Natural Capitalism*, Little, Brown and Company, Boston.

Henry, D. (2011), *Australia spends $11 billion more encouraging pollution than cleaning it up*, edited, Australian Conservation Foundation, http://www.acfonline.org.au/articles/news.asp?news_id=3308&eid=11731.

Ho, M.-W., S. Burcher, L. L. Ching, and others (2008), Food Futures Now, organic, sustainable, fossil fuel free*Rep.*, www.i-sis.org.uk/foodFutures.php pp, Institute of Science in Society, London.

Horne, D. (1964/2005), *The Lucky Country*, 5th ed., Penguin Group.

Howarth, R. W. (2014), A bridge to nowhere: methane emissions and the greenhouse gas footprint of natural gas, *Energy, Science & Engineering*, 2, 47-60.

IAASTD (2008), Synthesis Report*Rep.*, www.agassessment.org/ pp, The International Assessment of Agricultural Knowledge, Science and Technology for Development (IAASTD).

Indi, V. f. *Voices for Indi*, edited, http://www.voicesforindi.com, http://www.voicesforindi.com.

Institute, R. (2015), The Farming Systems Trial: Celebrating 30 years, www.rodaleinstitute.org.

Interface_Inc (2001), *Interface Inc*, edited, http://www.interfaceinc.com, http://www.interfaceinc.com.

Jackson, T. (2009), Prosperity Without Growth: Economics for a finite planet, Earthscan, London.

Jackson, W. (1994), *Becoming Native to This Place*, University Press of Kentucky.

Jotzo, F., and L. Kemp (2015), Australia can cut emissions deeply and the cost is low*Rep.*, Centre for Climate Economics and Policy, ANU, for WWF-Australia.

Katakis, M. (2014), A Thousand Shards of Glass, Simon and Schuster.

Keen, S. (2009), "No-one saw this coming?" Balderdash!, http://www.debtdeflation.com/blogs/2009/07/15/no-one-saw-this-coming-balderdash/.

Keen, S. (2011), Debunking Economics: The Naked Emperor Dethroned?, Second, revised and expanded ed., Zed Books.

Kennedy, M. (1988), *Interest and Inflation Free Money*, Permakulture Institut e.V., Ginsterweg 5, D-3074 Steyerberg, Germany, Steyerberg.

Kevin, T. (2004), A Certain Maritime Incident: The Sinking of SIEV X, 320 pp., Scribe Publications Pty Ltd.

Khan, S., R. Mulvaney, T. Ellsworth, and C. Boast (2007), The myth of nitrogen fertilization for soil carbon sequestration, *J. Environmental Quality*, 36, 1821-1832.

Klein, N. (2014), This Changes Everything: Capitalism vs. The Climate, Simon & Schuster.

Knox, M. (2015), *Supermarket Monsters*, Redback, Collingwood, Vic.

Kunstler, J. H. (1993), *The Geography of Nowhere*, Touchstone, New York.

Lal, R., J. L. Kimble, R. F. Follet, and C. V. Cole (1998), The Potential of U.S. Cropland to Sequester Carbon and Mitigate the Greenhouse Effect, Sleeping Bear Press, 121 S. Main St., Chelsea, MI 48118, Chelsea, MI.

Landcare, A. (2015), *Landcare Australia*, edited, http://www.landcareonline.com, http://www.landcareonline.com.

Lang, J. T. (1962), *The Great Bust*, Angus & Robertson, Sydney.

Lovins, A., and R. M. Institute (2011), *Reinventing Fire*, 334 pp., Chelsea Green.

Lovins, A. B. (1977), *Soft Energy Paths: Toward a Durable Peace*, Ballinger Publishing Company, Cambridge, MA.

Lovins, A. B. (2005), Energy End-Use Efficiency. www.interacademycouncil.net, InterAcademy Council, Amsterdam.

Lovins, A. B. (2011), *Reinventing Fire*, Chelsea Green Publishing, White River Junction, VT.

Manne, R. (2011), Bad News: Murdoch's Australian and the Shaping of the Nation, *Quarterly Essay*(43), http://www.quarterlyessay.com/issue/bad-news-murdochs-australian-and-shaping-nation.

Manne, R. (2013), Why Rupert Murdoch can't be stopped, *The Monthly*, (November 2013)http://www.themonthly.com.au/issue/2013/november/1383224400/robert-manne/why-rupert-murdoch-can-t-be-stopped.

Manning, R. (2004), Against the Grain: How Agriculture Has Hijacked Civilization, North Point Press, New York.

Martin, P. (2013), Hey, big spender: Howard the king of the loose purse strings, *Sydney Morning Herald*, http://www.smh.com.au/federal-politics/political-news/hey-big-spender-howard-the-king-of-the-loose-purse-strings-20130110-2cj32.html.

McAdam, J., and F. Chong (2014), Refugees: why seeking asylum is legal, NewSouth Publishing, Sydney NSW.

McCoy, A. W., and B. Reilly (2011), Washington on the Rocks, *Tomgram*, http://www.tomdispatch.com/blog/175383/.

McDonough, W., and M. Braungart (2002), *Cradle to Cradle*, 193 pp., North Point Press, New York.

McKibben, B. (2005), *The Cuba Diet*, in *Harper's Magazine*, edited,

McKinsey&Company (2007), Reducing U.S. Greenhouse Gas Emissions: How Much at What Cost?*Rep.*, McKinsey & Company, New York.

McKinsey&Company (2008), An Australian Cost Curve for Greenhouse Gas Reduction*Rep.*, McKinsey & Company.

McLean, I. W. (2013), Why Australia Prospered: the shifting sources of economic growth, 296 pp., Princeton University Press, Princeton, NJ.

McLeay, M., A. Radia, and R. Thomas (2014), Money in the modern economy: an introduction*Rep.*, 10 pp, Bank of England.

McMalcolm, J. (2013), It's Boom or Bust for Australia's Manufacturing Sector, *Business Review Australia*, http://www.businessreviewaustralia.com/leadership/134/It039s-Boom-or-Bust-for-Australia039s-Manufacturing-Sector.

Meadows, D. H., D. L. Meadows, J. Randers, and W. W. Behrens III (1972), *Limits to Growth*, Universe Books, New York.

Meadows, D. H., J. Randers, and D. L. Meadows (2004), *Limits to Growth: the 30-Year Update*, Chelsea Green, White River Junction, VT.

Megalogenis, G. (2012), The Australian Moment: How we were made for these times, 371 pp., Penguin.

Menadue, J. (2015), Democratic renewal, vested interests and the subversion of the public interest?, *Independent Australia*, https://independentaustralia.net/politics/politics-display/democratic-renewal-vested-interests-and-the-subversion-of-the-public-interest,7948.

Milman, O. (2014), Tony Abbott adviser warns of threat of 'global cooling', *The Guardian*, http://www.theguardian.com/environment/2014/aug/14/tony-abbott-adviser-warns-of-threat-of-global-cooling.

Mobbs, M. (1998), *Sustainable House*, Choice Books, Marrickville, NSW.

Mollison, B. (1999), Permaculture Two: Practical Design for Town and Country in Permanent Agriculture, Reprint edition ed., Tagari Publications, Tyalgum, NSW 2484, Australia.

Mondragon *Mondragón Corporación Cooperativa*, edited, http://www.mondragon-corporation.com/ENG.aspx, http://www.mondragon-corporation.com/ENG.aspx.

Muller, D. (2015), Press Council chief fires parting shot at News Corp, *The Conversation*, https://theconversation.com/press-council-chief-fires-parting-shot-at-news-corp-44841https://theconversation.com/press-council-chief-fires-parting-shot-at-news-corp-44841.

News, P. (2015), *Positive News (UK)*, http://positivenews.org.uk.

O'Malley, N. (2012), Fighting the right: conservatives find Republican party line hard to follow, *Sydney Morning Herald*, http://www.smh.com.au/world/fighting-the-right-conservatives-find-republican-party-line-hard-to-follow-20120713-221ch.html?page=1.

Oakland, I. (2015), Agroecology Case Studies, http://www.oaklandinstitute.org/agroecology-case-studies.

Olding, R. (2015), Right-wing extremism equal to Muslim radicalisation: academics and police, *Sydney Morning Herald*, http://www.smh.com.au/national/rightwing-extremism-equal-to-muslim-radicalisation-academics-and-police-20150716-giduqp.html#ixzz3g7WdXe8c.

Parenteau, R. (2015), Get a TAN, Yanis: a timely alternative financing instrument for Greece, *New Economics Perspective*, http://neweconomicperspectives.org/2015/02/get-tan-yanis-timely-alternative-financing-instrument-greece.html.

Pascoe, B. (2014), *Dark Emu. Black seeds: agriculture or accident?*, 176 pp., Magabala Books Aboriginal Corporation, Broome, WA.

Pearson, N. (2017), A job half undone, *The Monthly*(June), 8-11.

Perkins, J. (2004), Confessions of an Economic Hit Man, Berret-Koehler, San Francisco.

Persky, J. (1989), Retrospectives: Adam Smith's Invisible Hands, *Journal of Economics Perspectives*(4), 195-201.

Pett, J. (2009), *What if it's a big hoax*, edited, Cartoon Arts International, USA Today, https://www.nytsyn.com/cartoons/.

Phillips, A. A. (1950), The Cultural Cringe, *Meanjin*, 9(4), 299-302.

Pizzigati, S. (2013), The Rich Don't Always Win: The Forgotten Triumph over Plutocracy that Created the American Middle Class, 1900-1970, Seven Stories Press.

Ponisio, L. C., L. K. M'Gonigle, K. C. Mace, J. Palomino, P. d. Valpine, and C. Kremen (2014), Diversification practices reduce organic to conventional yield gap, *Proceedings of the Royal Society B*, 282(1799), doi:10.1098/rspb.2014.1396.

Popper, K. (2002), The Open Society and It's Enemies, Routledge.

Powell, J. L. (2012), Why Climate Deniers Have No Scientific Credibility - In One Pie Chart, *DeSmogBlog*, http://www.desmogblog.com/print/6662.

Rabinovich, J., and J. Leitman (1996), Urban planning in Curitiba, *Scientific American*(March), 46-53.

Randle, M., and R. Eckersley (2015), Public perceptions of future threats to humanity and different societal responses: A cross-national study, *Futures*, 72, 4-16, doi:10.1016/j.futures.2015.06.004.

Ray, P. H., and S. R. Anderson (2000), *The Cultural Creatives*, Harmony Books, New York.

Reich, R. B. (2011), *The Limping Middle Class*, in *New York Times*, edited, New York, NY, http://www.nytimes.com/2011/09/04/opinion/sunday/jobs-will-follow-a-strengthening-of-the-middle-class.html?src=rechp.

Roberts, N. (2015), Australian houses are just glorified tents in winter, *The Canberra Times*, www.canberratimes.com.au/action/printArticle?id=996902241.

Robertson, T. (2015), We need to talk about radicalisation, *Independent Australia*, https://independentaustralia.net/article-display/we-need-to-talk-about-radicalisation,7492.

Roos, G. (2014), For want of industry policy, our living standards are set to fall, *The Conversation*, https://theconversation.com/for-want-of-industry-policy-our-living-standards-are-set-to-fall-23317.

Rowbotham, M. (1998), *The Grip of Death*, Jon Carpenter Publishing, Charlbury, Oxfordshire.

Rudd, K. (2009), The Global Financial Crisis, *The Monthly*, (February)http://www.themonthly.com.au/issue/2009/february/1319602475/kevin-rudd/global-financial-crisis.

Sage, P. (1999), The Purple Sage Project*Rep.*, Victorian Women's Trust, http://vwt.org.au/1998/11/purple-sage/.

Schultz, J. (2016), Captains don't always know best, *Griffith Review*, 51, 7-10.

Shuman, M. (2015), The Local Economy Solution: How Innovative Self-Financing "Pollinator" Enterprises Can Grow Jobs and Prosperity, Chelsea Green.

Simons, M. (2010), The inside story on Fraser's resignation, *Crikey*, http://www.crikey.com.au/2010/05/26/the-inside-story-on-frasers-resignation-abbott-appealed-to-him-to-stay/.

Solutions, B. (2015), *Beautiful Solutions*, edited, https://solutions.thischangeseverything.org/#, https://solutions.thischangeseverything.org/#.

Soos, P. (2014), Do the crime, do the time? Not if you're a banker in Australia, *The Conversation*, https://theconversation.com/do-the-crime-do-the-time-not-if-youre-a-banker-in-australia-33548.

Sparrow, J. (2015), Maurice Newman v the UN: logic behind the crazy, *The Drum (Australian Broadcasting Corporation)*, http://www.abc.net.au/news/2015-05-11/sparrow-maurice-newman-v-the-un/6460160.

Stone, G. (2005), *1932*, 429 pp., Pan Macmillan Australia, Sydney.

Taylor, M. (2014), Global Warming and Climate Change: What Australia knew and buried...then framed a new reality for the public, ANU Press, http://press.anu.edu.au?p=303951, Canberra.

Toohey, B. (1994), *Tumbling Dice*, 348 pp., William Heinemann Australia, Melbourne.

Trust, V. W. (1999), The Purple Sage Project*Rep.*, Victorian Women's Trust, http://vwt.org.au/1998/11/purple-sage/.

Trust, V. W. (2007), Our Water Mark*Rep.*, Victorian Women's Trust, http://vwt.org.au/2007/11/water-mark/.

Turnbull, S. (2003), Network governance, *Corporate Governance International*, 6(3), 4-14.

Turnbull, S. (2007), A framework for designing sustainable urban communities*Rep.*, 15, http://papers.ssrn.com/abstract=960193 pp, International Institute for Self Governance.

Verrender, I. (2014), Think Whitlam ruined our economy? Think again, *The Drum, ABC*, doi:http://www.abc.net.au/news/2014-10-27/verrender-think-whitlam-ruined-our-economy-think-again/5842866

Verrender, I. (2015), A royal commission into banks could end two scandals, *The Drum (ABC)*, http://www.abc.net.au/news/2015-08-17/verrender-a-royal-commission-into-banks/6701420.

von Weizsäcker, E., A. B. Lovins, and L. H. Lovins (1997), *Factor Four: Doubling Wealth, Halving Resource Use*, Allen & Unwin, St. Leonards.

Watch, H. R. (2015), Human Rights Watch: World Report 2015, http://www.hrw.org/world-report/2015/country-chapters/australia?page=1.

Weisbrot, M., D. Baker, and D. Rosnick (2005), The Scorecard on Development: 25 Years of Diminished Progress*Rep.*, Center for Economic and Policy Research, www.cepr.net/index.html, Washington D. C.

Whitzman, C. (2015), City planning: we can learn from Vancouver, Portland, *The Drum, ABC*, http://www.abc.net.au/news/2015-04-10/whitzman-we-can-learn-from-vancouver-portland/6383772.

Wicks, P. (2015), 'Ag-gag' laws expose Coalition's freedom of speech hypocrisy, *Independent Australia*, https://independentaustralia.net/politics/politics-display/ag-gag-laws-expose-coalitions-freedom-of-speech-hypocrisy,7751.

Woods, J., and P. Lewis (2015), Hate privatisation? There's nothing new about that, *The Drum, ABC*, http://www.abc.net.au/news/2015-02-11/lewis-and-woods-voters-still-sceptical-of-privatisation/6083982.

Wray, L. R. (2012), Modern Money Theory: A Primer on Macroeconomics for Sovereign Monetary Systems, Palgrave Macmillan.

Zinn, H. (1980), *A People's History of the United States*, 729 pp., Harper Perennial Modern Classics.

About the author

Dr. Geoff Davies is a scientist, author and commentator. He is a retired Senior Fellow (now a Visiting Fellow) in geophysics in the Research School of Earth Sciences at the Australian National University. In 2005 he was awarded the inaugural Augustus Love medal for geodynamics by the European Geosciences Union. He was selected in 1992 as a Fellow of the American Geophysical Union. He has authored over 100 scientific papers and two scientific books.

He has been delving into economics for over 15 years and commenting on society for longer.

See more at his web site: betternature.wordpress.com/about.

Other books by Geoff Davies

The Seventh Generation series

(The Great Council of the Six Nations of the Iroquois is reputed to have included one member whose role was to speak for the seventh generation unborn.)

1. *Economia* (ABC Books, 2004). Critiques the archaic theories and practices through which economies are managed, or mismanaged, and develops a new vision that grows out of modern systems concepts. This is the original critique of mainstream economics and development of the new framework of complexity. '... *a joy to read for visionaries and sceptics alike,*' - Hugh Stretton.

2. *The Nature of the Beast* (betternature.wordpress.com/my-books/nature-of-the-beast/, 2012)

3. *Sack the Economists* (BWM Books, 2013). The disastrous flaws in mainstream economics, and how economies can serve our total wellbeing. Brief, updated, focused account. '*With delightful wit and insightful analogies, geophysicist Geoff Davies dissects the inconsistencies — and the inanities — of mainstream economics,*' Sam Pizzigati.

4. *The Rise and Failure of the Radical Right* (BetterNature, 2017). The right-wing ideology of the past 40 years has failed. It was always going to fail. Australian politics has been dragged far to the right since 1980, but now the radical right's grip on power is finally slipping. We are poised for a major political re-alignment.

5. *Desperately Seeking the Fair Go* (BetterNature, 2017).

Professional science books

Dynamic Earth (Cambridge, 1999)

Mantle Convection for Geologists (Cambridge, 2011)

www.ingramcontent.com/pod-product-compliance
Lightning Source LLC
Chambersburg PA
CBHW071905290426
44110CB00013B/1281